Learn Human-Computer Interaction

Solve human problems and focus on rapid prototyping and validating solutions through user testing

Christopher Reid Becker

BIRMINGHAM - MUMBAI

Learn Human-Computer Interaction

Copyright © 2020 Packt Publishing

All rights reserved. No part of this book may be reproduced, stored in a retrieval system, or transmitted in any form or by any means, without the prior written permission of the publisher, except in the case of brief quotations embedded in critical articles or reviews.

Every effort has been made in the preparation of this book to ensure the accuracy of the information presented. However, the information contained in this book is sold without warranty, either express or implied. Neither the author nor Packt Publishing or its dealers and distributors, will be held liable for any damages caused or alleged to have been caused directly or indirectly by this book.

Packt Publishing has endeavored to provide trademark information about all of the companies and products mentioned in this book by the appropriate use of capitals. However, Packt Publishing cannot guarantee the accuracy of this information.

Commissioning Editor: Sunith Shetty
Acquisition Editor: Devika Battike
Content Development Editor: Joseph Sunil
Senior Editor: Ayaan Hoda
Technical Editor: Sonam Pandey
Copy Editor: Safis Editing
Project Coordinator: Aishwarya Mohan
Proofreader: Safis Editing
Indexer: Rekha Nair
Production Designer: Jyoti Chauhan

First published: September 2020

Production reference: 1180920

Published by Packt Publishing Ltd.
Livery Place
35 Livery Street
Birmingham
B3 2PB, UK.

ISBN 978-1-83882-032-9

www.packt.com

To my son, Helios, for showing me how learning every day is part of growth, and to my wife, Voula, for listening to me and supporting the process.

– Chris R. Becker

Contributors

About the author

Christopher Reid Becker is a senior UX designer/lead curriculum architect (UX/UI) at 2U Inc. He comes with extensive experience in building web-based software and commercial projects accessing design thinking, human-centered user research, UX strategies, UI best practices, and interaction design to build relevant, usable, and useful human-computer interactions.

About the reviewer

Philippe Renevier Gonin has been an assistant professor at the University Nice Sophia Antipolis, France, since 2005. Philippe teaches web technologies, software engineering (architecture and development), and **Human-Computer Interaction (HCI)**.

On the research side of things, Philippe works on connections between user-centered design (that is, users and task models) and software engineering (such as component architecture and UI development). For his projects, Philippe often develops software and tools in Javascript/HTML/CSS and Java (Android).

Packt is searching for authors like you

If you're interested in becoming an author for Packt, please visit authors.packtpub.com and apply today. We have worked with thousands of developers and tech professionals, just like you, to help them share their insight with the global tech community. You can make a general application, apply for a specific hot topic that we are recruiting an author for, or submit your own idea.

Packt.com

Subscribe to our online digital library for full access to over 7,000 books and videos, as well as industry leading tools to help you plan your personal development and advance your career. For more information, please visit our website.

Why subscribe?

- Spend less time learning and more time coding with practical eBooks and Videos from over 4,000 industry professionals

- Improve your learning with Skill Plans built especially for you

- Get a free eBook or video every month

- Fully searchable for easy access to vital information

- Copy and paste, print, and bookmark content

Did you know that Packt offers eBook versions of every book published, with PDF and ePub files available? You can upgrade to the eBook version at www.packt.com and as a print book customer, you are entitled to a discount on the eBook copy. Get in touch with us at customercare@packtpub.com for more details.

At www.packt.com, you can also read a collection of free technical articles, sign up for a range of free newsletters, and receive exclusive discounts and offers on Packt books and eBooks.

Table of Contents

Preface   1

Section 1: Learn Human-Computer Interaction

Chapter 1: Introducing HCI and UX Design   9
  Prologue   9
    HCI challenges   10
  Introducing HCI and UX design   11
    Challenge 1 – Capturing conceptual relationships – binary and beyond   11
    Following the leader – HCI pioneers   14
    Operating in the HCI sandbox   14
  Why HCI?   16
    Documenting HCI jargon   16
    Challenge 2 – Highlighting and collecting all HCI jargon   17
  Exploring HCI jargon and their acronyms   17
  Exploring the history of computers   19
    Very early history – the 17th century   19
    Early history – the 17th to 19th centuries   19
    Recent history – the 20th century   21
    The 21st century – the internet, smartphones, cloud computing, and IoT   24
  Evolving from T-person into a π person   25
    Hermeneutic loops   27
  The author's perspective   28
    HCI is a vocation   29
    Challenge 3 – What do you know about a lawnmower?   29
  The HCI professions   30
    Challenge 4 – Self-guided questions   33
  Summary   33

Chapter 2: Human-Centered Design Principles   35
  Understanding the HCI ethos   36
    Challenge 5 – Questions refresher   36
    The heart of HCI technology   37
      Usability factor   38
      Accessibility factor   38
      Time-on-task factor   40
    The holy trinity (mirepoix) of HCI   40
    Some HCI professions   42
    Challenge 6 – Profession of interest   44
    Challenge 7 – Software naming and shaming   45

Challenge 8 – Human needs identification table	46
Case 1 – the crosswalk	50
Challenge 9 – Observing humans and technology	50
How software shapes its users	52
How HCI is standing on the shoulders of giants	54
HCI principles are rooted in humans, technology, culture, and data	59
User research – gathering data on humans	60
Iterative solutions and agile development	61
Summary	63
Chapter 3: Interface Design Values	65
Solving a problem with computer software	66
Positive software example – the alarm	66
Negative software example – text messaging	67
Using computer software to build software	68
Text editors	69
Challenge 10 – Technology coding challenge	70
Human-centered software origins	70
Design and development tools	73
HCI design roles	74
Code, roles, and tools	75
Coding – markup syntax and object-oriented syntax	77
Hypertext markup language	78
Cascading style sheets	79
Object-oriented programming	80
Continually better software	80
Summary	83

Section 2: How to Build Human-Centered Software

Chapter 4: Human-Centered Thinking	87
Understanding the HCI designer's role	88
Challenge 11 – User research – a design mindmap	88
Challenge 12 – Product and software inspiration	91
Challenge 13 – First computer experience	92
The long tail of software design	93
The short tail of software design	96
Considering the developer's role in software design	97
Challenge 14 – A 2x2 matrix – your code experience	99
Using agile development cycles	102
The waterfall design and development process	102
Design thinking, agile design, and the development process	104
Agile design cycle	105
Design thinking and the agile development process	107
Executing prototypes first as a design ethos	108

Paper prototypes   109
Challenge 15 – Sketching and prototyping challenge   111
Interactive and clickable prototypes   112
Challenge 16 – Clickable paper prototype with the InVision app   113
Native and coded prototypes   114
Validating with users   118
Stage 1 – idea validation   119
Stage 2 – usability validation   120
Stage 3 – market validation   122
Challenge 17 – Prototype validation   123
Summary   124

Chapter 5: Human-Centered Methods for User Research   125
Gathering research data on our users   126
The human side of data collection   130
Exploring qualitative user research methods   131
Qualitative method 1 – observation – fly-on-the-wall method   132
Challenge 18 – Observation – fly on the wall   133
Qualitative method 1.1 – micro-observations   134
Qualitative method 2 – moderated observation   134
Challenge 19 – Moderated observation script   135
Qualitative method 3 – user interviews   136
Open question types   137
Probing questions types   138
Challenge 20 – Interview candidate script   140
One-to-one interview sessions   141
Challenge 21 – One-on-one interview   142
One-to-many interview sessions   143
Qualitative method 4 – user recording, tracking analysis, and interview   144
Challenge 22 – Observation recording   146
The numbers side of data collection   146
Examining four quantitative research methods   147
Quantitative survey method   148
Challenge 23 – Quick-and-dirty survey   149
A/B testing (split testing)   150
Challenge 24 – A/B survey results   153
Usability analytics   154
Challenge 25 – Analytics data gathering   155
Quantitative method 4 – accessibility compliance   156
Challenge 26 – Accessibility for all via ANDI testing using WCAG 2.0   157
Using qualitative and quantitative data   158
Summary   158

Chapter 6: User Insights for Software Solutions   161
Synthesizing data into action   162
Part 1 – analysis of user research data   162

Collection and organization of user research data 163
Mining the user research data 164
Sorting, clustering, and categorizing the user research data 164
Part 2 – user insights 165
Identifying user insights 165
Rooting action to deeper user purpose 167
Challenge 27 – The deep purpose of people challenge 168
Identifying and writing user insights 169
Challenge 28 – IDEO's POV mad lib 170
Challenge 29 – IDEO's POV mad lib iteration 171
Aligning a solution to users 172
Summary 174
Chapter 7: Storytelling and Rapid Prototyping 175
Prototyping first 176
Challenge 30 – Idea/concept generation 178
Laseau's funnel 179
Dot voting 180
2x2 opportunity matrix 181
Paper prototyping (low fidelity) 182
Challenge 31 – Paper prototype sketching 185
Clickable prototyping (mid-fidelity) 187
Challenge 32 – Clickable paper prototype 188
Challenge 33 – Clickable wireframe prototype 189
Motion prototyping (high fidelity) 190
Frontend prototyping (low to high fidelity) 192
Challenge 34 – Frontend clickable prototype 193
The prototyper (developer) 194
System diagramming 195
Challenge 35 – System diagram 196
HCI interface best practices 197
Challenge 36 – Researching HCI user interface best practices 197
Challenge 37 – Researching software tips and tricks 198
Interface design guidelines 199
Challenge 38 – Researching popular user interface guidelines 200
Software prototyping tools 201
Summary 201
Chapter 8: Validating Software Solutions 203
Establishing a software hypothesis 204
Challenge 39 – Software hypothesis 206
Informal user feedback 207
Challenge 40 – Informal feedback guerilla user testing 208
Formal user feedback 209
Formative assessment and user feedback 211
Expert feedback 211

Self-feedback and reflection 213
Critique feedback 213
Summary of user feedback 214
Challenge 41 – Formal user feedback 214
Validating prototyping solutions 215
Challenge 42 – Prototype validation 217
Executing usability tests 218
Challenge 42 – Prototype usability testing challenge 220
Iterating software solutions 221
Challenge 43 – Iterate your prototype challenge 222
Summary 223
HCI resources 223

Section 3: When to Improve Software Systems

Chapter 9: Improving Software Systems with Data 227
Designing software for all users with universal design principles 228
Challenge 44 – Research universal design principles 230
Applying usability for all users 231
Learnability 233
Efficiency 233
Memorability 234
Low error rate 235
User satisfaction 235
Utility 236
Valuing accessibility 237
Disability impairments 237
Cognitive impairment 238
Challenge 45 – Research Miller's law 238
Mobility impairment 239
Hearing/auditory impairment 240
Visual impairments 240
Challenge 46 – Screen reader tool 241
Designing useful interfaces 242
Summary 243

Chapter 10: Human-Centered Solutions 245
Exploring open source software culture 245
Open source projects 247
Bootstrap (Twitter) 248
Angular 248
Node.JS 248
NPM (Node Package Manager) 248
React Native (Facebook) 249
VS Code (Microsoft) 249
Challenge 47 – Research an open source project and contribute 250
MVC, not MVP 251

Iterative loops for improving software, which improves culture   254
Summary   256
Chapter 11: Extending HCI   257
  Contributing to software development as a collective community   258
    UX, UI, frontend dev, backend dev, PM, business, and ops   260
    Team handoff and responsibility   263
    Communication tools – Zeplin, Figma/XD/Sketch, InVision   265
    Challenge 48 – Add a Zeplin.io project   265
  Exploring how great solutions should be shared and scaled   267
    Challenge 49 – Software scale research   267
  Evangelizing to your team and sharing common goals   269
    Challenge 50 – Educate yourself   269
    Diversify your team's skills   270
  Demonstrating how you care   271
  Summary   272
Chapter 12: The Future of HCI   273
  Designing software is an awesome responsibility   274
    Challenge 51 – SWOT analysis of a software feature   276
  Creating solutions that are net positive for culture   278
  Evaluating what is off-limits   281
    Challenge 52 – Zones of interest and worthwhile pursuits   282
  Empowering computers   283
  Designing software for the future   285
    Education software (embedded systems)   286
    Collaboration software systems for work and creativity (ubicomp and seamless interactions)   288
    Communication/media software systems (digital affordance and seamless interactions)   290
    Automation software systems (ubicomp and embedded systems)   291
    Logistics/analytics software systems (knowledge data)   292
    Democratic power software systems (ubicomp and security)   294
    Challenge 53 – Which software future?   296
  Summary   297
Other Books You May Enjoy   299
Index   303

Preface

Human-Computer Interaction (HCI) is a field of study that researches, designs, and develops software solutions that solve human problems. This book will help you understand various aspects of the software development phase, from planning and data gathering through to the design and development of software solutions. The book guides you through implementing methodologies that will help you build robust software.

In this book, you will learn why human-centered methodologies are winning in software development, and how to develop unique insights into your users through practical research processes you can try from home. You will then embark on how to translate your human understanding into software solutions through validation methods and rapid prototyping, leading to usability testing. In the end, you will learn how to build and deploy a software prototype that will allow you to test and iterate your human-centered solution as well as tell a better story about why we implement human-centered values into software solutions. The practice and skills will be contextualized through the book with historical figures, mistakes, and successes from the software industry. The concepts and stories will sharable and resonate throughout your software development path.

By the end of this book, you will be well versed in HCI strategies and methodologies to design effective **User Interfaces (UIs)**.

Who this book is for

This book is for software engineers, **User Experience (UX)** designers, entrepreneurs, or anyone who is just getting started with user interface design and looking to gain a solid understanding of HCI and UX design. Readers who are budding software engineers, UX designers, UI engineers, entrepreneurs, graphic designers, and others looking for a solid understanding of how to approach digital products, and people who are curious, self-driven, and motivated to take their education in their own hands, will also all benefit from reading this book. Who will benefit the most is a person willing to be enthusiastic about learning new things and self-guided in mining their past knowledge to gain new perspectives. This book will deliver the best experience if you meet the following prerequisites:

1. Have familiarity with HCI, UX, UI, **Interaction Design (IxD)**, visual design, computer science, or other related software building professions
2. Want to know how to build better software

3. Are curious about how computers work
4. Are open to new ideas

What this book covers

Chapter 1, *Introducing HCI and UX Design*, outlines the goals the reader will work toward throughout the book, as well as an introduction to the author's perspective. It will frame the space and professions that the knowledge in this book is relevant to and will ask some key questions that will guide the reader throughout their journey.

Chapter 2, *Human-Centered Design Principles*, focuses on the explosion of software made possible through the introduction of the internet in 1990. It will also explore samples of how the principle is applied to software, and explore various tools we can use.

Chapter 3, *Interface Design Values*, focuses on the tools and approaches used by software teams to tackle various problems.

Chapter 4, *Human-Centered Thinking*, talks about how design and development cycles lead to better outcomes.

Chapter 5, *Human-Centered Methods for User Research*, focuses on qualitative and quantitative user research methods that you will be able to apply in your own projects.

Chapter 6, *User Insights for Software Solutions*, shows us how user research data builds trust and relationships. It will show us how to align our software solutions according to the users' needs.

Chapter 7, *Storytelling and Rapid Prototyping*, acts as a review of how systems diagramming and user input builds testable experiments.

Chapter 8, *Validating Software Solutions*, demonstrates how we can employ human-centered methods to gather user testing data. It also shows us how to use data to capitalize on our solutions.

Chapter 9, *Improving Software Systems with Data*, outlines the process of validating the usability and accessibility of a software solution. Throughout this chapter, we will look at how we can reinforce our software solutions with the help of data.

Chapter 10, *Human-Centered Solutions*, showcases software solutions as a feedback loop to culture. It also shows us how to use the past to capitalize on and improve our solutions.

Chapter 11, *Extending HCI*, continues by discussing education, team values, and the design community. It shows us why HCI is valuable for teams, and why we should evangelize the value of human-centered design to each team member.

Chapter 12, *The Future of HCI*, explores embedded systems, ubiquitous computing, and seamless interactions that are pushing the future of HCI into new frontiers.

To get the most out of this book

Successful software is used by billions of humans around the globe. Understanding how to approach, model, and generate software solutions that your users need and want will make you more employable, and make the software you analyze, design, and code work better for your users. This book does the following:

- Introduce the reader to HCI and UX by discussing the origins of the profession and why learning HCI is essential for the 22nd century.
- Review how HCI is connected to a long history of humans making tools to solve problems.
- Articulate how HCI considers when the software will help its users.
- Discuss how HCI starts with valuing humans, and how, just as software improves, so do humans evolve too.
- Execute qualitative and quantitative methodologies for establishing humans as a feedback loop in the software design process.
- Implement a rapid prototype through software to create human-centered solutions and validate these solutions through quantitative testing methods.
- Articulate the possibilities of software's reach into the future.

Software/hardware covered in the book	OS requirements
Figma/Abobe XD/Sketch or equivalent UI/vector software	Mac - Catalina PC - Windows 10 Browser - Chrome
Google Chrome and Google Drive applications	Mac - Catalina PC - Windows 10 Browser - Chrome
The InVision app	Mac - Catalina PC - Windows 10 Browser - Chrome
VS Code or equivalent text editor software	Mac - Catalina PC - Windows 10 Browser - Chrome

Download the color images

We also provide a PDF file that has color images of the screenshots/diagrams used in this book. You can download it here: https://static.packt-cdn.com/downloads/ 9781838820329_ColorImages.pdf.

Conventions used

There are a number of text conventions used throughout this book.

Bold: Indicates a new term, an important word, or words that you see onscreen. For example, words in menus or dialog boxes appear in the text like this. Here is an example: "We will discuss a wide set of **Human-Computer Interaction** (**HCI**) topics that address how to design, build (code), and test the vast amounts of software that ultimately run the world."

 Warnings or important notes appear like this.

 Tips and tricks appear like this.

Get in touch

Feedback from our readers is always welcome.

General feedback: If you have questions about any aspect of this book, mention the book title in the subject of your message and email us at customercare@packtpub.com.

Errata: Although we have taken every care to ensure the accuracy of our content, mistakes do happen. If you have found a mistake in this book, we would be grateful if you would report this to us. Please visit www.packtpub.com/support/errata, selecting your book, clicking on the Errata Submission Form link, and entering the details.

Piracy: If you come across any illegal copies of our works in any form on the Internet, we would be grateful if you would provide us with the location address or website name. Please contact us at copyright@packt.com with a link to the material.

If you are interested in becoming an author: If there is a topic that you have expertise in and you are interested in either writing or contributing to a book, please visit authors.packtpub.com.

Reviews

Please leave a review. Once you have read and used this book, why not leave a review on the site that you purchased it from? Potential readers can then see and use your unbiased opinion to make purchase decisions, we at Packt can understand what you think about our products, and our authors can see your feedback on their book. Thank you!

For more information about Packt, please visit packt.com.

Section 1 - Learn Human-Computer Interaction

This section is a starting place for considering and thinking about people (humans), technology (computers), and how we interact. We will discuss a wide set of topics that address how to think about, design, and even code the vast amounts of software that run our interfaces and ultimately run the world. Throughout the next 12 chapters, we will discuss how our lives have been fundamentally reorganized around technology and software interfaces.

This section comprises of the following chapters:

- Chapter 1, *Introducing HCI and UX Design*
- Chapter 2, *Human-Centered Design Principles*
- Chapter 3, *Interface Design Values*

Introducing HCI and UX Design

1

Learn Human-Computer Interaction is a starting place for considering and thinking about people (humans), technology (computers), and how we interact. We will discuss a wide set of **Human-Computer Interaction** (**HCI**) topics that address how to design, build (code), and test the vast amounts of software that ultimately run the world. Throughout this chapter, you will be introduced to the foundations of HCI, which will set the stage for growing your skills and joining HCI practitioners on software design teams.

The topics you will learn about in this chapter are as follows:

- Prologue
- Introducing HCI and UX design
- Why HCI?
- Exploring HCI jargon and their acronyms
- Exploring the history of computers
- Evolving from a T-person into a π person
- The author's perspective
- The HCI professions
- Self-guided questions

Prologue

The core of this book covers three pillars:

1. **HCI skills, theory, and historical context:**
   Use of stories, contextual examples, and some brief history of widening your HCI knowledge.
2. **HCI Activities and practical challenges:**
   A series of hands-on methods to deepen your HCI understanding.

3. **HCI Community resources and source materials:**
   A vast set of knowledge and experience that I could never surpass but am happy to share and grow with you as you read in the share your experience:

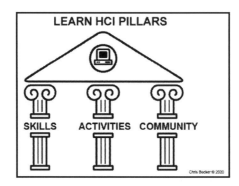

As the author of this book, my background comes from the Design point of view via **user experience** (**UX**)/graphic design/human-centered research into computers rather than via computer science, mathematics, engineering, or computer coding, however, I have gained much of this knowledge over time. Therefore, the content of the book will focus more on the human component of HCI over the computer component.

However, the framing of skills and considerations are designed to improve either side. So read on.

Since you have continued reading, you are along for the ride, and we will start out by considering HCI from the beginning and why HCI inside software has become successful.

HCI challenges

Throughout this book, you will be given a series of challenges designed to get you to practice the skills and knowledge necessary to apply HCI in the world. Each challenge will take between 10 min up to 2+ hours. I highly recommend you create a folder in Google Drive or on your computer to store your work and label all your files. Activities will combine physical making (paper, pen, pencil, sticky-notes, etc) to more digital executions (Google Docs, Adobe XD/Figma/InVision) and will combine together over time. Take the challenges seriously as they can be applied to your HCI portfolio as well as be tangible representations of the skills and experience outline in this book.

As you continue to grow your HCI skills, understand that there is a lot to take in and no one book will capture the entire field. I promise to help you establish a solid foundation but you must also take this information I am covering and run with it.

Do not be scared to mark up this book with your notes, sketches, doodles, and underlines. Dog-ear pages, take a highlighter to quotes, tear out pages as long as it helps you approach HCI. Learn HCI is a learn-by-doing document and should be treated that way. The goal is to gain new skills in HCI.

Introducing HCI and UX design

In the beginning, there was nothing but darkness, and then there was light, a binary relationship understood by all—zero (0) and one (1). *Binary* means related to or composed of two things. Binary relationships dictate a vast majority of our decisions: up or down, left or right, yes or no, like or don't like. Let's practice thinking about some binary concepts through a challenge. The challenges in this book are designed to get you to practice the HCI skills and knowledge necessary to function as an HCI practitioner in the real world. Each challenge will take between 10 minutes and 2 hours to complete.

Challenge 1 – Capturing conceptual relationships – binary and beyond

Setup:

1. *Get out a sheet of paper or a Google Doc/Word doc.*

Part 1: Binary concepts:

1. *Think of some binary relationships in your own life.*
2. *Write them down.*

    Binary relationships:

    _____ *versus* _____

Part 2: Other relevant concepts:

1. *Think of other conceptual relationships (such as logic/emotion, frontend/backend, and so on).*
2. *Write them down.*

    Relevant concepts:

    _____ + _____

Part 3: Write a short paragraph (~300 words) on why "concepts" are valuable to HCI designers:

- *Lots of concepts are useful to HCI designers and the creation of great software.*
- *Documenting these over time will help you use many of the concepts we will discuss in the future.*

If you do not like writing in books, you can do the following instead:
1. Create a Google Drive/Computer folder in which to create docs to capture any challenge/activity issued throughout this book.
2. Follow along and label your docs with the book chapters and the challenge title, using something similar to the following syntax, for example, `01-Binary-Relationships.doc`.

The binary relationship in computing is expressed in a system of numerical notation that has two digits (zero - 0 and one - 1) or ON and OFF. Binary is how a computer operates a transistor, where "0" represents no flow of electricity, and "1" represents electricity is allowed to flow. In this way, numbers are represented physically inside the computing device, permitting calculation. A computer processes 1s and 0s in the trillions allowing the creation of software to be possible which is deeply connected with the practice of HCI. Computers utilize this essential binary truth to create something entirely new: computation. Computation is the ability of a computing machine (comprising both software and hardware) to evaluate a binary logic to produce a variety of solutions based on the computational outcome. Binary is the root of all computer processing. Luckily for you and me, binary code has been made easier to program over time through computer programming languages including HTML, CSS, C++, JavaScript, and so on, and we will be discussing how an HCI designer can use tools and computer coding languages to build software solutions throughout this book.

At its core, a computer is just crunching away a bunch of 1s and 0s. When the software systems and user interfaces we use and design get more complicated, it's still just 1s and 0s. The computer in all its forms has limitations, and how we use this binary processing power is also constrained. The constraints of the computer are incredibly useful as they start to define what is possible and impossible with computer technology. We will discuss in greater detail some of these computing constraints, including size, modes of interaction, connectivity, and others, as we explore all the possibilities of designing technology as an HCI designer.

HCI is a vast field of multidisciplinary study, as shown in the following diagram:

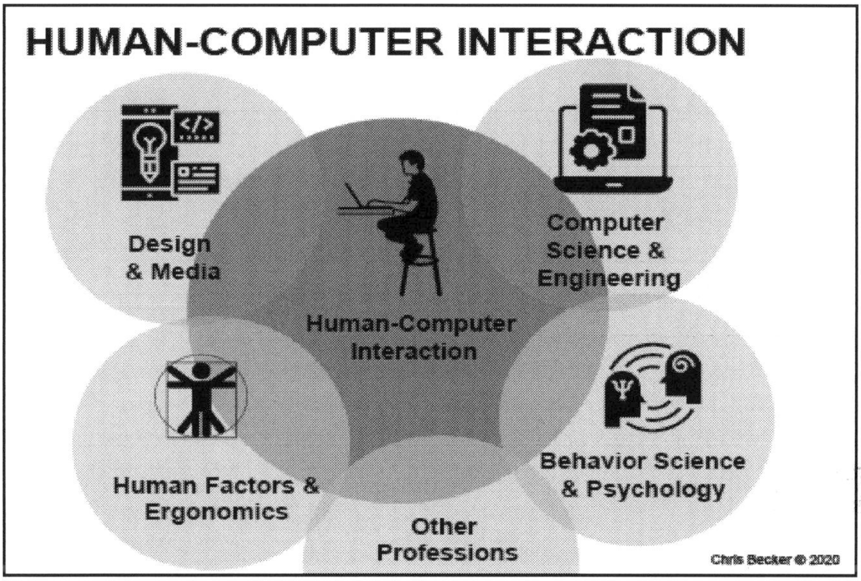

The areas of study in the field of HCI include the following:

- **Computer science and engineering**: The computer component, including the concepts, theories, and coding languages that allow us to build computer software.
- **Behavioral science and psychology**: The human component, including the concepts, theories, behavior, and ways people think about systems.
- **Design and media** (**product design**, **visual design**, **and content**): The design and interaction component including methodologies, theories, concepts, and best practices that make up the products that are used by people.
- **Human factors and ergonomics**: The interaction component of HCI, including the concepts, best practice, form factors, and physical constraints of products so that people can use them without any injury.
- **Other professions**: HCI also extends into professions such as information architecture, informatics, cultural anthropology, user research, education, and business, which all overlap with HCI.

HCI focuses on the design of computer technology and the interaction between humans and computer software systems. HCI is situated at the intersection of computer science and engineering, design and media, human factors and ergonomics, behavioral sciences and psychology, and several other fields of study and research.

Personal computing started turning up in homes and offices during the 1980s, as computer technology started to get smaller, faster, and cheaper. These sophisticated electronic systems started to become widely available to the general public for the first time. The explosion of the usefulness of computers, as well as the need to create human-computer interactions that are easy and meaningful, has lead to the adoption of HCI not just among academic institutions but generally by all of society.

HCI has been essential in propagating the idea of interaction between a user and a computer. HCI further investigates how the experience between a user and a computer should model human-to-human communication and foster an open-ended dialogue. We will discuss this in greater depth later in the book, but at its core, HCI believes in the computer as an extension of human empathy and our ability to infuse software solutions with human values to ultimately makes those solutions more valuable and scalable in our culture.

Following the leader – HCI pioneers

HCI has many thought leaders and academic institutions that continue to add to the canon of knowledge. Throughout the book, I will be referencing and pointing you to designers and authors to pay attention to. For example, **John M. Carroll** (`https://jcarroll.ist.psu.edu/`) is a faculty member at Penn State's College of Information Sciences and Technology, an author, and a founder of the field of HCI with many good things to say about how HCI design has come to develop and mature. I highly recommend reading some of his thinking and paying attention to the other founders of our field.

Operating in the HCI sandbox

HCI is a sandbox in which we get to play. The reality is that technology is not limitless; the HCI designer operates inside technological constraints. The constraints of the computer give us some rules and boundaries that we will define and help you define yourself. Your computer sandbox is made up of your HCI tools, your thoughts on HCI, your ideas for software, and the software you will create:

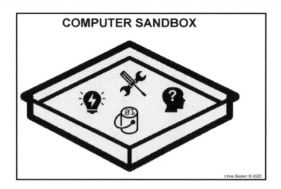

How you choose to manipulate these rules and technology constraints is where your creativity, ingenuity, and pure curiosity about humans and computers can thrive and influence people's lives and professional practices.

Learn Human-Computer Interaction will help you define your computer sandbox as you build your knowledge of HCI, your HCI tools, activities, understanding of your users, how the computer works, and more. An expectation as you continue to read this book is that you are willing and able to jump into the HCI computer sandbox. The edges of your sandbox are undefined at the moment, but we will start by defining some boundaries and then rolling around in the sand. I promise that while reading this book, we will not make you "comb the desert" to find what you are looking for, but it will require some effort on your part.

Watch *Spaceballs*, a Mel Brooks film, in order to gain context on the "comb the desert" reference: https://www.imdb.com/title/tt0094012/.

However, if you are willing to get your hands dirty, we will dig some holes in the sand and uncover many HCI skills. Some skills are right on the surface of your sandbox, and others will require some digging, but the outcome of your journey nonetheless will be to build your digging skills and improve yourself as an HCI designer.

Why HCI?

The profound impact of computing stands among humankind's greatest achievements alongside the wheel, refrigeration, and sliced bread. The publication of this book itself in both printed and digital formats would be rendered impossible without computation. The reality is that our world is full of technology run by computers. They are here to stay, so let's figure out how they impact our lives and how we can design with them and for them. A big part of understanding computers is that humans make them for other humans and, therefore, can be changed based on how humans evolve. Technology moves at an incredible speed, and the way it impacts our society, our behaviors, and our education are sometimes hard to understand; however, this is HCI's role. We will explore the vast set of opportunities that can come out of harnessing technology and how to keep up with the rapid change.

Documenting HCI jargon

HCI jargon is a collection of unique words or expressions that are used by people in our particular profession and are difficult for others to understand. Here are a few HCI terms to get you up to speed:

- **Operating System (OS)**
- The mouse
- Windows
- **Graphical User Interface (GUI)**
- **What You See Is What You Get (WYSIWYG)**

If you want to learn more HCI jargon with some history, check out https://www.cs.cmu.edu/~amulet/papers/uihistory.tr.html.

There are hundreds of terms in HCI and if I listed them all here, you would be overwhelmed and bored out of your mind, as this is not a glossary book nor is it an almanack for HCI. I highly recommend reviewing the HCI community jargon and boning up on technical terms at https://www.interaction-design.org/literature/book/the-glossary-of-human-computer-interaction and https://uiuxtrend.com/ui-ux-glossary-jargon/.

Challenge 2 – Highlighting and collecting all HCI jargon

Setup:

1. *Get out materials and a highlighter or marker.*

Part 1: Highlight the text:

1. *Use a highlighter and mark up words, terms, and technical content that you don't understand.*

Part 2: Create a jargon collection:

1. *Use Google to search for these terms if you need more help and create a Word doc or spreadsheet and start adding the highlighted jargon.*
2. *Collect the HCI jargon terms you encounter in a Google doc/Word doc that you can go back and review.*

 Being an expert will not happen overnight. You need to get practice with the technical jargon and HCI terminology. Help your memory out by making a list and highlighting terms throughout this book.

Part of learning HCI is "talking the talk," as well as "walking the walk," but for now, being able to understand that jargon will be essential to growing your skills. I encourage you to start using some HCI jargon in everyday descriptions of computers.

Exploring HCI jargon and their acronyms

This book contains technical jargon by nature. I will do my best to add resources and a glossary of terms, but some will be on you to figure out. I promise this book will not be a multithreaded annotation like David Foster Wallace's "*Infinite Jest*," but we will help you grow your HCI language.

The goals of HCI jargon are to do the following:

1. Establish a shared language for building human-centered solutions.
2. Build a shorthand for skills and industry terms.
3. Identify and navigate the growing job market utilizing HCI skills.

This can also be seen in the following diagram:

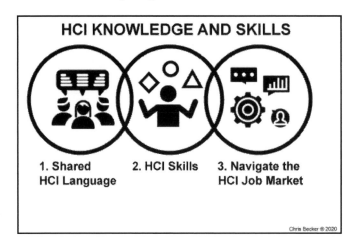

Millions of people around the planet build computer hardware and software. As a group, we can create software with computers faster due to our shared vocabulary for describing, discussing, and ultimately building solutions. It is nerdy. HCI jargon is a way to introduce you to the community to give you a shared language and allow you to talk the talk as you walk the walk. The language we share is relatively new and revolves around technology and computer systems. Lean into your nerd self and know that as a group, it is us nerds that change the world through technology.

 If you are new to technical jargon, we recommend using a highlighter to identify and recognize terms, make a personal list to help your memory, and try using them in your everyday discussions as you share what you are learning in this book with your friends, loved ones, or colleagues.

With this in mind, we'll take a quick look at the history of computers to establish where a majority of this jargon comes from. This will help us proceed toward growing our curiosity about computing and is essential for building your knowledge as well as your HCI credibility.

Exploring the history of computers

Without computers, HCI would not be a profession. Software that HCI designers work on is steeped in history and knowing the foundations will allow you to take steps into the future more confidently, therefore, let's rewind a bit and understand how we got here.

Very early history – the 17th century

Since the beginning of civilization, there is proof of human beings' ability to quantify and record their interactions. The computer is the outcome of millennia of knowledge, all now combined into handheld devices that allow us to quantify our existence. The long tail of human accomplishment and innovation that have brought us to today are too numerous to count, but we have been able to advance faster than any other time due to our ability to harness the accomplishments of our forefathers in computing history.

In the Enlightenment era, we had logician Gottfried Wilhelm Leibniz (a 17th/18th century German philosopher and mathematician) who invented and refined the binary number system, which is the foundation of all computers. Computers have a long history and are rooted in machines that can do mathematics.

 For more history on Gottfried Wilhelm Leibniz, check out `https://www.iep.utm.edu/leib-met/`.

Early history – the 17th to 19th centuries

During the industrial revolution, we find an explosion of shared ideas accompanying banking, the stock market, and the industrialization of the workforce that led to the invention of many machines that helped increase productivity while decreasing the reliance on human capital to execute the work. Take mathematics; for example, it is tough to count large numbers and is a tedious process for any human being to do manually. Thus the invention of the mechanical calculator started with Wilhelm Schickard and Blaise Pascal during the 17th century.

During the 18th century, these adding machines were mechanical devices to help speed up bookkeepers' work. Adding machines and cash registers were the precursors to computers:

The preceding photo shows William S. Burroughs' (1855-1898) adding machine. The invention of the adding machines was aimed to accommodate human inability to memorize numbers and to take manually laborious tasks off our hands. In 1886, William S Burroughs founded the American Arithmometer Company. His first U.S. patent was a nine-digit keyboard and a printing mechanism that would print out the total of the computation, with the original model selling for $475. All machines were crank-operated until the first electric models were introduced in 1928. By 1935, the company produced 350 different models of adding machines, both electronic and non-electric. Adding machines and typewriters answered specific human tasks at the time that our computers have now fully taken off our hands through software programs and computation.

Moving through the 19th century, we arrive in the post-Depression era (the 1930s-40s). Machines continued to build on human limitations, but in 1934 the first programmable machine (a computer) was created by German Konrad Zuse - the Z1. The programmable computer is the foundation on which all computers today are rooted. A computer is transformed by the programs installed on each computer that execute a variety of different tasks. Programmable computers are connected to how we start thinking about what a computer can and cannot do. Today, there are millions of programs that do everything from help us write emails to managing computer networks. The software that is ubiquitous in our world is both generally used by all users such as word processing or internet browsers, to specialized software for specific users, such as 3D modeling or film editing software.

All computer programs are processed as bits. A bit is the smallest unit of data in a computer, a 0 or 1 of a transistor. See the following representation of 8 bits = 1 byte:

1	0	1	0	0	1	1	0
		—			—	—				
☒	☐	☒	☐	☐	☒	☒	☐
y	n	y	n	n	y	y	n

Transistors are organized in groups of 8, so each group can store a byte. All computer processing power and computer memory is a multiplication of 8. A kilobyte (KB) is 1,024 bytes, 1 MB is 1,024 kilobytes, and 1 GB is 1,024 MB, and so on. Computer storage, speed, and size have led to the proliferation of devices from personal computers to smartphones to smart TVs to internet-connected light bulbs. Now, why are binary logic and basic computer history important to this, you might be asking?

Since the 1930s, a lot of innovation has been directed into the production of computers, and we have become very reliant on them for some time. During World War II, computers were used by the Allies (USA, Britain, France, the Soviet Union, and Poland) to break German communication encryption codes. Alan Turing and his team helped break the Enigma code and helped the Allies win World War II. Computers allowed organizations to speed up human data processing skills.

Recent history – the 20th century

The post-World War II economies created many opportunities and the 1950s-1980s saw an explosion in computing technology and computer software creation. The movement of the computer out of specialized clubs and enthusiasts' groups and into the hands of the masses is not arbitrary. Computers are useful, and humans will spend money on valuable products. Just like the adding machine helped people execute math faster, the personal computer is that same idea times a thousand.

The computer was once used only by a small set of researchers, scientists, and academics. Luckily for us, computer enthusiasts broke down those ivory towers and democratized computer programs, which are useful for everyday people. For example, I am part of the generation that had computers in my classroom for the first time. I learned to type on a typewriter first before using word-processing software on a Macintosh IIci. My generation was one of the first to be taught 21st-century computing skills as part of my base education, including access to computers to learn to type, play games, learn math, and do art. The computer in my elementary classroom is the foundation of why I continue to work with computers to this day.

The addition of digital literacy in K-12 education is inseparable from computer software and its ability to permeate the systems we use and learn from impacts our own innovative skills. As computers came down in price and in size, their usability increased to the point where even school children could learn and execute a program interface without learning computer programming languages like MS-DOS. The use of the computer was made essential to operate in the modern world. The power of the computer in our society is nothing but remarkable. Still, you already know this because you are here attempting to grasp and manipulate how humans engage with technology.

When computers started being used, they were the size of entire rooms. Over time, they got smaller and faster. The Xerox **Palo Alto Research Center (PARC)** became a catalyst for many of the ideas that propelled computers into the homes of billions of users. The Xerox Alto systems pioneered the power of a GUI and were used for a variety of research purposes into the fields of human-computer interaction and computer usage:

Research computers at Xerox PARC inspired Steve Jobs and Steve Wozniak and others to design a GUI for Apple computers. Some HCI pioneers that came out of Xerox PARC are the following:

- **Butler Lampton** (1943-present): A computer scientist and founding member of Xerox PARC who was instrumental in developing the Xerox Alto in 1973 with a three-button mouse and GUI.
- **Charles "Chuck" Patrick Thacker** (1943-2017): A computer scientist who helped create an OS that allowed users to interface with a computer and a computer mouse through a GUI. The GUI was implemented by Steve Jobs and Steve Wozniak and their colleagues at Apple into the 1984 Macintosh.
- **Alan Kay** (1940-present) is a pioneering computer scientist well known for his work on object-oriented programming and Windows-based user interfaces.
- **Mark Weiser** (1952-1999) was the CTO at Xerox PARC and is considered the father of ubiquitous computing (*ubicomp*).

In September of 1991, Mark Weiser wrote *The Computer and the 21st Century*. At the precipice of the creation of the World Wide Web, these thinkers, engineers, and designers started to understand something profound about the computer. They began to see the potential of computers not just as useful tools but as drivers of culture. They would become the new drivers of the modern world.

As computers came down in size and started to use software that was more friendly and accessible, they quickly became instruments for education, business, and government. In the 1980s and 1990s, the personal computer took off and companies such as Microsoft, HP, Xerox, IBM, Apple, and so on started creating consumer-friendly hardware and software that could be portable in the form of laptops. Portability allowed users and workers to be unchained from their desks and move freely throughout the office or the world. This freedom was then augmented by being able to be connected at all times through the internet.

There is a robust history of all the factors and technologies that came together to produce the internet that we will quickly discuss to get us all on the same page.

The 21st century – the internet, smartphones, cloud computing, and IoT

The origins of the internet has its roots in Cold War government research going as far back as the 1960s and programs like DARPA but in 1991, Tim Berners Lee invented the World Wide Web and thus the consumer internet, allowing computers to communicate over a network through **HyperText Transfer Protocol (HTTP)**. The world was then fundamentally altered. Using **HTML (Hypertext Mark-Up Language)**, websites could publish their content for all the world to see through a web address. HTML was limited as a coding language and was then augmented by **Cascading Style Sheets (CSS)**, which impacted the look and feel of a web page, and then **JavaScript (JS)**, which impacted their behavior. This built the foundation for modern web pages that both function well *and* look good. The internet is loved by many because of a combination of standardized computer code (HTML/CSS/JS) plus a way to quickly deliver content around the globe through **content delivery networks (CDNs)**:

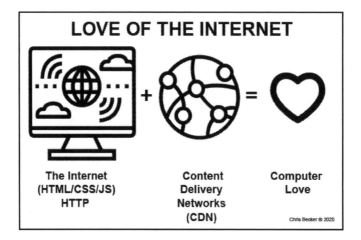

The internet fundamentally altered our existence. You could write a library of books on the impact the internet has made on the world, so I won't go into it too much; however, the expansion of computer networks and the ability to communicate with anyone around the globe has modified our ability to consume knowledge. The ability to serve content via a CDN around the planet has a profound impact on the number of people we can reach, but also on the content they can consume.

Computers thus moved from devices of business to points of access and entertainment. Connecting users around the world through computer networks have altered how we communicate, exchange ideas, and think. The acceleration toward smaller and smaller computers exploded alongside the expansion of the internet, and the communication technologies of Wi-Fi and cellular technology. This has resulted in the acceleration of smartphone technology, cloud-based application infrastructure, and the proliferation of the **Internet of Things (IoT)**. IoT is the ability of everything to be networked and connected to the internet, which allows all things to communicate and collect data. All this change has occurred in half a century. The potential of what the next half-century has to offer is where we will pick up the torch. As the personal computer and the software designed to operate it have permeated our jobs, our education, and our media lives, we start to understand that computers are like Pandora's box – once opened, you can't put anything back in. There is no undoing computer technology; we can only ride the wave and learn how to approach our technology systems so that they reflect our human values.

This is not a history book, but some context-setting with the history of HCI and the language that has sprung out of the computer domain is necessary. Let's discuss the role you will play.

Evolving from T-person into a π person

By picking up this book, you are committing to becoming a T-based person. A T-person is based on two factors, the horizontal and the vertical, as shown here:

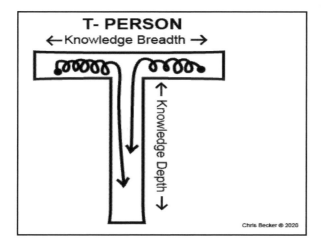

The horizontal factor represents the breadth of knowledge. This is the knowledge that can be obtained through life experience, curiosity about people, and cultural education, and is the knowledge that can produce insight. Insight can then travel down the vertical stem of the T, which represents the depth of knowledge, and becomes connected to speciality knowledge. Depth of knowledge is a concept that applies to any specific domain, for example, a **General Practioner** (GP) represents the horizontal bar, whereas a cardiologist (the specialist medical skill of understanding the heart) would represent the stem of the T. Being skilled at your profession requires considering what your breadth and depth of knowledge concern.

For HCI, this means having and understanding an extensive knowledge about humans and computers, which allows you to then funnel those experiences down into specific skills relevant to your software development roles, and hopefully wider society. As an HCI designer if you have a breadth of knowledge without any depth in the skill you will carry a limited ability to be as sought after in our world. The saying, *A jack of all trades is a master of none* calls out the folly of focusing only on the breadth of your knowledge. Luckily HCI has many stems to focus on and create a depth of knowledge. This makes HCI practitioners more like π people. The number π (pi) is a mathematical constant and appears in many formulae in all areas of mathematics, physics, and computer science. It is approximately equal to 3.14159.

The shape of π is more sturdy than a T anyway, as it has multiple stems, and just like the number π the knowledge you can gain in HCI goes on and on just like π (pi). A π person has a stable two-legged base:

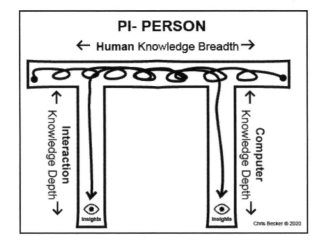

This book is committed to helping you grow your stems with specific skills in HCI. However, the nature of HCI is not just about in-depth specific knowledge only. To be human-centered, it will require growing your breadth of knowledge and improving your ability to approach the problem that the computer can solve with your user at the center. The goal of this book is to stretch your knowledge in all directions and help you develop your curiosity about just how we use computers.

Gaining depth in the stems of the topics of computers and interaction is no easy task, and knowledge of humans takes a lifetime to build. The reality is that gaining knowledge takes time. However, that time has to be dedicated and allocated so that the experience can be consumed, practiced, and ultimately redesigned. You will not become an expert instantly, and reading this book alone will not guarantee that expertise, though it will hopefully help to move the needle a little. As you learn HCI throughout this book, you will find we use a hermeneutic loop.

Hermeneutic loops

Hermeneutics is a thinking framework that loops through synthesis and analysis, based on the idea that multiple parts build a whole. For example, the book you are reading now is made up of chapters. The whole of *Learn Human-Computer Interaction* cannot be understood by reading just one chapter. Each chapter is sequentially designed for the book as a system and becomes additive in its analysis. Over time, you will synthesize each chapter with those that came before it as you learn HCI, thus revealing the whole. You will practice this hermeneutic learning loop through activities and practice with reading and engagement:

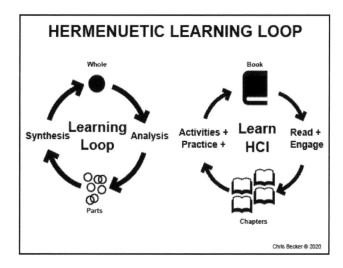

As a framework, hermeneutics has its roots in the beginnings of western philosophy and is a process that you can use to think and talk about knowledge and understanding. The word has its origins in the ancient Greek word for interpretation.

The loops we are on are continuous and will last far beyond the completion of this book. However, using a hermeneutic loop will be a useful framework as you progress and increase your HCI skills.

At the end of each chapter, you will find a summary that you can use to synthesize the conversations, activities, and practice into the whole of your HCI experience and knowledge. As part of growing your HCI knowledge, you will be expected to do a few things along the way to expand your skills. HCI requires a lot of practice:

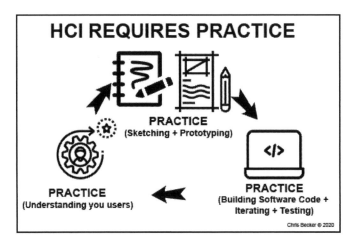

The hermeneutics loop is all about practice, and we will use this practice to grow our skills and learn more about HCI. As a designer who also has made HCI their practice, I will be giving some of my own perspectives as well as sharing systems and tools used by the HCI community.

The author's perspective

I am a designer. My education is in human-centred design, and my professional experience is in design education. These things, along with my work experience as a UX designer as well as a UX/UI curriculum architect, have given me some knowledge worth sharing. HCI is a lot to wrap your arms around. One book will not make you an expert; however, the professions that are the by-product of HCI skills are also growing and are more of a vocation than merely an occupation, and I hope you will continue on this path.

HCI is a vocation

A vocation is a job that is particularly worthy and rewarding to a person and typically requires great dedication and passion. I suppose my great dedication to the UX/UI practise has a part in me writing this book, but it also is why I come back to the HCI watering hole. Great dedication requires time, effort, *and* enthusiasm. Hopefully, you possess these factors. The time it will take you to consume this book will not make you a designer, but the information given can be executed with effort and enthusiasm over time. This practice will allow you to improve, and with improvement comes mastery. We will put you on the path to mastering some HCI skills. Still, there is always something new to learn, a new technology to consider, a new coding language to adopt, a new way to communicate complexity, a new way to think, and a new way to solve a problem with and for other people.

Challenge 3 – What do you know about a lawnmower?

Setup:

1. *Get out a sheet of paper or open a Google doc.*
2. *Set a timer for 15 min.*

Part 1: What is your lawnmower knowledge?

1. *Write down everything you know about a lawnmower.*
2. *Include brands, use, value, cost, mechanics, and so on.*

Part 2: Review your knowledge:

1. *Review your lawnmower knowledge and recall.*

 HCI will work on a wide range of content. Your ability to become an expert quickly in the software problems you are solving will help you throughout your career. The value an HCI designer brings is their thinking and skills.

Often, students have never put a second thought into a lawnmower. I then follow up with: *"What if your client is John Deere?"* How much do you have to know about lawnmowers now? A heck of a lot. The modern John Deere corporation is a global manufacturer with thousands of employees and thousands of products or **stock-keeping units** (**SKUs**). The role of HCI skills, software, and user interfaces in the success of John Deere or any other company is not to be understated. I do not work for John Deere. However, as an HCI designer, I know that I can use my human-centred research skills, software prototyping abilities, and user-testing processes to get excited about improving the human-computer interaction between a lawnmower and a user. I also know that interacting with a computer to buy, operate, or to fix a lawnmower will ultimately have an impact on the business of John Deere. John Deere, or any other company, solve very human problems with their products, and computers play an essential part in making them successful.

HCI is not only relevant to, but *crucial* to any business and the ability to use user research to identify problems, understanding their users' experiences, diagnosing what needs improvement, and helping communicate the values of human-centred thinking to their business and their users are the reasons why you should want to learn HCI. Throughout this book, I will extend my love for HCI, the human-centred design process, and continue to show you how you will be able to apply this ethos to your current and future jobs.

The HCI professions

Thousands of new job titles have been created to accommodate the skills that have been created associated with computers and the essential roles they play in modern business. Rapid technological change is modifying the skill requirements for most jobs. HCI is responsible for some of this technological change. As the computer has come to dominate modern business, the role of the products and services that support humans' use of computers has also skyrocketed, which has to lead to the shift in roles and job titles that are filling modern businesses.

According to the US News Report (2018) on "100 Best Jobs", a software developer is the #1 job role, with a median salary of $101,000 and a projected 255,000 openings in the US alone. The best software developers are well-versed in HCI skills and use them to work with teams that focus on users as they build great software. Whether you are coming to HCI from the computer science space or the human design space, there are a plethora of job roles that have not even been invented yet that will be ripe for humans with HCI skills to fill.

HCI is birthed from the academic landscape where computer science departments had to rapidly grow to meet the demand for the jobs and skills required as computers multiplied their influence on our world. A large number of people who worked with HCI and computers or built software were not formally trained in HCI. Take Steve Jobs, for example; he was an enthusiast who saw the potential of a personal computer and knew he could put smart people around him who also believed in the human-centred opportunity to allow the computer to blossom. HCI has a formal place in academia, but also if you were to study all the fields that make up the discipline over the four years of school (or six years with a Master's degree), you would still probably not touch on all these fields.

For example, I have an HCI-adjacent degree with a Master's in Fine Arts (MFA) in Media Design from the Art Center College of Design. The overlap here is between design thinking, human-centred research, and interaction design. The reality is the fields of HCI are broad and deep for a reason. HCI practitioners in the "real world" work in teams. No one team member can be an expert in all the HCI fields. This is a good thing, as great technology and software are a by-product of the diverse thinking possessed by a team.

Another reason HCI covers such a wide field of disciplines is that they have all been impacted by the computer themselves. The computer is a fantastic feedback loop operating on the ideas we are considering. The ability to combine knowledge from computer science into psychology and then carry that over to user experience is how we allow the computer to reinforce our understanding. The knowledge shared between a team that all have sufficient understanding of their fellow team members' skills can create a catalyst for better human-centred solutions. The field of HCI is made up of many growing professions:

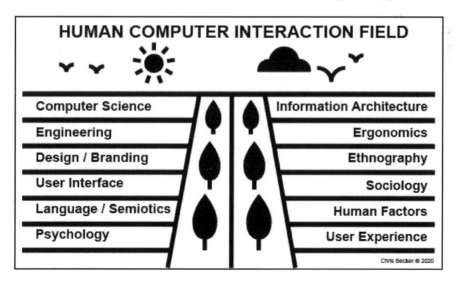

These professions include the following:

- Computer science professions
- Information architecture professions
- Computer engineering professions=
- Ergonomics professions
- Design/branding professions
- Ethnography professions
- User interface professions
- Sociology professions
- Language/semiotic professions
- Human factor professions
- Psychology professions
- User experience professions

In the business landscape, this results in job titles that span a super wide range of job opportunities. From user experience designer to systems architect, to frontend/backend engineer, the reality is that HCI skills have never been in higher demand than they are today. Every company from Ford to Fage Greek Yogurt has software systems, web pages, business practices, and customers who interface with their products or services through a computer.

The concepts, skills, discussions, and activities explored in this book will grow your skills in HCI. It is an electric field, and we will cover what we can. However, it will not cover every topic in great depth (otherwise the book would be thousands of pages and frankly unusable), therefore we are going to take a journey through HCI that gives you an in-depth overview with some critical skills to dive into and identify areas where you can continue to grow.

As you continue reading, it will be essential to maintain some questions in mind. Let's look at those now.

Challenge 4 – Self-guided questions

Setup:

1. *Create a Google doc/Word doc.*

Part 1: Write down your answers:

1. *Write down short answers to the following questions:*

    - *Why do you love computers?*
    - *Where have you already started digging into your HCI sandbox?*
    - *Where do you want to start digging next?*
    - *Why do you want to grow your HCI skills?*
    - *What do you want to get out of joining the HCI community?*
    - *Where are you in your HCI journey? (initial growth, expanding growth, or maintaining sustained growth?)*

Part 2: Review your HCI questions:

1. *Keep these questions handy and return to and review the answers as the book covers them.*

Being able to ask great questions is essential for your career, and being able to answer some of these throughout this book is our goal.

Summary

Throughout this chapter, we discussed how our lives have been fundamentally reorganized around the computer and how this book, *Learn Human-Computer Interaction*, provides a way to approach, address, and capitalize on this change. We looked into a brief history of computing and how HCI will change you into a π person. We also looked into the relevant opportunities present in the job market.

HCI is a lot to wrap your head around, and this chapter allowed us to get excited about the potential of leaning into our knowledge and putting it to practice in our own lives and jobs. We covered an introduction to HCI, which included why we care about this profession along with some HCI topics that came from our quick history of computing. All this information is hopefully growing your π person qualities as you develop your HCI interests and direction towards an HCI profession.

In the next chapter, we will focus on the explosion of software made possible through the introduction of the internet in the 1990s. We will also explore some HCI design principles to sample how these principles are applied to software.

2
Human-Centered Design Principles

Human-computer interaction (**HCI**) is more significant than just a set of skills or professions. There is a shared set of human values that bind all of us who participate in the execution of software. HCI skills apply to our roles as we produce software products, websites, or any other computer-related solutions. The collection of skills we are learning and practicing is also part of a bigger picture that joins together with the long line of designers, developers, technologists, and creators who have made humanity better with their ideas and contributions.

Throughout this chapter, we will be covering human-centered design principles that support the HCI profession. **Human-centered design** (**HCD**), sometimes called **user-centered design** (**UCD**), is a design process that focuses on the user throughout iterative design cycles. The design process allows design teams to create useable, useful, accessible, and potentially delightful user experiences over time. At its core, HCI attempts to solve the underlying issues experienced by their users and not just the symptoms. The goal of this chapter is to give you the skills to identify symptoms and seek out the deeper issues that exist with your users.

The topics you will be learning in this chapter are as follows:

- Understanding the HCI ethos
- How HCI is standing on the shoulders of giants
- Designing continually better software

Understanding the HCI ethos

Before we dive deep into the HCI ethos, you must dive into your interests in the interactions between humans and computers, which starts with some self-reflection. HCI requires a lot of personal interest and fortitude to keep learning. I recommend you dig deep as we grow our HCI skills.

Challenge 5 – Questions refresher

Setup:

Get out a sheet of paper or create a Google doc/Word doc.

Part 1: Write down these questions:

Add each question to your page:

- *Why do you love computers?*
- *Where have you already started digging into your HCI sandbox?*
- *Where do you want to start digging?*
- *Why do you want to grow your HCI skills?*
- *What do you want to get out of joining the HCI community?*
- *Where are you in your HCI journey (beginning growth, middle expansion growth, or end maintaining growth)?*

Part 2: Answer each question:

Write a short answer to each question.

Try asking these questions to your friends and colleagues to see whether their answers are similar to yours.

Now that you have some questions to ask yourself throughout your HCI journey, let's discuss why HCI matters. HCI is the practice of designing computer technology, focusing on the interaction between humans and computers.

Between 2019 to 2020, US adults spent an average of 3+ hours on their devices or small computers a day (https://www.emarketer.com/content/us-time-spent-with-mobile-2019). This is close to 10 percent of a 24-hour day. Given that humans need to sleep, we can assume that they were only using their computer during waking hours, which is on average 16 hours, taking into account a normal 8 hours a night of sleep, and so the amount of time spent on their phones alone came close to 20 percent of their waking hours using a phone interface. Smartphone computer usage has a staggering average: 3 hrs 35 mins/day, which is equal to 1,291 hrs 22 mins a year:

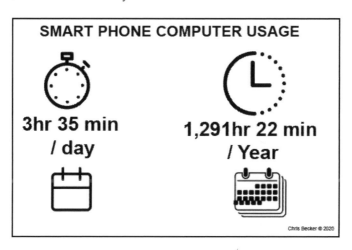

Over a lifetime, the amount of time a user spends on their computers working, playing games, or scrolling through Instagram might make your stomach turn. The prevalence of computers plus the massive scale of devices has driven down the cost of computer hardware, as well as exploded the market for software. As the price has gotten cheaper, the access has gone up. According to Worldometer (https://www.worldometers.info/computers/), in 2015, we reached 2 billion personal computers. The ability for 2 billion people to use computers is a product of HCI designers making software worthy of users' attention and helps them solve problems, communicate, and operate in the modern world, as well as is representative of the intrinsic human value that technology creates.

The heart of HCI technology

As computers have rapidly moved into existence, so has the care we should be taking in building software for our users, which is at the heart of HCI. There are three major factors that an HCI designer should consider when designing software, websites, or products.

Let's cover the three primary considerations:

- Usability factors
- Accessibility factors
- Time-on-task factors

Usability factor

Usability is related to the ease of use of a product or website. Designing products, interfaces, or software that are usable or unusable is a spectrum. Usability is typically scored and based on a set of software design features based on a set of human-centered tasks. The useability of a software product can only be defined together with the context of the user. Usability has to determine what a user wants to do in their environment. Testing users is the only way to determine the level of usability for a design solution.

For an official definition of usability, refer to the official ISO 9241-11 definition (`https://www.iso.org/obp/ui/#iso:std:iso:9241:-11:en`).

Accessibility factor

Accessibility as a factor defines how a software product can be used by the widest audience possible in the widest set of environments possible. HCI designers should design software solutions that accommodate the needs of all potential users in all scenarios. Accessibility (`https://www.interaction-design.org/literature/topics/accessibility`) is not only closely aligned with people who have a disability, such as color-blindness (affecting 1 in 12 men and 1 in 200 women, ~4.5% of the entire population) or physical disabilities (1 in 4 adults in the United States, or ~26% of the entire population) but also encompasses anyone facing physical barriers, such as being forced to multitask or using a screen outdoors. The UX/UI Möbius strip is a continuum of usability and accessibility considerations as we design solutions for people:

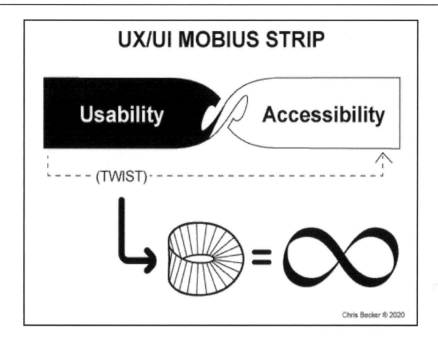

The Möbius strip (https://www.math.hmc.edu/~gu/curves_and_surfaces/surfaces/moebius.html) is a unique shape—it can be constructed by cutting a long strip of paper, putting a half twist in it, and gluing the ends of the strip together. The resulting object has one continuous shape; if you were to take your finger and draw along the flat space of the strip, your finger would touch both sides of the paper and loop around. It is quite a simple shape that is continuous, just like usability and accessibility. A product that is usable but not accessible ignores the totality of the humans that can be affected by not considering their accessibility needs. Throughout this book, in order to avoid having to always write usable and accessible together, we need to understand that these terms are connected, and if we say something is usable, we include the accessibility factor.

For example, if we test a software solution for its usability, then, of course, accessibility to part of that test. A product, service, or interface that is not accessible is not usable.

Usability and accessibility are cornerstones in Universal Design (http://universaldesign.ie/What-is-Universal-Design/), a goal of HCI solutions. There are many books and articles on Universal Design, but the main idea is that a designer should consider the diverse needs and abilities of their users throughout the design process. Universal Design creates products, services, and environments that meet users' needs.

Time-on-task factor

A unique factor for any computer is time. Time is a function of the required user task plus the context/interface plus the environment. For example, if the job is to fill out a form to receive information about a product, then time is defined by how long it takes your user to complete the form successfully. The form completion then needs to be understood on which modality—smartwatch, mobile phone, tablet, computer, smart TV, smart speaker, and so on—along with the time of day and under which environment. Concentrating on time requires HCI to deeply understand our users and respect their time when designing solutions.

Because not all tasks require the same time, it is essential for HCI designers to understand the job that is being done by the user before evaluating the time required to accomplish the desired task. Time is an important factor in determining the usability of a software solution. If an HCI designer values their users' time, they will design solutions that use up the appropriate amount of time to solve a problem.

The user has time expectations and the software system has time requirements. For example, search in a web browser for the Google search engine. The time it takes a user to type/speak the search item and hit **Google search** is relatively small. This request activates the system time requirements by the Google search engine, which has to receive the "query," parse the content, cross-reference it between keywords, and then return a list of content related to the search query back to your web browser. Hopefully, this is also fast, but system time requirements are reliant on communication speeds and internet connectivity. The time required by the system is interconnected to other systems that supply the software data and thus impacts the time expectations of a user. When an HCI designer considers time-on-task, they should consider the entire software and technology system in order to deliver the best user experience.

The holy trinity (mirepoix) of HCI

HCI skills are linked to these three factors, and we will be using them throughout our process in growing our HCI skills. If you like to cook, you can think of usability/accessibility/time-on-task like the mirepoix of HCI. Mirepoix (`https://www.marthastewart.com/268585/mirepoix`), the holy trinity of cooking, is the combination of carrots, onions, and celery, for those you that don't know your French cuisine. The mirepoix of cooking is translatable to the mirepoix of HCI:

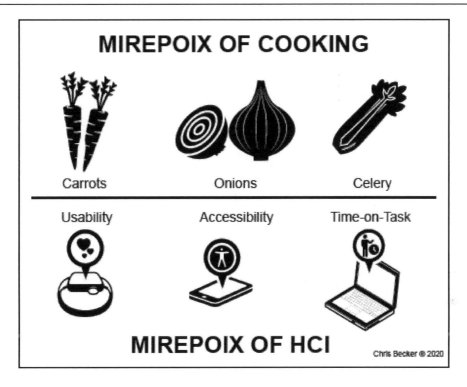

A wide variety of dishes, stocks, soups, stews, and sauces use the combination of these three ingredients for their flavor base. Usability/accessibility/time-on-task is also at the core of all HCI solutions and, like mirepoix, make all sorts of user interfaces, products, services, websites, and software better.

 Note: HCI and cooking conceptually have a lot in common —they both combine a lot of different skills to create experiences and treat users with dignity. I will be using the chef analogy throughout this book, so if you are reading this before eating, be warned!

The ability to use and improve your root HCI skills is essential as all the professions that stem from HCI hold these skills necessary. The occupations that utilize HCI skills when designing and building computer technology are multidisciplinary. The explosion of technology systems, the internet, and application services has resulted in tons of demand for people who can execute software and web solutions.

Some HCI professions

It is required that those working in professions that use HCI skills are experts in usability/accessibility/time-on-task; otherwise, they would be producing solutions that are not used by their users. The HCI profession opportunities that stem from HCI skills include the following:

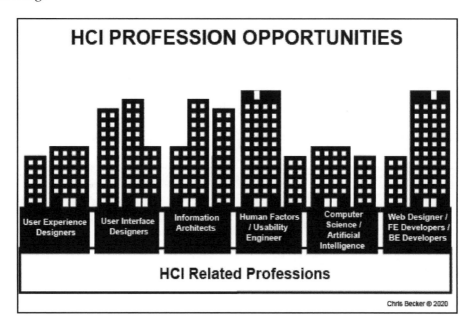

This can be further explained with the following list:

- **User experience designer (my background)**: Research and design products and services using a design process that places user satisfaction with a product at the center. A UX designer improves the end-to-end experience of a product by considering the usability, accessibility, and desirability of a solution. Includes other user experience professions, such as service design, learning experience, user-centered research, user strategy, UX writing, and so on.
- **User interface designer (designer/frontend engineering)**: Design and invent user interfaces for software, machines, and digital products. The goal of user interface design is to make the user's interaction as efficient and straightforward as possible, in terms of accomplishing user goals within an HCD. Includes other user interface professions, such as visual design, graphic design, content strategy, UI copywriting, branding, and so on.

- **Information architect**: Design and research structural information solutions. Utilizing the art and science of organizing and labeling information content. Information architecture applies architecture design principles to the structure, logic, and content of our digital landscape to support usability and findability. Includes other information architecture professions, such as system architecture, information strategy, information security analyst, and so on.
- **Interaction designer**: Design and invent interactive digital products, environments, and services through the consideration of human behavior, environments, and technology. Interaction design applies a broader consideration, exploring how a user might interact, including human-to-human interaction as well as HCI. Includes other interaction designer professions, such as prototyper, interaction strategy, sociology, psychology, and so on.
- **Human factors/usability engineering**: Research and design software using psychological and physiological principles of engineering. The goal of human factors is to reduce human error, increase productivity, and enhance safety and comfort, with a specific focus on the interaction between the human and the thing of interest. Includes other human factors/usability professions, such as ethnography, anthropology, material science, architecture, and so on.
- **Computer science engineering**: Design and code as they apply the principles of software engineering to computer software. Includes other computer science professions, such as network administer, SEO specialist, information technologist, computer network architect, and so on.
- **Artificial intelligence engineering**: Use the advances in artificial intelligence programming systems to design human-inspired artificial intelligence software from cognitive and emotional intelligence and understanding human emotions into software systems. Includes other artificial intelligence engineering professions, such as machine learning specialists, language/semiotic, data scientists, business intelligence developers, and so on.
- **Web designers/developers (frontend/backend/applications)**: A programmer who specializes in the development of internet software solutions using a client-server model. The applications typically use HTML/CSS and JavaScript. Includes other developer professions, such as webmaster, **frontend (FE)** development, **backend (BE)** development, full-stack developer, solutions architect, and so on.

Of course, these are many more roles, and some that have not yet been invented that will continue to rely on the HCI skillset to address the needs of a rapidly changing technological world.

Any UX designer/HCI designer/or product designer must read *The Design of Everyday Things* by *Don Norman*:

`https://www.amazon.com/Design-Everyday-Things-Donald-Norman/dp/1452654123`

At this point, you may not know where in the HCI sandbox you fall, and that is okay. I know many professionals that are uncomfortable with labeling themselves as well. They possess the HCI ethos but at the same time, don't want to get pigeonholed. If you are brand new to HCI, this is an excellent opportunity for you to consume all the HCI skills equally and start to identify what fits you best. If you already have some HCI experience, reviewing and adding to your skills is equally important and might help you deeper identify which profession in HCI you should be focusing on. During the process of this book, if you have a unique aptitude for a specific skill or activity of the HCI design process, make a personal note, as that helps drive your future learning, and gives you an idea of which HCI topics you would like to pursue deeper. Before we move on, let's do some self-reflection.

Challenge 6 – Profession of interest

Setup:

> *Get a sheet of paper or create a Google doc.*

Part 1: Professional interest:

> 1. *Write down the profession(s) you are most interested in.*
> 2. *Write down the profession(s) you are least interested in.*

Part 2: Answer why:

> *Write down why you are interested or not interested in these HCI professions.*

 Questions can be revisited and should be repeated over time.

Because of the large number of professions in HCI, there is a lot of ground to cover, and even more to consume to be knowledgeable in HCI, and knowing what resonates with you is vital for future decisions.

HCI is the study of how humans interface with computers. Computers have gotten more sophisticated, smaller, faster, and much more powerful over time, which is part of the reason why HCI and professionals (such as yourself) are trying to grasp, understand, and hopefully design better. In the past, HCI focused on the desktop computer and the interaction paradigm of the mouse and keyboard. Other paradigms exist and will be discussed throughout this book.

The reality is that we have all used software that is frustrating, encountered a web page where we couldn't complete a task, or used an application that made you say out loud "Why does it work like this?! No?! Is that just me?". As the author, I am relying on the fact that a big part of why you have picked up this book is because you too have found yourself in this position, and now you want to do something about it.

Challenge 7 – Software naming and shaming

Setup:

> *Create a new Google Doc.*

Part 1: Bad software experiences:

1. *Write down any software experience that was memorably bad.*
2. *What was the last interface that annoyed you?*
3. *Why was it so bad, and how did it make you feel?*

Part 2: Share the bad software experience:

> *Share your bad memories with friends, colleagues, or on social media.*

 I believe we cannot fix terrible interfaces until we name and shame as many of them as we can. If you want to share yours with me, add yours to Twitter and tag me @cbecker.

Recognizing that the world is not perfect and the computer is not complete, is precisely where you should be. You have identified a problem like a teenager with a pimple on their nose, and it is less important to point out the problem and more important to go about cleaning up the factors that led to the problem in the first place.

At its core, we use our understanding of computers, design, and interaction to solve human problems first. The **H** comes first for a reason. Designing solutions for human beings is at the center of all HCI thinking, and we want to design for everyone the best we can. Humans want usable solutions (usability), and we want as many people as possible to use our solutions (accessibility) so that they can accomplish their tasks (time-on-task) and hopefully repeat the process and share its value with more and more users. We are repeating the cycle and value for HCI designers to solve software solutions.

The process starts with understanding humans, and a big question to ask is "*What do users (humans) need?*".

Human needs come first. This is an essential ethos in HCI and HCD. Our ability to relate why a computer can help a user with their needs is connected deeply with understanding their needs first. Users are our primary responsibility, and we want to make sure we know them deeply before relying on the computer to solve their problems. To give us a starting place for thinking about users' needs, let's document some needs to start.

Challenge 8 – Human needs identification table

Setup:

- *Create a Google doc with a table for listing human needs.*

Part 1: Human needs:

1. *Set a timer for 10 mins.*
2. *Write down as many human needs you can think of.*

Part 2: Human needs from the computer:

1. *Set a timer for 5 mins.*
2. *Write down as many human needs from a computer.*

An example of what your human needs table might look like is as follows:

Part 1: Make a list of human (user) needs (write down a many needs as you can).	• (list needs)	• (list needs)
Part 2: List human needs from a computer.	• (list (user) needs) >	• (list (user) needs)

 Use Google Sheets to make a quick list.

Some human needs are enormous—for example, the need to be loved. Technology cannot necessarily solve this user's need. I'm sorry to let you know, but your smartphone does not love you back; however, it does assist in users communicating and transmitting messages that convey love. Love is a human quality, and when software developers consider the user's needs and understand that software is about connecting one person to another, then the ability to convey emotion is an essential feature. The connection that phones make with others using the software it controls places more emphasis on the software to be usable, useful, delightful, and beloved because it is being relied on by its users to communicate their emotions. Because the use of these devices helps users express emotions, its result in users personifying glass and aluminum to say things such as "I love my phone" is nothing short of remarkable. Making it highly usable and accessible, and tasks for sending emotions quickly and easily plays an essential role in this emotional transfer. Done? Great! Congratulations, you are on your way to focusing your human needs barometer.

Throughout this book, we are going to grow your ability to sniff out users' needs and ultimately find ways to meet them with a software interface. I hope that you captured many more user needs than the 20 slots provided, and if you made a Google sheet, you could continue to add to them. There are thousands of user needs. As you can imagine, not all needs are immediately solvable through computer technology; for example, the human need to transport from point A to point B through teleportation. Teleportation is not yet a viable technology, although it would be cool.

Users still need to get from point A to point B, and there is a technology that exists that is designed to assist in solving that need—for example, Google Maps. Many users are unaware of when they are interacting with a usable and accessible software solution but will say things such as "I can't leave the house without my phone" or "I love my phone." Relying on a software solution over time creates computer love:

We will discuss user needs in greater depth; however, the vast landscape of user needs is inherently dynamic. The needs of today are not necessarily the needs of tomorrow, which is the opportunity we have as HCI designers. HCI is uniquely adept at solving problems within these changing user needs. Our growing knowledge of computers and their impact on users is made possible because we can ask:

How can a computer help solve this user (human) need?

We start by understanding that humans design computers. It is not an alien technology gifted from a far-off world. We made it, and we can remake it when and if we want. Computers and the internet, a network of interconnected computers, operate in the service of human needs. The creation of software interfaces is the expression of how technology can help solve users' needs.

For example, email. Mail has existed as a communication standard for millennia. In Greece, Pheidippides, a Greek soldier, ran between Marathon and Athens (40 kilometers) to deliver a message (which very well could have been the first letter delivery) of the defeat of Persian foe at the Battle of Marathon. Tragically, he died from exhaustion. This is the modern-day story and justification for marathon races, but at its core, humans need to communicate.

Whether it be Pheidippides with an announcement of "*νικῶμεν!*" ("Hail, we are the winner!"), to papyrus scrolls, to parchment decrees, to letters from the wild, wild west, to modern-day Instagram Stories, the through-line is that human beings have always invented ways to communicate more effectively. Email became a dominant driver for introducing consumers to a new way to communicate: the internet. Email used the efficiency of computer networks to advance how we communicate. It fundamentally changed how businesses and computer users operate.

Email did not replace the role of handwritten letters, although it may have diminished its prominence in users' needs to communicate. Email and its many iterations are the extensions of humans' need to talk. Email as a solution for communication through the internet is also a compelling case as its ability to be widely adopted by users and corporations. Its mass appeal has also spawned a whole new set of problems. An email is not a perfected communication modality, and it is just another version propped up through technology and advanced through software. The ease of use and convenience of email has lead to its overuse.

Users are regularly over-communicated with through email. We had to invent terms for unwanted email: spam. Spam is often a legal term used to describe an electronic promotional message sent to a consumer without the consumer's prior request or consent. Spam makes up a large percentage of all emails and is frankly annoying (`https://www.spamlaws.com/spam-stats.html`). This is a function of how the system is designed. Spam email is made possible because computers can automate email messages and propagate them across billions of email addresses. HCI has had deep hooks into understanding the power of technical communication solutions and how it impacts the speed and efficiency of how we keep in touch. As spam increases, so does the inability of our email software to handle the sheer volume of communications. The nuisance of unwanted email has resulted in many different iterations and software solutions, from Gmail, to Apple Mail, to Microsoft Outlook, and others. The reality is that the problems emails solved created a whole set of new issues that were hard to anticipate.

These new problems are linked with and multiplied by the volume they make a user capable of. Office work is not necessarily about email, but the pure dominance of the communication software has resulted in workers being conditioned to consider email "work." Email is one of the many technologies that require HCI professionals; with them, it wouldn't exist, and it could potentially be an even worse experience. I am not suggesting email is a perfect experience by any means, but it has gotten better over time because of the diligent work of others.

The success of email is the outcome of software designers thinking deeply about what users wanted from their email communications. In 2020, it has never been easier to write a sufficient email. Software such as Gmail will actively help you write an email as you type, applying AI learning algorithms and language processing to complete common email sentences. I am sure that at this very moment, talented designers and technologists are dreaming up ways to eliminate writing an email at all. You will just have to think about writing an email and "poof," an email will be sent. We will invent new technologies to address the old, and the implications of these ideas will be discussed through an HCI lens. Will a mind-reading email tool replace email? NO! Just as email didn't eliminate writing letters; however, there will be many other considerations, and the skills we will build in HCI will prepare you for inventing, designing, and implementing these new technologies.

The reason HCI can address any new technology is fundamentally linked to the idea that it is a tool, or, more accurately, a tool aggregator. Computers may have been created as a tool for counting, and now you can run hundreds of programs for executing countless tools. The computer as a tool has shaped our world profoundly, and not just through email. Let's discuss a case where software has shaped us.

Case 1 – the crosswalk

One of the best skills an HCI designer should continue to grow is their ability to observe humans not only in their environments and how they behave but also how they use technology. Humans operate strangely and are not always predictable. We know this because we observe uncommon behavior and unique patterns. As an HCI designer, your ability to recognize and observe patterns in humans requires a lot of practice; therefore, let's practice observing with the next challenge.

Challenge 9 – Observing humans and technology

Setup:

1. *Create a Google doc or get a sheet of paper to document your observations.*
2. *Create a table with the following headings:*

   - *Total number observed/Total number observed on a computer/smartphone.*
   - *What were they doing?*
   - *What did you learn about your users?*

Part 1: Intersection observation:

1. *Go to an intersection in your town or city, preferably where a lot of people are walking across the street.*
2. *Get out a notepad and set a timer for 10 mins.*
3. *Count how many people you see using a computer/smartphone as they cross the street:*
   Tally the total number of people you observe in 10 mins.
   Tally the number of people on their phones.
   Take notes on those that were using their phones.
   What did you observe them do?

Part 2: Observation documentation:

I recommend taking photographs, video recordings, and notes on your observations to review later.

Try and blend in so that people using the crosswalk don't see you documenting them.

Is it safe to cross the street while using your smartphone? NO! Was everyone using their phones for critical tasks? NO! Have humans quickly been shaped by their technology that they increase their own risk? YES, absolutely! Our tools are continually developing us. This is both a scary concept as well as an excellent opportunity. How a smartphone is shaping its users is entirely unknown and being studied by researchers far more qualified than myself. However, the skill of observing humans is essential not only to identify user needs but also as a feedback loop into how our computer technology impacts our users' behaviors. The truth about computers is that they are learned and socially mediated, and therefore, they can be unlearned or retrained.

I have a young child who is currently younger than 1 year old, and he is learning to control his body by practicing standing up, moving his arms, and grabbing things. He is learning. He watches me and my wife for cues and starts to mimic our behavior. Everything a human being learns is done through experience. Everything is learned. Humans and their use of computers are also in the constant learning feedback loop. We are using a smartphone on a crosswalk, although not advisable, because we observe others do it successfully and then modify our social behavior based on those observed rules. Will my child use a smartphone on a crosswalk? Hopefully not, but unless there is training or more learning built into smartphones, it will be a hard behavior to retrain.

How software shapes its users

The challenge in how a tool shapes humans continues to return to a user-centered approach: does the tool meet user needs first? Identifying how a tool is useful will help articulate why it was created in the first place. However, knowing that our users are malleable and shapable needs to be considered with great care. HCI skills will allow you to gain insight into how computer tools shape us and how we can ultimately shape computer software so that it hopefully doesn't damage us. It is a constant dance, and the reason we want skilled HCI practitioners building these technologies is that we need to trust the people who design our software. We need to know that technology has our best intentions in mind and at their core, they are human-centered.

Software tools are dominant in our culture and need to be taken seriously, which is the goal of HCI. We do know that human beings are highly habitual creatures. Habits drive behavior, and behavior is reinforced through a software interface. We will discuss software habits more deeply as we get into understanding our users. As technology changes, so do the habits. Take your observation challenge of observing users cross the street. Before the smartphone, I am sure you could observe humans do other things while crossing the street. Back in the day, I am sure people were reading the newspaper, using their Sony Walkman, or playing with a yo-yo as they crossed the road. The fact is that the smartphone is just a catalyst in occupying existing human behaviors. Our ability to tap into these behaviors as well as train our users to learn our interfaces can impact their lives for the better.

A valuable part of the HCI skills associated with this thinking is that we can be both reactive and proactive when it comes to technology. Technology moves fast, and we have to react to new interfaces, modalities, services, and so on. As practitioners, we also have agency over the creation process and the ability to invent new technology, new software interfaces, and new services. The HCI designer's balancing act occurs between the past and the future:

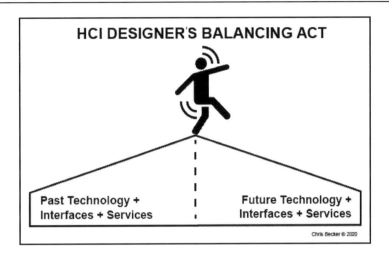

The balancing act we play is learning enough about how humans use existing technology to anticipate the future. At the core of this space between what is happening now with technology and what is happening in the future are some truths:

- **Humans (users) need interfaces to be usable.**
- **Humans (users) want to have access at all times.**
- **Humans (users) learn everything through experience.**

For example, the on and off button is an interface that allows a user to control a device. The interface is a byproduct of users' need to control technology. A computer, for example, has an on and off button because it is operated through electricity. The power runs the hardware and produces a visual representation of the data that is stored within the mechanical memory of the computer as binary code, as we discussed earlier. On early computers, on and off were represented by 0 and 1—the binary relationship where a 0 is off and 1 is on:

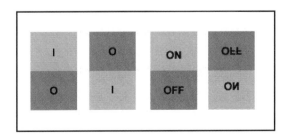

These graphic shapes were also designed in our products and became interface buttons. Over time, the 0 and 1 individual symbols were combined to create the power icon interface. The combined shapes got more sophisticated. They then used LED lights to help the user understand when the computer was on or off, represented by the power icon displaying visual feedback:

Without electricity or battery power, the on and off button is an unnecessary interface. As computers become omnipresent in our world (ubiquitous computing), the prevalence of a usable on and off button interface has diminished. Many of our modern computers and phones make it downright complicated to turn them off. This is not arbitrary as the users' need to turn off their technology is not required. We can argue the human value of this, but that will come later.

The dominance of computer technology in our modern lives is because we have increased our need for it to operate. We have intertwined our human needs with technology. We use technology to get around, find food, communicate, earn money, engage in trade, have fun, be entertained, read, and even lose or gain weight, and more. If we are going to continue, we might as well work hard to make sure our solutions are usable at a minimum. However, the goal is not to solve the minimum of human needs with technology, but rather to delight our users in how we have deeply considered their needs.

How HCI is standing on the shoulders of giants

I will be quoting many HCI designers and other technology thought leaders, as well as making reading suggestions. There is no way for me to be comprehensive about HCI; the field is too big. Many before me have done an exceptional job, and it would be arrogant of me to attempt to relate or even regurgitate their ideas. I recommend making a list of thinkers along the way and following these thought leaders on Twitter. Many of them contribute to the community, and reading what they have to say will not only inform your work but also help you relate to others around you.

I highly recommend reading the following books:

- *The Design of Everyday Things* by *Donald Norman*: Every HCI designer should have read this book as it lays out the origins of UX and discusses thinking about design as a system (`https://www.amazon.com/Design-Everyday-Things-Revised-Expanded/dp/0465050654`).

- *Don't Make Me Think* by *Steve Krug*: If you plan to work on digital interfaces, this is essential for not making mistakes (`https://www.amazon.com/Dont-Make-Think-Revisited-Usability/dp/0321965515/ref=sr_1_1?dchild=1keywords=don%27t+make+me+thinkqid=1589496009s=bookssr-1-1`).

- *About Face: The Essentials of Interaction Design* by *Alan Cooper*: This book sets the gold standard for learning interaction design concepts (`https://www.amazon.com/About-Face-Essentials-Interaction-Design/dp/1118766571/ref=sr_1_1?dchild=1keywords=About+Face%3A+The+essential+of+Interaction+Designqid=1589496046s=bookssr-1-1`).

- *Designing for the Digital Age* by *Kim Goodwin*: A fantastic reference book for just about every digital deliverable throughout the software design process (`https://www.amazon.com/Designing-Digital-Age-Human-Centered-Products/dp/0470229101/ref=sr_1_2?dchild=1keywords=Designing+for+the+Digital+Ageqid=1589496074s=bookssr-1-2`).

- *Ruined by Design* by *Mike Monteiro*: A more philosophical conversation with designers about the role we play, the decisions we make, and the world we want to exist in (`https://www.amazon.com/Ruined-Design-Designers-Destroyed-World/dp/1090532083/ref=sr_1_1?dchild=1keywords=Ruined+by+Designqid=1589496103s=bookssr-1-1`).

Computers and technology are intimately intertwined with our lives. Because of this, paying attention to pop culture, movies, documentaries, and TV can make you a better HCI student and a better designer:

- The *Lo and Behold* documentary by *Werner Herzog*:
    - An excellent documentary about the internet, software, and the way the world has changed. Werner Herzog is both fun to listen to and has some great insights.
- *Objectified* by *Gary Hustwit* (Twitter: `@gary_hustwit`):
    - An insightful documentary about product design and the things that we use in our world.
- *Design + Thinking* by *Mu-Ming Tsai*:
    - Design Thinking has been popularized by IDEO and distributed across the design industry to be used as a process at IBM down to design.

- *Her* by *Spike Jonze*:
  - An authentic look at humanity and a not-too-distant future where computers and artificial intelligence are intertwined.
- *Steve Jobs* by *Danny Boyle*:
  - A unique look at the founder of Apple post mortem.

HCI is a broad field with lots of movers and shakers in each specialty. As we continue to grow our HCI skills, there are several thought leaders that, as an HCI practitioner, you should be aware of. This list is by no means exhaustive but should give you the right starting place to continue to explore. I highly recommend you highlight any names you don't recognize and do some research along the way. This book is an amalgamation of all of these thinkers' thoughts, and I am sure that some have been left out. The reality is that HCI covers a lot of different professions, which is both a good thing and a hard thing to review:

Computer science is the study of computers and computational systems:

- Alan Turing: The founder of the artificial intelligence field
- Steve Wozniak: The Apple co-founder (Twitter: `@stevewoz`)
- Mark Weiser, XeroxPARC: The inventor of ubiquitous computing (ubi-comp)
- Alan Kay: Pioneer in object-oriented programming
- Bill Gates: Microsoft founder and pioneer in BASIC programming (Twitter: `@BillGates`)

Computer engineering involves the design and development of computer systems and sophisticated digital logic devices:

- Guido van Rossum: Python inventor (Twitter: `@gvanrossum`)
- Ryan Dahl: Node.js inventor (Twitter: `@ry`)
- Jordan Walke: React inventor (Twitter: `@jordwalke`)
- Tim Berners Lee: The inventor of the internet (HTTP and HMTL) (Twitter: `@timberners_lee`)
- Larry Page: The founder of Google and search indexing (Twitter: `@Iarrypage`)

Design/branding is all about creating a brand identity and all the visual communication elements that allow a brand to exist in the world. Branding is the larger ethos that allows all of a company's services, products, interfaces, and marking materials to be cohesive:

- Jonathan Ive: Industrial designer/product lead at Apple
- Dieter Rams: Product designer at BRAUN
- Tim Brown: Former IDEO CEO and author (Twitter: `@tceb62`)

- Debbie Millman: President of Sterling Brands (Twitter: `@debbiemillman`)
- Stefan Sagmeister: Graphic designer (Twitter: `@sagmeisterwalsh`)

The **user interface** is the point of HCI and communication in a device. It is the study and design of how humans and machines interact:

- Jef Raskin: Macintosh project founder; provided a vision of a computer whose legacy would be low-cost and high-utility, and have groundbreaking friendliness
- Bill Moggridge: Industrial designer and inventor of the first laptop. IDEO founder, father of interaction design
- Luke Wroblewski: Currently a product director at Google and author on UX/UI (Twitter: `@lukeW`)
- Wilson Miner: Product designer, currently at Strip, helped create the Django web framework (Twitter: `@wilsonminer`)
- Rachel Been: Currently a designer, creative director, and art director at Google on the material design team (Twitter: `@rachelbeen`)

Language/semiotics is an investigation into how meaning is created and how meaning is communicated. *Semiotics* is a crucial tool to ensure the intended meaning of iconography and other interactive concepts:

- Charles W. Morris: Wrote *Foundations of the Theory of Signs* and defined semiotics as grouped into three branches:
  - Semantics
  - Syntactics/syntax
  - Pragmatics
- The Belgian Mu group: A collective of semioticians who wrote a series of books and developed a theoretical approach toward visual rhetoric and visual semiotics that involved classifying images according to their differences from plastic and iconic norms.

Psychology is the scientific study of the mind and its control of behavior:

- Lillian Evelyn Moller Gilbreth: American psychologist, industrial engineer, consultant, and educator
- Paul Fitts: Came up with Fitts' law, a predictive model of human movement
- Fredric Bartlett: Pioneer in cognitive psychology
- Donald Broadbent: Developed cognitive psychology

Information architecture is the design of information systems and environments, applying lessons and architectural practices to the field of data:

- Richard Saul Wurman: Inventor of TED talks and advocate for LATCH (Twitter: `@rswurman`)
- Ted Nelsen: Information technology pioneer, inventor of the terms hypertext and hypermedia (Twitter: `@TheTedNelson`)
- Peter Pirolli, Xerox PARC: Inventor of the informavore concept
- Peter Morville: Author of *Information Architecture and The World Wide Web* (Twitter: `@morville`)
- Christina Wodtke: Information architecture specialist and Stanford lecturer (Twitter: `@cwodtke`)

Ethnography and sociology are the systematic studies of people and cultures:

- Sudhir Venkatesh: Urban ethnographer at Facebook (Twitter: `@avsudhir`)
- Barrie Thorne: Professor of Gender and women studies at UC Berkeley
- Paul Willis: Princeton University – Sociology and Cultural Studies
- Phil Francis Carspecken: Indiana University – Critical Theory
- Marshal McLuhan: Author of *The Medium is the Message*, media theorist, and philosopher

Human factors and ergonomics is the scientific discipline of researching and exploring the understanding of interactions among humans and other elements of a system:

- Stuart Card, Xerox PARC: Looks at human factors into HCI, author of *The Psychology of HCI* (`https://g.co/kgs/QYPRi4`)
- Frederick Winslow Taylor: American mechanical engineer who sought to improve industrial efficiency
- Neville A Stanton: Fellow at the Institute of Ergonomics and Human Factors
- W. E. Hick: Looks at experimental psychology and ergonomics
- Dr. M. M. Ayoub: Pioneer in ergonomics and material handling

User experience is the design of products or services, considering a person's emotions and attitudes about using a particular product, system, or service:

- Donald Norman: The UX godfather and author of *The Design of Everyday Things* (Twitter: `@jnd1er`)
- Steve Krug: UX author of many books, including *Don't Make Me Think* (Twitter: `@skrug`)

- Alan Cooper: UX author and founder of Cooper Design (Twitter: `@MrAlanCooper`)
- Kim Goodwin: UX consultant and author of *Designing for the Digital Age* (Twitter: `@kimgoodwin`)
- Jesse James Garrett: UX author and founder of the Adaptive Path strategy and design consulting firm (Twitter: `@jjg`)

Design strategy/systems design is the overlap of the design process and business interest between corporate strategy and design thinking. Corporate strategy is a method that businesses use to identify, plan, and achieve objectives and goals, typically long-term goals:

- Bill Buxton: Principal researcher at Microsoft Research. A pioneer in the HCI field (Twitter: `@wasbuxton`)
- Jarod Spool: The co-founder of Center Centre, one of the most knowledgeable communicators on the subject of user experience (Twitter: `@jmspool`)
- Aarron Walter: VP of Education at InVision (Twitter: `@aarron`)
- Whitney Hess: UX strategist (Twitter: `@WhitneyHess`)
- Nick Finck: UX educator (Twitter: `@nickf`)

There are many many more that I could recommend, but start here and expand outward. Designing beloved software is very, very, very hard, so listening to those that have done it successfully is essential. I am just one designer, and I have learned a lot from these people. The reality is that the HCI field is too vast to be covered in one book or by one author. This is an excellent thing as you have the opportunity to consume a lot more content than just what this book has to offer. The role of any HCI practitioner is to continually learn, and who better to learn from than seasoned designers and software engineers?

HCI principles are rooted in humans, technology, culture, and data

Marshall McLuhan, a well-known Canadian philosopher and media theorist, is famous for saying *"The medium is the message,"* a phrase coined in his book *Understanding Media: The Extensions of Man*, published in 1964. McLuhan discusses how the role of television impacted culture. How we communicate, how we organize our homes, and how to tell stories have all fundamentally been altered by television technology. It is not a stretch to say that the computer and the internet have had an equally large impact on humankind.

The medium is the computer, and our role as an HCI designer is to distinguish and define the message it produces, as well as identify how users fundamentally reorganize their lives around its participation. The HCI designer role is sophisticated stuff and should not be taken lightly. We have the potential to make software that can impact the world, and if we care about humans, the technology they use, the culture they impact, and the hype it ultimately creates, we can infuse HCI into every nook and cranny of the world.

User research – gathering data on humans

As we discussed at the beginning of this book, computers traffic in data with a 0 or a 1. The origins of the computer are rooted in counting, and what makes working with computer technology unique is that we can use that data record to feed back to our work. As HCI designers, we will use lots of data to help in our decision making for our users. Data is a constant cycle in the pursuit of gathering information through qualitative and quantitative methods. We will dig much deeper into some of these methods, but the essence of collecting data is so that we can understand humans and the systems they use. Before we create any solution, HCI looks for opportunities and user needs from data. We then create a solution and use our computer systems to feedback data on how the solution is working. The data cycle created by computers and HCI designers improves our computer software solutions:

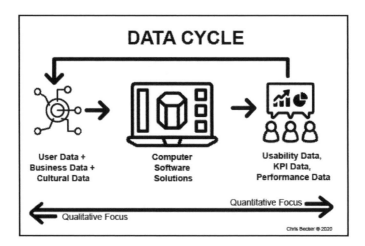

Data helps us learn about humans. Humans are complex. We do not think or use logic in the same way that a computer is programmed, and because of this discrepancy, HCI designers have a lot of work on their plates to figure out what we know, what we think we know, what we don't know, and what we want to know.

There has been a lot of data about humans collected over time, and HCI's goal is using data to make decisions. Allowing data to feed back into our software solutions is about distinguishing the signal from the noise. Like a radio tuner trying to find the most definite signal, HCI tunes our skills to apply the most apparent solutions. Data helps us, and we cultivate our data-gathering skills to build better, more useful software.

Software, like data, is accomplished over time. With time comes change, and our technology documents this change. As technology changes us, we also need to change our software, and this is a constant cycle that we will keep discussing at length.

Iterative solutions and agile development

As technology becomes embedded in our lives, humans come to expect it to be there and to help solve their problems. The only way computers can adapt and disappear into our world is through thinking of them as changeable. A computer is fundamentally an idea, and ideas can be manifested into multiple implementations. As HCI designers, we can implement technology through creating various iterations. Modern software design follows an iterative design cycle:

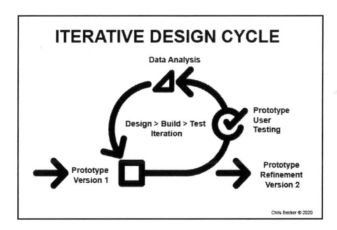

Iterative design is a methodology based on a cyclic process of prototyping (design and build), testing, analyzing, and refining a product, software, or technology over time. As we discussed, our users are always changing, and this makes solving their problems hard to pin down. Luckily, computer software is programmable code, and code can be updated dynamically. In the past, software was only iterated on physical hard drives, floppy disks, or compact disks. However, with the internet and modern software platforms such as GitHub and application platforms such as Apply (`https://www.applyds.com/the-platform`), or Google Android, we can update software quickly.

If you have ever had an application on your phone update overnight or required a new version to be downloaded, you have participated in iterative software design. The HCI professionals that brought you those applications are continually refining, improving, and hopefully making your software better for you. The iterative process is essential to understanding HCI, and gathering data on how our software solutions are working for our intended audience will help us as we iterate. We will be going into iterative methods much deeper in this book, but understand that *we don't have all the answers*; we are making our best guess and using all the available tools and data to create software that solves our users' problems, but as we discussed earlier, users change. We learn to adapt and change our software along with them through iterations, both big and small.

The core of this book is not about project management; however, the iterative design cycle is built into software design through an agile methodology. The agile design cycle is a product management process for producing quality software products:

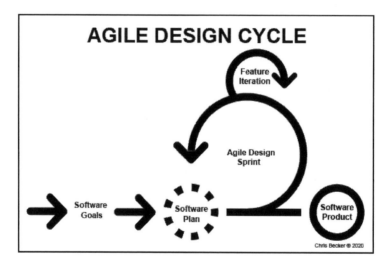

Agile development is an approach to software design and development where requirements and solutions evolve through a collaborative effort within a cross-functional team. Agile development applies iterative design to its software solutions with the customers (users) at the center of feedback and changes. The essence of agile development is that it continuously improves a software product. There is no *done*! Software can and should always be tested and iterated based on user feedback. There are many books on how agile works in software development, but know that HCI is particularly aligned with this process.

HCI wants to build and continue to improve human experiences with computers through software that develops over time through iteration, which is why agile is a better process for us. Iterative solutions with our users at the center allow us to understand we solved a problem and will enable us to not rest on our laurels but continue to polish and refine our solutions.

Summary

Throughout this chapter, we discussed how HCI applies to our lives and the bigger picture. We looked at HCI as a field of study and the history of building systems by highly accomplished professionals. We focused on the explosion of software made possible through the introduction of the internet in 1990 and discussed that HCI is a by-product of a lot of knowledge. The HCI foundations covered this chapter will have set you up to build your own HCI ethos through learning not just from me but also from all the other HCI giants that have come before us. The knowledge they have passed along has given HCI a broad set of principles that continue to grow through user research and the endless amount of software that can and will be created and improved through agile and iterative solutions.

HCI is a big field of study, and this chapter allowed us to start applying some new knowledge and follow some other thinkers that make up HCI's deep past as well as its rich and fertile future.

In the next chapter, we will focus on the origins of HCI and how software and software development is an evolving process, along with some tools and methods for approaching software solutions.

3
Interface Design Values

As a growing **human-computer interaction (HCI)** practitioner, you now get to share a set of human values that bind all practitioners together in the execution of great software. Hopefully, you are learning HCI to join this community of practitioners that care about the community and want to improve the world through software. We only want you to join us if you care about the things you might create.

Interacting with a computer requires lots of trust from your user. If you stand back from software technology, software design can fundamentally impact our day-to-day lives in both positive and negative ways. As you continue to grow your HCI skills, wrapping your head around the bigger picture of how technology impacts society (your users) will improve your ability to design solutions that address their needs. You will learn why HCI designers are valuable for their human-centered perspectives within software development.

In this chapter, you will be learning about the following topics:

- Solving a problem with computer software
- Using computer software to build software
- Human-centered software origins
- Design and development tools
- Coding – markup syntax versus object-oriented syntax
- Continually better software

Solving a problem with computer software

Software is connected along a large spectrum of possible solutions, from those that are not so helpful to those that are very helpful to its users. The problem-solving spectrum has given software design a lot of value in the world:

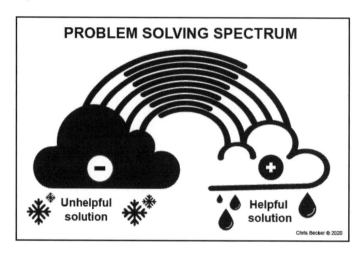

Software is a process, and at the heart of why we design and develop software is that it is based on the opportunity to solve a problem. Problems, fortunately, are an endless stream. Unfortunately, there are no finite solutions, as some problems have multiple answers. Software design and development is one of the many ways to solve a human problem, and as we use software to solve problems, we need to be aware of the role software and computers can play in helping address and ultimately become a strong candidate for helping to design solutions to those human problems.

Positive software example – the alarm

Software technology has been designed and created to carry out everyday tasks. Take waking us up with an alarm. An alarm is a fairly simple application that has great benefits for helping its users both get up on time and generate good waking habits. Waking up on time allows users to get to work on time, get up early enough to bathe, or eat a nutritious breakfast. The alarm can be scheduled and adjusted automatically for timezones or changes in daylight saving time. The alarm is made habitual and with consistency in helping its user wake up, it is trusted to do its job and thus creates trust from its user in the technology itself.

Because a user can trust an alarm software to wake them up over and over again on time, that trust translates into users trusting software to manage their bank account, keep their house locked, or share legal documents overseas. As users allow software to infiltrate a wider and wider set of experiences in their day-to-day lives, the ability of HCI designers to maintain this valuable trust is essential and can be impacted by all the other software that exists in the ecosystem. If all alarm applications malfunctioned tomorrow, the world would be adversely impacted. I don't believe it would be catastrophic, but you bet there would be some missed flights, traffic jams, or possibly some users that might lose their jobs due to being late. The reality is that humans have come to trust, and thus become reliant on, software to wake us up.

Negative software example – text messaging

Software technology that has been designed and created to do everyday tasks can also create unintended consequences. Take text messaging as an example. This is a fairly simple communication application that can have great benefits for helping users communicate through short, typed messages, rather than using their voice or other forms. Text messaging applications are not bad in all use cases, but when done in tandem with operating a vehicle, it can have terrible consequences.

 1 out of every 4 car accidents in the United States is caused by texting and driving (`https://www.edgarsnyder.com/car-accident/cause-of-accident/cell-phone/cell-phone-statistics.html`).

The trust that we discussed in the positive example of the alarm clock application has an effect on why users have their smartphones on them while driving. The relatively easy use of text messaging apps, plus their size and the ability to be connected at all times, has lulled users into trusting in their ability to text while they drive. The negative outcomes of that software's trust can be deadly. Users trust their software technology more than their vehicle technology, and in 2020, we are not limiting texting applications from working in cars but rather adding more technology to cars that allow users to do more of this kind of behavior. I imagine Elon Musk is a notorious text-and-driver, which is why he is adding so much autonomous vehicle technology to his vehicles. If and when automobiles can drive themselves, it is even more of a reinforcement in the trust we as users have bestowed on the creators of the software.

The responsibility of software is vast, which is what makes it an exciting field to design for. It is fundamentally a creative endeavor. Solving problems is exciting, and learning how the software we design can be used in the service of solving problems is why millions of people get up and diligently go about their work. A large piece that binds us all together is that we are solving human problems, and to do that well, we need to value who we are designing for. Let's discuss how we use tools to be more creative in our methods of solving human problems.

Using computer software to build software

As we move deeper into creating software, one thing you will start to see is the multitude of software and programming domains that exist in the services of building software. At its core, software is computer programming code. There are thousands of programming languages that have been created since the first programmable computer.

For the purposes of this discussion, we will focus on coding languages for the web, those rooted in **HyperText Mark-Up Language (HTML)**, **Cascading Style Sheets (CSS)**, and **JavaScript (JS)**, which are the three foundational coding languages for producing billions of web pages and web applications that populate the internet. The role and popularity of these languages are quite remarkable; we all use the same code to produce web pages.

If you have tinkered around with programming or have some skill with designing for the web, you will know that all computer code is a series of rules (syntax) written on computer software that allows us to compile and execute the commands defined in our code. For the web, HTML/CSS/JS is stored on a server (web address) delivered via an internet connection (CDN) and visualized by an internet browser software (for example, Chrome) that compiles the code and visualizes the web user interfaces based on how the pages are coded:

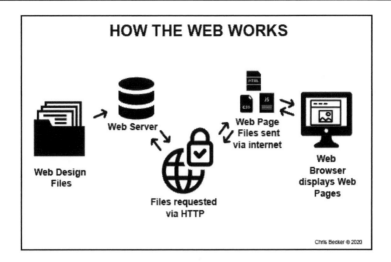

To design these web pages, we use text editor software to write and compile our code. The origins of HTML was a markup language intended for writing research content at the CERN research laboratory where Tim Berners-Lee and his colleagues worked. As the internet exploded, so did the use of coding languages and the standardization that allows us to create software via the web.

Text editors

Text editor computer programs edit plain text. Text editor software ranges from simple programs such as Microsoft's Notepad to more complex versions, such as Macintosh's Atom. Each software is designed to manipulate plain text as you write a coding language syntax (HMTL, CSS, JS, or others). The text editor can then save coding files, such as `.html`, `.css`, `.js`, and so on. The text editor software gets more complicated, which allows users to write a multitude of coding languages as well as include extensions, spell checking, debugging, and terminals control to speed up the process for the user who is writing computer code. Writing computer code is a very specialized skill, and we use software designed to help us code faster or make fewer mistakes. Trust me, it is easy to make mistakes while coding. Computer software to help you write computer code is only as good as the person wielding it. Like a novice sushi chef using a Japanese Ginsu knife, if you don't have good knife skills, it is not recommended to pick up the sharpest knife as you will probably cut yourself. If you are brand new to coding, stepping into software dedicated to those that live and breathe code can be frustrating. I recommend starting with text editor software tools that do not overwhelm you. Sublime or Visual Studio Code is the right starting place. You can learn a lot about how code works from others, as well as with practice.

Challenge 10 – Technology coding challenge

Setup:

1. *Sign up for Codepen.io.*
2. *Go to* `https://codepen.io/.`
3. *Create an account.*
4. *Explore web code syntax examples.*

Part 1: Code with a text editor:

> *Download a text editor.*
> *Recommended text editors are Sublime* (`https://www.sublimetext.com/3`) *or Visual Studio Code* (`https://code.visualstudio.com/`).

 Use the software tutorials to get familiarized with unique coding features.

The reality is that HCI will traffic in code. You do not need to have a Ph.D. in computer science; however, if you reject learning any code, you will be limited in your abilities to solve problems. You had better be willing to get your hands dirty in computer software such as text editors and learn about the possibilities and limations of code if you want to build anything for your users. We will discuss software used for thinking about and creating software interfaces much more, and over time, we will dig deeper into coding, so find your favorite text editor. I challenge you to write some code or at least practice using software to build software. Since we will be using software to build software, let's create a foundation on how to use any software effectively in HCI.

Human-centered software origins

As we discussed, the computer's origins are rooted in solving human problems—for example, doing mathematics. Much of software is linked with and obsessed with counting, and whether it be social media likes, views of web pages, or how many photos you take a day, we create software that helps users manage the things we create from our software.

The origins of designing computer software are intimately tied to caring about the people who will use our solution in the first place. The role of HCI is birthed out of these human-centered ideals. We hold that we can solve users' problems with technology, but first come to understand what they need.

As Silicon Valley grew and software scaled into our world, the role of designing software well also changed. The education of computer scientists, engineers, and designers came into play as their skills are being used to execute software design. HCI is a reaction, a way of improving the way we think about, evaluate, design, and deploy software.

HCI reflects the needs of users, and to do this well, it also has to reflect these skills in how it is taught. For example—IDEO, the international design consulting firm responsible for early innovations such as the Apple computer mouse—has helped educate the world about human-centered design and design thinking. It developed a methodology for communicating with their clients how they go about their design process. The design thinking methodology was ultimately a process of education. IDEO recognized this, and its founder, David Kelley, helped create The D-School in 2004 at Stanford (The Hasso Plattner Institute of Design: `https://dschool.stanford.edu/`).

Double Diamond design thinking is a design process that follows a human-centered ethos—**research** > **empathize** > **define** > **ideate** > **prototype** > **test** > **deploy**—as shown here:

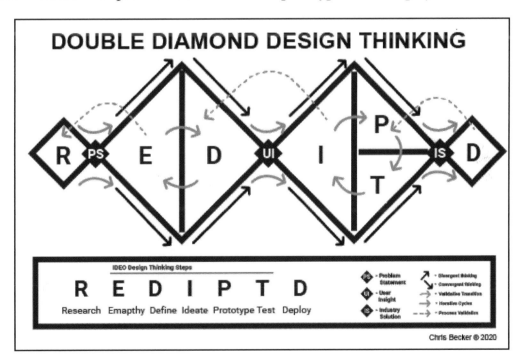

Caring about your users as you design software can be done in many ways, but applying design thinking during the education of design has then influenced the way countless software design firms go about their work. Arguably the grandfather of UX, Bill Moggridge, a co-founder of IDEO and the industrial designer of the first laptop computer (the Grid Compass), understood early on that a laptop computer would only be as good as the software that ran the screen. Bill Moggridge helped pioneer the field of interaction design and applied integrated human factors into the design of computer software and hardware.

 I recommend reading many of the books, articles, and points of view of IDEO and its founders: Tom and David Kelley, Bill Moggridge, and Tim Brown.

Without designers that showed caring about your user is essential in the software and hardware design process, the computer could be a very different technology. Human-centered design is like a bonfire that should never to go out. Without the older generation of software designers, new generations of designers, and education, all keeping the human-centered ideal alive, our technology could quickly stop serving our users first. Software solutions have been contributed to by older generations, new generations, and education, which all help keep HCI a burning-hot profession:

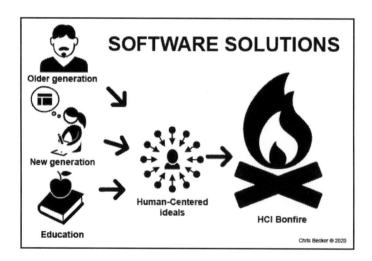

Solving problems is very hard, and if HCI doesn't hold our users as having paramount importance, we will not be able to solve their problems with simple, elegant solutions. Now that you understand some ideals that underpin HCI, let's discuss the variety of tools that exist for design and development.

Design and development tools

There are thousands of computer programs all dedicated to solving unique user problems through the computer. The role of tools in our world is connected to executing a specific task. In the past, we defined a profession based on its tool usage. A miller milled grains with stone tools, a baker made bread with the milled grain using ovens, and so on. Technology also has specialized tools for the roles in the process.

There are two significant specializations in software design:

- **DESIGN**: All the roles and tools that go into visualizing a software solution
- **CODE DEVELOPMENT**: The functions and tools that go into coding the software design

This is better represented using the following diagram:

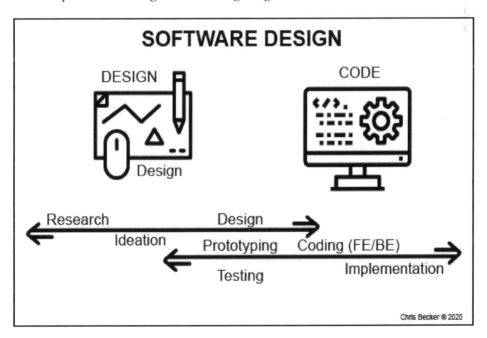

Let's start with design. The design piece of software design has many roles and tools (tools are always changing; as well as outlining some roles, this review will be a reflection of some of the roles and some of the primary tools used in 2019). The roles have a more extended standing than the software tools; however, specialized roles call for specialized tools.

HCI design roles

Roles are unique as they also morph and change, so these are a reflection of the UX/UI/HCI roles in the early 2020s. The following table covers a number of HCI roles and tools used in the field (note: technology tools are always changing):

Role Title	Tools	Mark Interest w/ (X)	Role Title	Tools	Mark Interest w/ (X)
User Researcher	Surveys, web/product analytics, Excel, Tableau, Adobe Design software, and so on		Usability Analyst	Heuristics evaluation, user testing (HotJar, Click Testing, A/B Testing, and so on), surveys, web/product analytics, and so on	
Information Architect	OmniGraffle, Microsoft Visio, SmartDraw, Mural.io, PowerMapper, FlowMapp, Mindmapping, Adobe Design software, and so on		Accessibility Expert	Design software, Excel, user testing Software (HotJar, Click Testing, A/B Testing, and so on), web/product analytics, and so on	
Information Designer	Framer.js, D3.js, Adobe Design software, Excel, R-coding, web/product analytics, and so on		Search Engine Optimization/Web Analytics Specialist	Web/product analytics, Excel, and so on	
Interaction Designer	Sketch, Adobe Design software (XD, Ae, Ps, and Ai) InVision, Figma, Axure, Principle, Framer, and so on		Content Strategist	Sketch, Adobe Design software (XD, Ai, and Ps), InVision, Figma, Axure, Principle for Mac, Framer.js, and so on	
User Interface Designer	Sketch, InVision, Adobe Design software (XD, Ai, and Ps) Figma, Axure, Balsamic, and so on		Visual Designer	Sketch, Adobe Design software (XD, Ai, and Ps), InVision, Figma, Axure, Principle for Mac, Framer.js, and so on	
Prototyper	Sketch, InVision, Framer, Swift, React, Principle for Mac, Adobe Design software, web code, Zeplin.io, Webflow, Proto.io, Origami, and so on		Technical Copywriter	Design software, Excel, user testing software (HotJar, Click Testing, A/B Testing, and so on), web/product analytics, InVision, Zeplin.io., and so on	

| User Experience Designer | Web/product analytics, Excel, OmniGraffle, Sketch, Adobe Design software, InVision, Figma, Axure, Principle for Mac, Framer, Mural.io, and so on | | Project Manager | Trello, Jira, Adobe Project Manager, Excel, Gantt Sheet, Mural.io, web/product analytics, and so on | |

Of course, there are a lot of tools used on the design side.

Review UX design tools at `https://uxtools.co/` and `https://www.prototypr.io/tools`.

Code, roles, and tools

The code part of software design has equally as many roles and tools/coding languages. (Tools are always changing; as well as outlining some roles, this review will be a reflection of some of the roles and some of the primary tools used in 2019.) The roles have a more extended standing than the software tools; however, specialized roles call for specialized tools:

Role Title	Tools	Mark Interest with (x)	Role Title	Tools	Mark Interest with (x)
Requirements Analysis	Surveys, web/product analytics, Excel, GitHub, Jira, Google Docs, and so on		System Architect Engineering	Text editor, web/product analytics, Excel, GitHub, Jira, Google Docs, and so on	
Program Developer	Text editor, web/product analytics, Excel, Google Docs, GitHub, Jira, Excel, AirTable, NPM, Codepen.io, TypeScript, Chrome Dev Tool, and so on		Frontend Software Engineer	Text editor, web/product analytics, Excel, Google Docs, GitHub, Jira, Excel, AirTable, NPM, Codepen.io, TypeScript, Chrome Dev Tool, and so on	

Software Process Engineer	Text editor, web/product analytics, Excel, Google Docs, GitHub, Jira, Excel, AirTable, NPM, Codepen.io, TypeScript, Chrome Dev Tool, and so on		Test Engineering	Text editor, web/product analytics, Excel, Google Docs, GitHub, Jira, and so on	
Backend Software Engineer	Text editor (MySQL, Ruby, PHP, Java, Python, and so on), web/product analytics, Excel, AirTable, GitHub, Jira, NPM, Codepen.io, TypeScript, Chrome Dev Tool, and so on		Quality Assurance Testing	Text editor, web/product analytics, Excel, Google Docs, GitHub, Jira, and so on	
Project Manager	Text editor, web/product analytics, Excel, GitHub, Jira, NPM, Codepen.io, TypeScript, Chrome Dev Tool, and so on		Software Delivery	Text editor, web/product analytics, Excel, GitHub, Jira, NPM, VanillaJS, Plain JS, Angular JS, jQuery, Bootstrap, and so on	
Software Prototyper	Text editor, Framer.js, Swift, Flinto, Webflow, React, web/product analytics, Excel, AirTable, GitHub, Jira, NPM, Codepen.io, TypeScript, Chrome Dev Tool, and so on		Unit Testing	Text editor, web/product analytics, Excel, GitHub, Jira, and so on	

A challenge in discussing all these roles and all these tools in one book is that it could end up being tens of thousands pages long, which this book is not. Therefore, we will not be covering every role in the software design process. However, we will be discussing the skills and ideas that underpin all the roles and tools that are used to design great software. Furthermore, each of these roles could call for their own book and be focused on over time. If you already have a leaning toward one role or another, now is an excellent time to start marking them with your level of interest. Teams build great software, and no one is good at the whole process. Look through the tools and roles list and highlight/check off the roles you are considering pursuing deeper. Comprehensively covering all of these roles would be a fool's task as these roles and tools are a reflection of what is available in 2019, but as we have been discussing, technology moves fast, and so do the tools and roles it takes to produce software. The design and development parts of software systems are unique, making HCI a vast sandbox, but understanding the pieces of the process you want to dig deeper into will keep you honest and focused.

Now that you have a loose idea of what roles make up HCI, we will dive deeper into it, so let's discuss the role of code.

Coding – markup syntax and object-oriented syntax

As we discussed earlier, we are going to use web coding languages as our proxy for talking about the thousands of coding languages. Let's start by discussing markup languages. HTML is a markup coding language. The coding language is designed as a way to annotate a document in its syntax to be called out from the content text. Markup coding languages come from the concept of writing on a paper draft, which is traditionally written on with a red marker by an editor. In digital media, this "markup text" was coded into HTML tags, thanks to Tim Berners Lee and his colleagues. Markup languages such as HTML are the basis for structuring web software. HTML is considered a semantic coding language.

Semantics is the study of language meaning and the interpretation of words, signs, and sentence structure. Reading comprehension is largely determined by semantics as it defines how we understand others, and even what decisions we make as a result of our interpretations. A semantic example of a brick can be used to build a wall, just as a pixel can build an interface. The HTML bricks are defined through tags in the markup, which we use to define content that becomes a graphic user interface on a semantic web page:

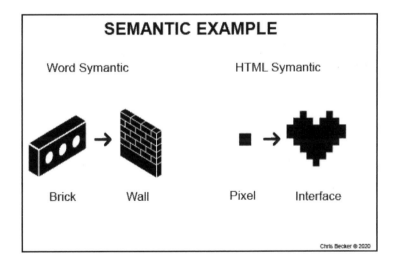

For example, a brick is an object that has meaning in the world; it has a size, a material, and a shape. The standard brick dimension (in the USA) is H: 2 1/4 in., W: 3 3/8 in., and L: 7 5/8. A brick and its size are semantic because of their standardization and consistency of use as a building material.

The reason I am using a brick to explain the use of semantics is that the internet and all software using a screen is assembled with the bricks of the internet—pixels. Pixels are the visual building blocks we use to solve our software problems though screen interfaces. The HTML bricks are then defined into markup <tags> that we use to define a document.

Hypertext markup language

In HTML, a <p> tag indicates a paragraph; because people know what paragraphs are from writing, this tag is semantic. The <p> tag is also presentational as all browsers will display any content tagged with <p> content </p> with that value from HTML. The more time you spend time with HTML tags, the more semantic they become to the developer. The following example is of HTML paragraph markup:

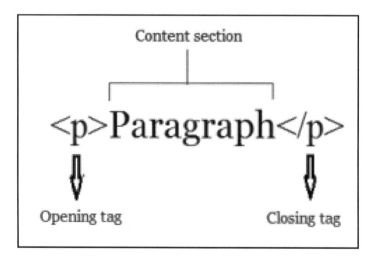

Markup languages are defined by syntax with defined rules for spelling and grammar of the programming language. Computers are programmed and are therefore inflexible machines. The code is written in a way that must be in the exact form that the computer code expects. HTML utilizes a tagging syntax and must have an <open tag> and a </closing tag> in most scenarios. Learning any coding language starts with understanding the rules. With HTML, for example, you learn the tags that build a web page interface. Learning all these tags, as a developer, can help you build a web page interface faster. There are thousands of HTML tags.

Cascading style sheets

One thing that we find with computer science and computer coding is that languages tend to rely on each other. HTML is limited and can only define a predetermined set of tags that help establish the structure and content of a web interface. HTML is inherently limited and can be enhanced by CSS, allowing the styling code syntax to select HTML tags and give classes with properties such as color. HTML and CSS work together to stylize content:

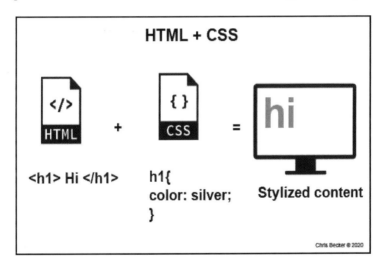

HTML and CSS can go a long way in visualizing a user interface via web browser software; however, the experience is limited in its behavior. This is where JavaScript comes into play and allows the software design to react to the user's actions and execute user commands for solving their problems. Sounds easy, right? Just like 1 > 2 > 3. However, building software, even with markup coding languages, gets complicated quickly, depending on what the user is trying to accomplish.

Object-oriented programming

One thing that makes coding hard is the idea of **object-oriented programming** (OOP). OOP is a unique type of programming that defines both data (types and structure) and behavior (operations and functions). Object-oriented coding syntaxes are modeled on a series of collaborating objects. An object is an entity that possesses both a state (or properties or attributes) and behavior. An example of a class could be a car and an object of that class are the manufactures of cars—Audi, Nissan, Volvo, and so on:

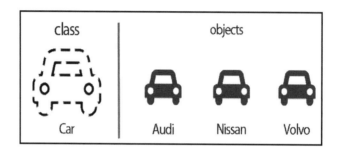

Significant object-oriented languages
include Java, C++, C#, Python, PHP, JavaScript, Objective-C, Swift, and so on. The reality is that our software is accomplishing more and more for our users, and this requires HCI professionals to understand what it takes to solve problems. Solving software problems is connected to the process of producing a coded solution.

Continually better software

Regardless of the computer code used to write a computer program, there are some ideas that make up every human-centered solution. Like we discussed before, humans change and, therefore, a software solution is not fixed but is rather highly dynamic. A software solution requires iteration. Iteration is the repetition of a process. The HCI design process produces a software solution and can be accomplished faster through designing, testing, and iterating that solution.

The design of any software has proven to be better with iteration. The very nature of software code being written by people speaks to why iteration is essential. Humans make mistakes, and with every mistake, we learn, but without the ability to iterate or correct these mistakes, they would persist in our software solutions. Luckily, code is not written in stone and is not impossible to change or iterate. Software is an idea, and we design coded solutions to prove that these ideas are working. If the coded solutions don't work, HCI professionals don't just wash their hands, they go and make improvements, fixing their solution and iterating them until they solve a user's problem.

Continually better software is accomplished through iterative passes, and software teams can also improve those iterations by participating in **continuous integration (CI)**. CI is a development practice where developers add to a shared repository frequently that integrates their code. Each integration can then be verified by an automated build and automated tests, allowing code to be shared across teams and improve the quality of each software build. CI is related to the CI/CD pipeline, which implements continuous delivery. Continuous delivery makes sure that the software checked in on the mainline is always in a state that can be deployed to users, and continuous deployment makes the deployment process fully automated. Iterating on software in a continuous delivery environment allows iteration to be baked into the design-development process as your user is continually receiving the benefits of iterative design.

Software iteration is a form of refinement. As a trained designer, one thing we always hold true is that learning is done by doing. You have to design something to see whether it works. The human-centered role in that is if you consider your user needs as you create a solution, it allows you to validate whether your solution is working. There is NO such thing as a perfect piece of software. This statement should be freeing. The goal of solving software problems isn't perfection, but rather responding to and iterating each solution over time. When you first create software, it sucks! It just does—you don't know enough, and you are making too many assumptions, but this is why iteration is so essential to the HCI design process. With iteration, you can quickly secure your solution. Iterative design cycles of design > build > test are continuous and essential to doing HCI effectively. One way to encourage iteration in software development is to bake it into the design process. This is where agile development comes into play. There are many, many books on agile and software project management; therefore, I will be brief.

Agile software development is a collection of frameworks including Scrum, sprints, extreme programming, and feature-driven development, as well as practices based on a set of shared software values. The focus of agile development is on how people do the work and how they work together. Agile separates itself from other approaches of software development by evolving solutions through collaboration. Software teams create self-organizing cross-functional teams that appropriate practices for their context. The agile design cycle puts iterative design into a plan over time:

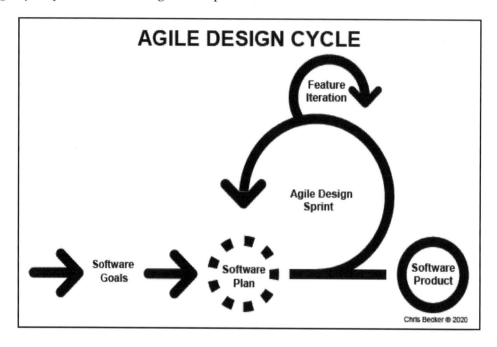

Agile software development fosters a community built on collaboration and the self-organizing team that produces software in sprint-based timelines. There is of course much more written and discussed on agile, including the 12 principles of agile, but I will leave that for you to explore on your own. The agile processes are widely practiced by software teams and have lots of nuances when it comes to clients/customers, design/user, and client/user relationships, and agile teams are not a monolithic group that you will experience over time.

Summary

Throughout this chapter, we discussed how HCI applies to software development and building programs from computers over time. The professions, skills, and tools used by small and large software teams are why HCI is a vibrant space to dive into.

We will continue to grow our HCI skills, and this chapter has covered how software is designed and coded to solve a problem. We solve these problems with tools and human-centered concepts that allow our solutions to not only be useful but also be relevant to our users. The reality is that there is a lot of software pulling our users' attention and because of this, we have covered how design and development tools are at the intersection of humans (users), technology, culture, and data. These vast considerations are approachable through executing solutions that are ultimately code and a majority of it is internet-based because our users spend so much time on the internet that the software expectations are really high. As HCI designers, our goal is to continually provide and improve software solutions through iteration and agile development methodologies, which we started to familiarize ourselves with.

In the next chapter, we will focus on part 2 of the execution of software design through HCI design and development: human-centered thinking through cycles.

Section 2 - How to Build Human-Centered Software

These chapters are a practical guide to how HCI implements the ideas, principles, and coding concepts reviewed in *Section 1*. How to build human-centered software will frame the tangible steps taken while developing software, and we'll also outline some of the methodologies for building human-centered software solutions. You will learn why human-centered methodologies are winning in software development, along with how to develop unique insights into your users through effective research processes that you can try at home.

We will dig into more of the pillars of *Learn HCI* by covering the following chapters:

- Chapter 4, *Human-Centered Thinking*
- Chapter 5, *Human-Centered Methods for User Research*
- Chapter 6, *User Insights for Software Solutions*
- Chapter 7, *Storytelling and Rapid Prototyping*
- Chapter 8, *Validating Software Solutions*

Human-Centered Thinking

4

Any great piece of software is built by a team, and the upcoming chapters will outline the roles and responsibilities for identifying and developing software solutions as a team. Design and development work with the users' best intentions in mind, which is a great concept but is only as good as how a team can execute those human-centered solutions. As we familiarize ourselves with the skills and concepts that allow us to execute HCI software design effectively, the ability of an HCI designer to understand the whole software design process, and all the team members who come together to make it happen, is a great starting place.

Throughout this chapter, you will familiarize yourself with the day-to-day practices of what a software team will be expected to execute when producing software. The HCI skills will also contextualize how a software team works through a human-centered design process to produce the best solutions for their users. The goal is to practice the design > build > test process, allowing you to get your hands dirty as we build our understanding of the design and the designer's role in software. Growing your HCI knowledge will be a process that you have to work at every day. Please use this book alongside the work of many other designers and thinkers and industry publications.

The topics you will be learning in this chapter are as follows:

- Understanding the HCI designer's role
- Considering the developer's role in software design
- Using agile development cycles – design > build > test
- Executing prototypes first as a design ethos
- Validating solutions with your users

Understanding the HCI designer's role

At this point, hopefully the value of software is clear to you and you understand that because computer software has the potential to solve human problems, it also has the potential to make companies money. Just look at Apple, Microsoft, Amazon, and IBM, all global Fortune 500 companies that at their core create software that solves users' problems and earns them and their investors a **return on investment** (**ROI**). Now, money is not the only benefit that software can provide, but as professionals who want make software better, we have to be armed with the knowledge that our skills and software considerations can impact the bottom line of any company for which we solve problems. The role of an HCI designer in any business should be considered essential, and your ability to understand your own value should translate as you grow your skills. An HCI designer has the ability to impact the ROI of any company.

Let's embark on how to translate our human understanding into software solutions before we can start. Let's explore what we know about humans in the first place. HCI starts by growing our user research skills. User research allows the HCI designer to improve their ability to understand, reveal, and ultimately solve human needs through software. An HCI designer's ability to apply user research skills can be the difference between building software that resonates with their users, which in turn drives business value, and software that falls flat and does not have an ROI. Regardless of an HCI designer's value to a business, we have even more opportunities to help our users when solving software design problems. Design can be defined as the ability to create, fashion, execute, and construct according to a plan. To start our plan, we will engage in some research and gain an understanding of design, and then apply it to HCI. Research is essential to HCI; therefore, let's explore what design means to you and how it is rationalized in the world of HCI.

Challenge 11 – User research – a design mindmap

Setup:

1. *Get out the required materials (Post-its, paper, and a pencil or a (web) mind-mapping software, such as* https://mural.co/ *(recommended),* https://coggle.it/, *or* http://www.mindlyapp.com*).*
2. *Take a Post-it note, or open a new mindmap canvas from the suggested software.*
3. *Set a timer for 10 mins.*

Part 1: Generate thoughts on the design:

1. *Spend a few minutes contemplating your day-to-day activities. Consider your habits: when you get up, when you eat, when you go to sleep, what products do you use, what technology you interact with, and so on.*

2. *Using Post-its (physical or digital), write down everything you use in a day that you think represents "design." Use one idea/thought on design per Post-it/digital note.*

For example, "Turn off my alarm clock" represents design because I can set it to go off according to plan. Here are some things to note:
- Do not edit yourself. Write as many thoughts that come to mind about what "design" is. If you think using a lamp is a design,   great! Write it down and move on to the next thought/idea.
- The goal is to generate as many thoughts about design as you can.
- When the alarm goes off, take a picture/screenshot of all your ideas on design.

Part 2: Organize/mindmap your thoughts on design:

1. *Get out a sheet of paper/create a new mindmap canvas of your ideas on design.*

2. *Set another timer for 10 mins.*

3. *Write "Design" on your paper/digital canvas in the middle and draw a circle around it.*

4. *Organize your ideas about design into categories around the central word.*

5. *Start grouping ideas on design together based on similarity (for example, Products: used a razor, used a toilet, used a coffee mug, and so on. Technology: used an iPhone, used a computer, used an ATM, and so on).*

6. *Add labels to your categories.*

7. *If a category is getting too large, see whether there is a sub-category or a sub-sub-category you can add (for example, Sub-category: Technology > iPhone apps. Sub-sub-category: Software > Design software > used Adobe Illustrator, Photoshop, and so on).*

8. *Create any connection points between Design in the middle and the categories and sub-categories on the outside.*

Part 3: Capture your mindmap process:

When the alarm goes off, take a picture/screenshot of your mindmap on design.

The goal is to connect all your ideas on design visually with categories, sub-categories, and connecting lines. When you making thinking visual, it is important to capture the process in order to share it with your HCI team or potentially in your personal portfolio.

Congratulations, you have now participated in design yourself: with a mindmap—a design tool for the brain that visually captures thinking. Mindmaps collect knowledge, help you remember connections, and create ideas through visual patterns. As a tool for HCI designers, they can also represent systems and visualize connections for seeing how things are interconnected. By imagining what you are thinking, you are also establishing an information hierarchy, creating parent-child relationships with your categories, and revealing information patterns that without visualization are harder to reveal. Practicing using mindmaps will help you as we dig into software systems and start to articulate the issues we are trying to solve. With practice, mindmaps can become a valuable tool, especially when done with a team or group or with your clients, as using mindmaps can be useful for more than just flushing out what design means to you throughout your day. But let's get back to your design results.

The reality is that everything is designed. However, not everything is designed well. That is to say, not all software is created by an HCI designer, but nevertheless, all things are designed. I hope your mindmap reflects the extensive use cases for design. When it comes to HCI, design is associated with software design. The technology systems establish the design of any software they operate inside, as well as the user interfaces that allow a user to interact with that software, and thus completes the value the design has for the user. The nature of software solving human needs is why it is designed and frankly why it should be designed well.

Take my alarm clock, for example—a Braun BNC005WHWH classic motion analog quartz alarm clock, designed by Dieter Rams:

As a product, it is designed because it exists. Remember, everything that is planned is designed. However, the Braun clock is designed well because it utilizes the **form follows function** principle. The travel clock also uses as little design as possible to communicate the clock's function. Form follows function is a concept within architecture and design. The premise is that the shape of a product, building, or object should primarily relate to its intended function or purpose. Products such as my alarm clock are designed with a refined simplicity in their application of form follows function, mastered by designers such as Dieter Rams and others.

The clock allows me (the user) to tell the time (analog) through a mechanical battery-powered motor. It also has limited software that will enable me to program an alarm noise through an on/off button and a volume control interface based on the time of the clock. The clock is designed to help the user keep time and to alert them to time, which is a feature of this particular clock. The product is also small and portable, which adds to its design qualities, and is reliable and easy to use. The role design plays in this product is baked into its entire DNA, and even for a product as seemingly ignorable as an alarm clock, it becomes relied upon not only for its simple design but also for the role the product plays in my life. There are thousands of alarm clocks to choose from, but as a designer, I use this product daily and nightly, and although small, it has come to represent a much bigger idea of design and its role in our lives to me. Now, you may not find my alarm clock that profound, and I wouldn't blame you; however, if everything is designed, being open to basking in the glow of something that has been designed exceptionally well will only help in your pursuit to design great human-centered solutions over time.

Challenge 12 – Product and software inspiration

Setup:

> *Get out a sheet of paper and/or create a Google doc.*

Part 1: Document product inspiration:

> *Write down five products that you think have an excellent design and why.*
> *Great product: _____ why: _____*

Part 2: Document software inspiration:

> *Write down five software applications that you think have a great design and why.*
> *Great software design: _____ why:_____*

I hope these products and software inspirations are represented on your design mindmap from *Challenge 11*. If not, go back and add them and refresh your mindmap.

The reason design has played a significant role throughout history is ultimate—design creates tools, and humans use tools. If we design better tools, then users will seek out tools that work better. When tools work better, we evaluate these tools to have a "better design." The exact same logic applies to software design except on a global scale. Great software exists, and it is trained in our users over time. How many of you learned to use a computer during grade school or before? I bet the vast majority of you reading this book have a hard time distinguishing education before and after computers. I am the product of a Macintosh computer strategy, where they placed their computers into our elementary school classrooms and beyond to teach computer skills. I technically learned how to type on an electric typewriter but quickly upgraded to the Apple IIci computers, which is my first computer memory.

Challenge 13 – First computer experience

Setup:

> *Get out a sheet of paper/create a Google Doc.*

Part 1: First computer memory:

> *Write down your first computer memory:*
>
> - *Computer hardware:* _____
> - *Computer model:* _____
> - *OS:* _____

The computer is deeply connected to our lives and our experiences from education through to daily tasks. Recognizing your personal history with software can help influence how you think and use the software.

Back in the day, when I was an early designer, I ultimately gravitated toward Apple products not because I was a designer but because I had learned on a Macintosh, and therefore, it became my go-to. Technology has both a long and a short tail.

The long tail of software design

Software technology, when designed with users in mind and helps solve users' problems, creates value for its users and has the ability to be long-lasting. The software can be connected to its user through the long tail of technology, which is supported by education and computer use over a lifetime:

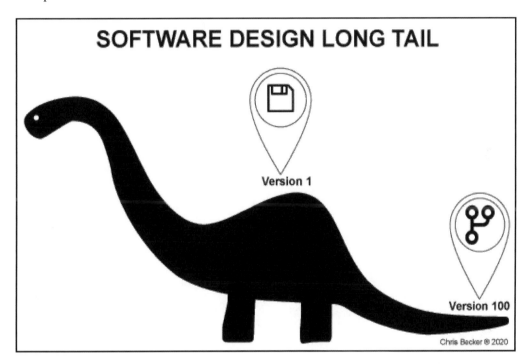

Consider how a baby born today will never know a world without a smartphone. Software companies such as Microsoft, Apple, Adobe, and others know that there is longevity in their software platforms if you can educate your users to use your software. That doesn't mean that software stays static or never changes, but it does equal a set of users who have potentially used their software for long periods. For example, I learned to use Adobe Illustrator when it was at version 6 in 1996. I will never forget this because of the rhyme in the previous sentence.

The following screenshot shows the user interface for Adobe Illustrator from V10:

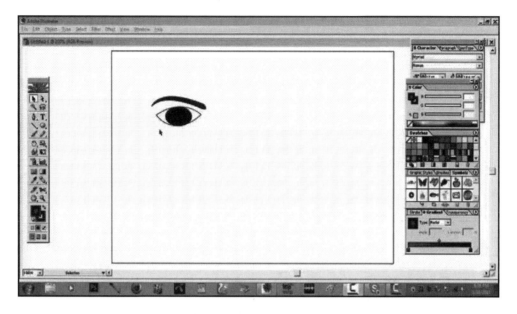

The following screenshot shows the user interface for Adobe Illustrator CC version 24.1.3:

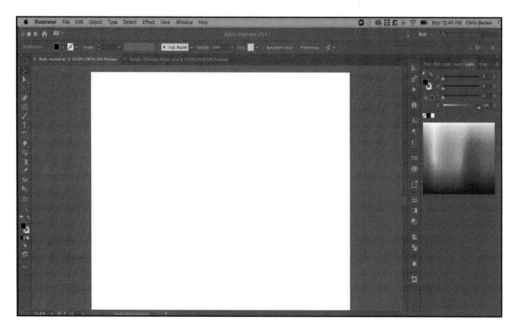

The software is very different from version 6. However, fundamentally, there are still some similar concepts in the computer drawing software, including shapes, bezier curves, the select arrow, the direct select arrow, cut, copy, paste, and artboards, which are all in the canon of features that I learned, and I would have a tough time unlearning them if they were suddenly changed due to software iteration. In the industry, we call people like me with long exposure to software "legacy users."

My father, Dr. Curtis M. Becker DDS, for example, is a retired dentist, and he purposefully keeps an older laptop computer running iOS 9 so that he doesn't have to upgrade his accounting software:

> *"The new software doesn't do what this old one can, and I'm too old to learn a new system. It works, so I don't change it."*
>
> *- Dr. Curtis M. Becker DDS*

Regardless of updates, the utility of the old software, to my father, holds more importance than the new features or improved workflow of the latest software updates. This sentiment from my father is not what the account team wants to hear, but the truth in software design is once you train your users to use your software, it is, after that, much harder to change that software because behaviors have been set. Users learn and then have to relearn a system if it is changed. Some users will be associated with the long tail of software and will speak up and not want updates or changes in features that they use all the time. The reality is that most users don't use all the features of your software.

The Pareto principle (`https://www.forbes.com/sites/kevinkruse/2016/03/07/80-20-rule/#90b3943814ba`), also known as the 80/20 rule, states that 80% of results in a system come from 20% of the causes. In software design, this means your user will spend 80% of their time using 20% of the software features. The long tail suggests designing features that will maintain that 20%. The role of the HCI designer is then intimately linked with knowing which 20% of a product to focus on. Easy right? The reality is the short tail of software design can pull focus.

Products such as my alarm clock are very, very hard to change once they have been designed, produced, and shipped to their final destination—in my case, my night side table. The same is not always true for software. What makes software unique is that it can be updated and modified over time, especially with the advent of the internet and modern internet-connected devices. This software can be updated remotely at will. In the past, you had to buy new versions of software, such as Adobe Illustrator 6 to 7, which we discussed. Today, software is always connected back to the mothership and can be patched, iterated, or changed overnight. We will talk more about iterative software strategies at much deeper length, but software is designed to be updated, which allows those that design it to improve it.

The short tail of software design

Software technology, when designed with users in mind, is not a static solution. The reality is that software requires updating to stay relevant with its users, whether it be to address new modalities (mobile, tablet, or watch technology) or new interaction models (touch screen, voice, or AR/VR). Software updates are part of the short tail of software design; the tail is short and moves in circles, and it creates cycles of design > build > test. The software design short tail is the iterative, quick-changing, and nimble solutions supported by the design > build > test methodology:

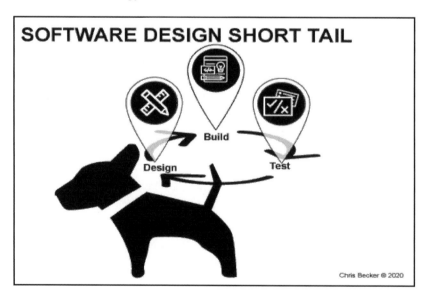

As we have discussed, HCI cares deeply about software design because that is where the need for our skills is applied. As far as design is concerned, there are a few designer roles that are specific to the software process.

HCI can help create the following roles:

- User experience designers (UX and UXD)
- User interface designers (UI, visual design, and frontend developer)
- Interaction designers (IxD, prototyper, and JavaScript developer)
- Information architect/information design (IA and InfoD)

These roles are not mutually exclusive; however, they each have unique specifics that maintain their independence as well as their unique position in the software design process. HCI skills underpin each of these software design roles, and many designers will wear many hats throughout the software design process because they possess these skills. At its core, each position is a designer, and when they are right, they are human-centered designers. The design values that run through our DNA apply to more than just software design but are particularly needed in these roles as the software is arduous, and it needs to be designed well.

However, UX/UI/IxD/IA is just one part of the total package, albeit a large piece, but the software is run by more than just design; there is also the hardware as well as the software code. An excellent user interface with a bad system is never going to create a great user experience. Software design requires balance. This is where development roles come into play.

Considering the developer's role in software design

Computer software is, fundamentally, code. Because software is executed as code, the role of a software developer is essential to the execution of any piece of software. Many HCI designers are the bi-product of computer science departments through university systems around the globe. Some developers have been trained through HCI departments or courses, but there is a significant number of developers who are just versed in the code side of the equation but lack the understanding of the human or design components of the software process. The reality is that there are lots of different types of developers, just as there are different types of people. My goal is to introduce you to a variety of developers and how they can make up aspects of the software design team. As HCI designers, we will be navigating and creating software solutions that will require getting our hands into code, and some of you may even consider yourself a developer looking to grow your HCI skills.

There are thousands of coding languages and the expectation is not to have memorized them but understanding the role code plays, and learning how to use code to solve software problems is something an HCI designer will do for their whole career.

As an HCI designer, your experience with code may range on a spectrum from no code knowledge to lots of coding knowledge. Over time, you will grow your coding knowledge range:

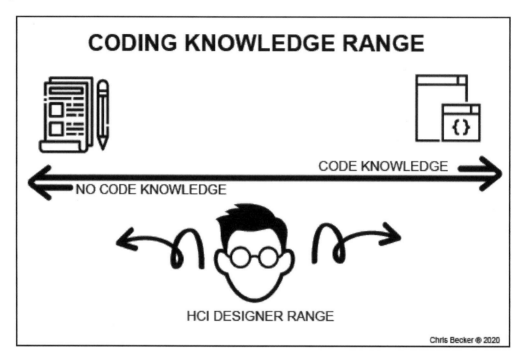

The goal is to allow you as an HCI designer to not be intimidated by the design or code or software. Fundamentally, coding is a skill used to solve problems, and when you can apply more knowledge to a solution, the better, faster, and more reliable your answers will be. It is impossible to be an expert on all the variations of code; however, you can be an expert at using design systems and code languages to execute human-centered software solutions, which is at the heart of being an HCI designer.

Because of the wide range of coding knowledge there is, let's start by analyzing our interests in code as we build our understanding of the developer's role in software design.

Software developers can be split into two camps:

- **Frontend developers**: Known as the client-side, a frontend developer is in the practice of producing HTML, CSS, and JavaScript for a website or web application.
- **Backend developers**: Known as server-side, a backend developer is where the software engineer or developer focuses on databases, scripting, and the architecture of websites. Backend server-side programming languages include Java, Python, Ruby, MySQL, shell script, and so on.

In reality, these camps are not neatly defined, and many HCI designers and software engineers span knowledge between these two camps.

Challenge 14 – A 2x2 matrix – your code experience

Setup:

1. *Get out a sheet of paper, or a digital canvas in Illustrator, Sketch, Miro, and so on if you're more comfortable.*

Part 1: Generate a 2x2 matrix:

1. *Get out a sheet of paper or a new digital canvas.*
2. *Create a 2x2 matrix (see illustration) and label the X axis* Software Development *and the Y axis* Code Complexity.
3. *Label the left side of the horizontal scale* Front End *and right side* Back End.
4. *Label the top side of the vertical scale* High *and the bottom side* Low:

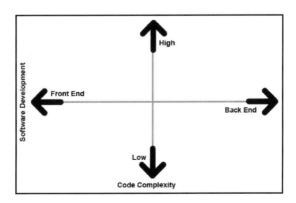

Part 2: Plot coding languages on the 2x2 matrix:

1. *With your 2x2 matrix, do some research using Google of frontend coding languages.*
2. *Plot the languages based on the matrix scales in blue:*
   - For example, HTML will be in the lower-left corner (frontend and low complexity).
3. *Do some research using Google of backend coding languages.*
4. *Plot the languages based on the matrix scales in red:*
   - For example, Python will be in the upper-right corner (backend and high complexity).

Part 3: Capture your process:

1. *Take a picture/screenshot of your matrix.*
2. *Place your initials next to the coding languages you know or are interested to learn about.*

 Your 2x2 matrix should try and cover the landscape of software development code opportunities. Add what you know off the top of your head first before doing research and adding coding languages you are not as familiar with.

Congratulations, you have now participated in more design and research yourself—a 2x2 matrix is used to reveal insights and findings on any two topics. Plotting ideas and data points on the matrix will help determine your own knowledge or lead to new insights about your level of interest in the development side of the equation.

After plotting your understanding of the world of software development, what have you learned? The reality is that code is complex and requires lots of studying to become good at it. HCI skills can also apply to may development roles. Use Google to look up each of the following job roles:

- Systems architect (IA and InfoD)
- UX engineer (web dev)
- User interface developer (frontend dev)
- Interaction developer (JS dev, prototyper, and **object-oriented-programming (OOP)**)
- Backend engineer (web dev)

These roles are not mutually exclusive as well; however, they each have unique specifics that maintain their independence as well as their unique position in the software design process. HCI skills underpin each of these software development roles, and many developers will wear many hats throughout the software design process because they possess these skills. At its core, each position is a developer, and when they are right, they are human-centered developers. The development values that run through our DNA apply to more than just software but are particularly needed in these roles as the software is arduous, and it needs to be developed well.

However, system arch/web dev/FE dev/interaction dev/BE dev is just one part of the total package that might write the code, but should also be code that is solving the right problem. Design and development are connected. A wonderfully coded button or software feature that is not needed by your user is a waste. Just like the design side, software requires balance. This is where design roles come into play. The better each team member understands their role and value, the better the team effort is at creating great software because software design and development is a team effort:

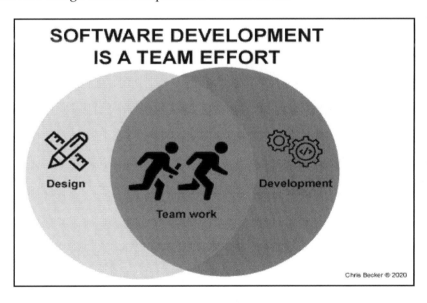

We are a team, and teams that run the race together get further. HCI skills such as design methods of mindmaps and 2x2 matrices are the tools that we hand off to each other. Software design requires a team with the ability to be able to sprint and hand off skills that keep each other running the race. The better each side understands and trusts their team members to handle that portion of the competition, the better the software will be. We will discuss more about this race next, but remember to keep practicing your design tools.

Using agile development cycles

How does HCI build great software? This is a tough question to crack. If it were easy, every piece of software would be great. Instead, it is tough and made even harder as humans adapt to technology, demanding more from our software interfaces, and embed software into their daily lives. There is some luck that goes into getting software right, and it is found at the bottom of caring about your user first. Any piece of software can be made even harder through the choices a team makes about the process of how they design and develop. The challenge is in how much risk versus reward a software team is willing to carry throughout the design and development process. Some software gets built with high risk, where all the assumptions and requirements are gathered up front. Then, all the features are designed at once, and all the elements are developed before everything is tested and launched into the world as a fully baked software solution.

The waterfall design and development process

The waterfall design process is a high-risk, high-reward method, and some businesses like a waterfall process. Although, be warned: the waterfall is a slippery slope:

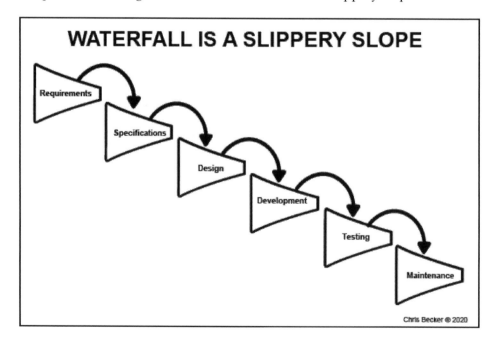

The waterfall methodology is used by businesses for the following reasons:

- **Defines a clear structure:**

   The waterfall approach focuses mostly on a clear, defined, linear set of steps. Its structure is simple; each project goes through these steps. Teams must complete an entire step before moving on to the next one.

- **Transfers information well through thorough documentation:**

   The waterfall approach emphasizes the comprehensive sharing of data as you move between each step. When applied to software design, each new step potentially involves a new group of workers. The emphasis is then placed on detailed documentation throughout a project's life cycle.

   Waterfall carries more risk throughout the process as any changes to requirements, updates in user needs, or issues during user testing can have the effect of returning to a previous step of the process. The risk of having to go back in the process can be highly expensive to a business, especially if teams who initially worked on that problem are no longer available—the risk of waterfall significantly outweighs the reward. However, there is a better way—agile software design and development.

- **Determines the end goal at the beginning:**

   The waterfall approach commits to an end product, goal, or deliverable at the beginning, and teams should avoid deviating from that commitment. For small projects where goals are clear, this step makes your team aware of the overall goal from the beginning, with less potential for getting lost in the details as the project moves forward.

The high-risk, high-reward method has chewed up and spit out many HCI designers and software teams, and for the experience, I would not recommend committing too heavily to the process.

Design thinking, agile design, and the development process

As we discussed earlier with the human-centered design and the design thinking process, iterative cycles are also essential to creating great software solutions. There are many ways to solve problems, but as a community, HCI and software design have utilized a few that we will review: design thinking, lean UX, and agile:

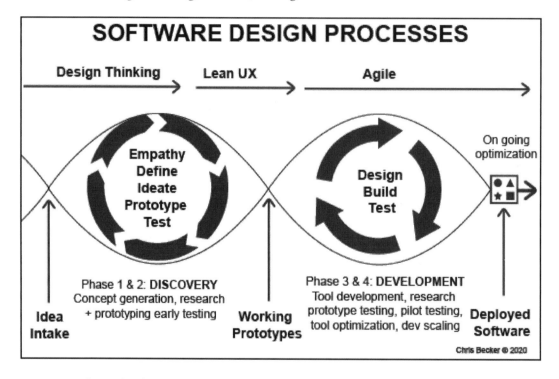

Learn more about this here: https://humanfactors.jmir.org/2018/4/e11048/.

Having an understanding of the roles these processes play in software development will improve your ability as an HCI designer, as well as look for proper teams. Design thinking and agile development go together because they fundamentally rely on the same concepts of design > built > test, as well as solutions, and are explored through building prototypes at the center of phase 1 and 2—discovery (ideation)—and phase 3 and 4—development (delivery). Let's quickly review the agile design cycle.

Agile design cycle

A process that can make software design less risky and that has been highly successful for software design teams is agile design and development. Agile is a series of software design and development methodologies that are rooted in iterative cycles. Agile values collaboration between self-organizing, cross-functional teams who evolve software over time. Agile looks to break software up into smaller, less risky parts through a collaborative team that then designs, builds (develops), and tests the software solutions over shorter timeframes known as **sprints**. Many software design teams prefer an agile cycle:

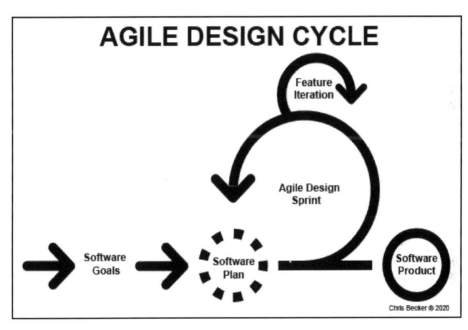

Agile development has become a popular software methodology because all the teams using agile stick to a number of values that help their teams produce software effectively:

- **Early and predictable delivery through prototyping:**

    Agile is executed with sprints lasting 1–4 weeks. A sprint is a time-boxed, fixed-schedule timeline where new features are delivered through prototypes, hopefully with a high level of predictability. Producing prototypes allows software solutions to be tested and supply data to ensure business value.

- **Schedule drive with predictable costs:**

  A sprint is a time-boxed assessment allowing the price of a software team to be predictable. The amount of work that can be accomplished during a sprint is determined through planning and team velocity.

- **Nimble to address change:**

  An agile software team through sprints stays focused on delivering a subset of the product's features. However, agile allows a team to refine and reprioritize the overall product backlog based on user feedback or changing business requirements.

- **Focuses on users:**

  Agile teams apply user stories to capture **key performance indicators (KPIs)** to define human-centered product features. Each feature incrementally delivers value through each sprint to both to the real users and to the business. User testing is baked into each sprint, allowing teams to gain valuable feedback throughout the iterative process. Testing not only commits to the agile methodology but testing early and often during any project can provide the ability to make changes as needed.

- **Focuses on user needs and business value:**

  Agile allows the client to help determine the priority of features, and the team understands what's most important to their users. This collaboration enables the most significant value between a user's needs and the client's business value.

- **It encourages transparency:**

  Agile methodology creates an opportunity for clients to be involved throughout the project, which requires clients to understand that they see a "work in progress" in exchange for this added benefit of transparency.

- **Incrementally improves quality:**

  Agile breaks down a project into manageable units; the project team can focus on high-quality design, development, and testing through collaboration. By producing frequent iterations and conducting testing, quality is improved by finding and fixing defects quickly and identifying expectation mismatches early on.

Agile is also made up of individual techniques that each agile team can use to their team's needs. Look up the following terms on Google and as an HCI designer, you should be able to speak to how each of these is used in software development:

1. **Scrum**
2. **Kanban**
3. **Lean UX**
4. **Extreme Programming (XP)**

There is much more to agile and many books have been written about it; however, this is not our goal. Therefore, I will leave it to you to pick up where I left off.

Design thinking and the agile development process

Design thinking and agile contain similar principles and define similar sets of roles and activities. The goal is to deliver solutions that drive growth and bring new value to users. Design thinking deploys techniques from user research and social sciences, such as ethnography and psychology, to help reveal human behavior, user needs, and task motivations. Design thinking relies heavily on a prototyping process that encourages teams to execute ideas quickly that can then be tested and validated:

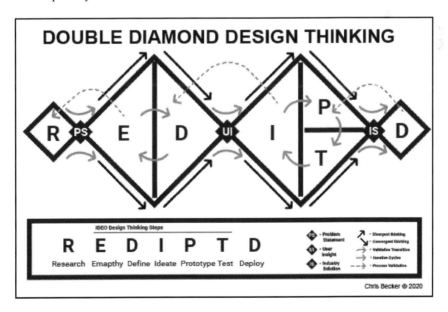

Agile development is also predicated on a quick turnaround process. The development team utilizes customer collaboration to respond and update a software product to changes in a market. Agile holds a goal to the market quickly. When agile development is executed correctly, a primary objective is satisfying users. However, if agile teams are only focused on incremental improvements, they can lose sight of the impact that their iterations will have on user experiences. When design and development teams work together, they can open up long-term revenue opportunities from repeat users.

The reality is that design thinking and agile are both processes and operate more like a Venn diagram than walled-off processes. A design and development practice is only as good as the team's willingness to learn and repeat the process. Design thinking and agile are highly practicable together, and software teams that practice them together will get better at building highly valuable software solutions for their users and clients.

The reason the design and development process becomes essential in HCI is that an HCI designer is destined to become part of the cross-functional teams that build software and who fit nicely into the design thinking and agile ethos.

 This book is not about project management, and there are many, many, *many* books on project management, which I encourage you to seek out. However, gaining a high-level understanding of the values in software design and development processes and when they are used will help you dig deeper and become a better HCI designer.

Executing prototypes first as a design ethos

It is evident in HCI that there are lots of people who come together to build software when the entire team is aligned under a design and development process; it offers fewer communication challenges but also allows organizations to share collective knowledge. When teams all speak the same language (design thinking and agile), they understand the same skills and share in the load for solving problems, which helps the team to move faster. This is where prototyping first comes into play.

A prototype is a usable sketch, a model of a product, service, or software built to test a concept or process. It is used to evaluate a new design by its users through rapid testing and iteration. Sometimes called rapid prototyping, it is a methodology used in a variety of design contexts, including product (physical), architecture, graphic design, electronics, and software programming, as well as others.

Prototyping is a vital part of web and application development. It consists of various phases of development with their respective set of functionalities. The prototyping-first approach lets the users experience aspects of the product with limited features during the development process.

Mainly, there are three types of prototypes, which are the following:

- Paper prototypes
- Interactive/clickable prototypes
- Native/coded prototypes

Paper prototypes

Although we have abundant software and technology at our fingertips, sometimes the best method is still paper and pencil. Paper prototyping is the drawing of software screens on paper as substitutes for digital solutions. Paper prototypes are viable because they can quickly represent different levels of complexity and fidelity. They continue to be widely used due to their speed and ability to help designers and developers think as well as validate solutions quickly with users. Whether a paper prototype is used as a demonstration of a potential feature or used for a usability test, the paper sketches can be quickly assembled to address a user's need and mimic a user's actions with a screen. Paper becomes a proxy for screen interaction and assumptions can be vetted quickly.

When trying to identify whether a solution is meeting a user's needs, there is a large set of assumptions a designer has to make. Through paper prototyping, they can quickly validate whether ideas are worth persuing into a more robust prototype.

For example, the content view is a standard feature for any software that has a record over time. A designer can build a paper prototype to validate quickly how the content might be viewed (in a grid or list view) and then promptly test which view has value with its users:

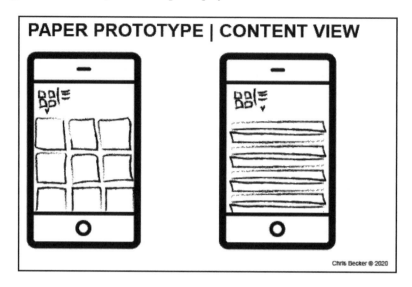

All prototypes should start as paper prototypes in some way. The more designers and developers use paper to validate their ideas, the faster they learn about what is working or not with their software. Every beginner should build paper prototypes first as there is so much to learn from making mistakes fast.

A huge value of paper prototypes is found if your idea doesn't actually work. Rather, the execution is cheap, and you can throw them away if they don't get used by your user. I can tell you, it feels really good to eliminate a lousy solution early. If you consider the value of reducing a lousy idea early in the process rather than allowing it to move into development—or worse, making it into the hands of all your users—then killing bad ideas at the paper stage saves thousands of dollars for your business.

Many will skip over pen and paper because it requires drawing. Sketching, unfortunately, is not a universal skill shared by all. As an HCI designer, you will benefit greatly from picking up a pen and paper more often. I know many designers and developers who say they can't draw. This is a failure of perception. Nearly everyone can draw; they choose not to practice or they equate drawing to realistic rendering. The goal of sketching paper prototypes is not about rendering but rather about speed. The reality of drawing is thinking, and if we want to think through the HCIs, it will take a lot of sketching. Let's practice.

Challenge 15 – Sketching and prototyping challenge

Setup:

1. Get out a sheet of paper (letter or A4 size) and a pen (sharpie preferred).
2. With a ruler, draw three mobile screens: 3 in. x ~6 in. boxes (the iPhone 11 screen is exactly 2.98 in. x 5.94 in.)
3. Label each screen as follows: 1. `Dropdown`, 2. `Dropdown open`, and 3. `Dropdown selected`.
   Bonus: Create a screen grid (2, 4, or 6 columns).

Part 1: Sketch three screens for a category dropdown:

1. With your pen/pencil, start on screen 1: `Dropdown`.
2. Sketch a button that has a dropdown (use rectangles or curved rectangles).
3. Add a category label (choose any category for your dropdown that you would like).
4. Move to screen 2: `Dropdown open`.
5. Sketch the drop-down button in the open position.
6. Include the categories of your choice.
7. Move to screen 3: `Dropdown selected`.
8. Sketch the drop-down button in the open position again.
9. Include the categories of your choice.

Part 2: Assemble paper prototype:

1. Get out some scissors.
2. Cut the screens into individual screen steps.
3. Stack your mobile paper screens on top of each other.
4. Flip through the screens to simulate the dropdown interaction.

Part 3: Document and share your paper prototype:

1. Take photographs of your completed paper version.
2. Document a video of you flipping through the paper interaction.
   Bonus: Share your paper prototype walkthrough with a friend/significant other for feedback.

Do not worry about your paper prototype being bad or appearing quickly put together. The faster the better. DO NOT agonize over a paper sketch prototype; it is an early idea worth quickly testing and should not carry the weight of a final solution. It is an object used to learn from and if it fails, it has not used up too much of your time.

Congratulations, you have now completed a paper prototype with three simple screens, a few drawn lines, and a pair of scissors. Your dropdown idea is ready to be tested by a user, and you can receive feedback on your drop-down button design, categories, and selection decisions. Paper prototypes, when used correctly, provide maximum learning for minimum effort. Do not assume that since you have created a paper prototype you have correctly solved a problem. Paper prototypes should be used to validate an idea or possible solution and if they are not used for testing, you are missing a fundamental learning opportunity.

Interactive and clickable prototypes

As you can imagine, paper prototypes can become harder to maintain as you add more and more features and screens. This is where interactive prototypes come into play. Known as clickable prototypes, they are the basic initial impressions of the product with a limited interface to perform certain operations. They may include some clickable buttons, links, or some dropdowns. Clickable prototypes can be produced through multiple iterations from low fidelity to high fidelity.

Low-fidelity clickable prototypes can use your paper prototype sketches and use a clickable prototype software to add some basic interactivity. Clickable prototypes can be made through Keynote, PowerPoint, Adobe XD, Sketch, the InVision app, Proto.io, Balsamic, and many others. The role this software plays is it allows a user to interact with a screen to move between screens of the designer software solution. Clickable prototypes mimic how the end product might work when coded, along with how the interface might behave. An HCI designer will want to build clickable prototypes early on, often to test our ideas throughout the process without having to develop those sequences before users have validated them. We can learn a lot by putting our software solutions in the hands of our users.

Low-fidelity prototypes can also use sketches that become digitized through wireframing. We will discuss wireframing much deeper. The early sketches we practiced in paper prototyping are a stepping stone into wireframing. Many digital software tools can be used to develop wireframes, and the role of wireframing is rooted in creating with speed so that we can create prototypes that can be put into the hands of our users.

A high-fidelity (*high*-fi or *hi*-fi) clickable prototype is a prototype that looks like and may work just like the finished product. It simulates the aesthetics of a proposed design and approximates the development behaviors and user interactions. They can include animations, transitions, and other advanced interactions. As they get closer and closer to a finished product, a high-fidelity prototype can also be coded where the product is closest to the final design in terms of content and functionality.

Over time, we will work toward building a high-fidelity software solution. There are many software tools in the UX/UI software design marketplace for building clickable prototypes. Go to `https://www.prototypr.io/` to explore more tools.

Challenge 16 – Clickable paper prototype with the InVision app

Part 1: Create an account with InVisionApp.com
(There are many clickable prototyping tools, but use InVision to start):

1. *Go to* `https://www.invisionapp.com/`.
2. *Create a new account.*
3. *Sign in to the InVision app.*
4. *Create a new prototype for a mobile phone (iPhone X, iPhone, or Android phone).*
5. *Label your prototype* `Mobile Dropdown Prototype`.
6. *Take pictures of your mobile sketches from* **Challenge 1**.
7. *Crop each screen photo to be 3 in. x 6 in. in size.*
8. *Label each photo to match the labels of your sketches (1.* `Dropdown`, *2.* `Dropdown open`, *and 3.* `Dropdown selected`).
9. *Drag and drop or upload your screen photos to your InVision prototype.*

Part 2: Connect your screens with hotspots and create a clickable paper prototype:

1. *Using the InVision app, select an uploaded filter.*
2. *The viewing screen brings up prototyping features.*
3. *Select* ***Build mode (B)***.
4. *Build mode allows you to add hotspots to areas on the screen and then mark where to target the interaction.*
5. *Connect your three paper-prototyped screens for your dropdown experience.*
6. *Include a hotspot to return your user from screen three to screen one, making sure our prototype does not have a dead end.*

Part 3: Share your paper prototype:

1. *Using the share button in the lower-right corner, share your prototype.*
2. *Share your prototype link on social media to get some feedback—on Twitter, tweet* @cbecker *#LearnHCIPackt and I will do my best to respond.*

 InVision is just one of many prototyping tools exploring prototyping. The InVision app has a shallow learning curve and it is quick to get your paper sketches into a clickable format. Practice will speed you up, so don't just use it once. Keep practicing.

Congratulations, you are now quickly advancing your abilities to quickly put ideas out in the world and start getting feedback on potential software solutions. You might be thinking *this dropdown is so simple and not worth a prototype*. However, the idea of prototyping is that it should become second nature and be folded into your design process and applied to how you think and make software. As I have said before, software solutions are very hard but can be made even harder if you make assumptions along the way without validating or testing them with your users. By prototyping and building solutions that can be manipulated by your users early on and often and are as cheap as possible, you will learn a lot and also fail a lot, but every cheap failure is an opportunity to get the solution correct over time.

Native and coded prototypes

Native prototypes are actual product-looking prototypes that resemble the idea of the product from a closer view. Users can perform more operations on native prototypes, just like fully fledged websites or applications. These are also the final prototypes from which the final product is built. Native prototyping is attempting to understand how a product works in the real world.

A software team should have solid development skills before attempting to design native prototypes. You should be able to prepare a useful prototype in just a few hours, rather than days or weeks, and without excellent development skills, coding the native prototype might take too long.

The type of prototype a software team builds should be determined by the skillset of the collective team, the timeline, the scope of the given project, and the questions that are trying to answer through creating solutions. If you are attempting to validate whether an idea will work with your users, then prototypes should occur toward the beginning of a project and be on the lower side of fidelity. If you are trying to see whether a product is ready for the market and should be released to all your users, this requires a higher fidelity:

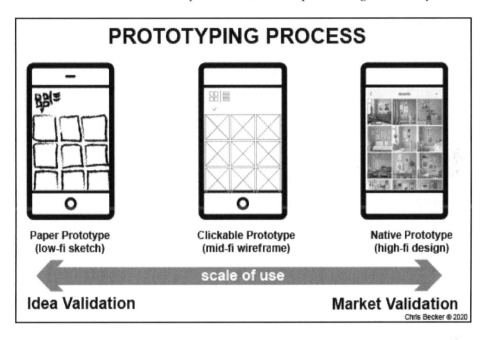

Regardless of the software process and the team that is designing and developing the software, if you are not prototyping, you are bound to make a mistake. Prototyping is a way of approaching a problem, rather than just a step in the process. By aligning a team into the value prototypes, they can become a type of language with your team.

For example, I worked on a prototype for an Apple campaign for Macintosh 30 in 2014 (1984-2014 = 30 years). The project was an interactive timeline project that was designed to commemorate the 30 years of Apple Macintosh computers. We were a small team of five designers—one UX (my role), two visual designers, one prototyper developer, and one motion designer. We worked through many ideas and concept prototypes. Each concept prototype took on a different name so that we as a team could keep track of our thinking as well as what we were pitching to Apple.

There were the following prototypes in order:

1. **The tray**: A prototype with an interactive tray at the bottom:

2. **The numbers**: A prototype with a minimal timeline by year number:

3. **The social dot**: A prototype that visualized the world and what people were watching by year:

4. **The web**: A prototype that highlighted all the Mac user by year as a web of interconnected dots:

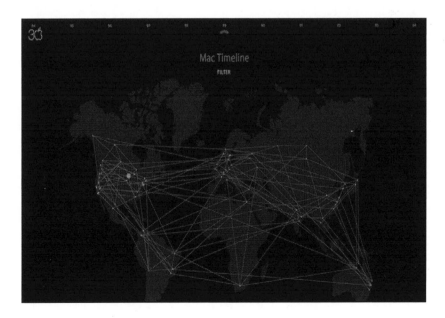

Why build all these different prototypes, you might be asking? Our team was tasked with exploring several options, and with each prototype we made, we moved the project closer to solving their problem. In the end, the timeline project used some of the concepts we prototyped, and during project pitching, we had a nice shorthand with the team for which prototype we were going to discuss. The reason why building prototypes also has enormous value for a software team is that through making an idea tangible, you can then test it with your users and validate one solution over another.

Validating with users

The reality is that an idea isn't worth anything, it is just a thought, but once that idea is executed and made tangible, that is where the rubber hits the road. Software is no different, just a set of ideas executed for a computer and a user. The key is knowing which ideas are worth executing. Since software has a massive range of possibilities and is the culmination of hundreds of ideas, the best way to understand whether those ideas are working is to validate them through user testing. Start by validating ideas quick and fast through prototypes, as we discussed previously.

Hopefully, your hundreds of ideas are not hundreds of features but rather a bunch ideas that go into executing a few features meaningfully for your user. Prototyping, as we just discussed, is about making ideas tangible, but without testing the execution of a prototype, it is pointless. To build a prototype is to create a model to test your software idea. Testing is immensely helpful to HCI designers and the software design process as a whole because the team can quickly identify what might work or what will fail all through testing.

Validating your ideas with users is a constant process, and the human-centered component of any good HCI practitioner allows them to want to test their solutions. Validating ideas can be a little nerve-racking as no one want to fail. Although you hear Silicon Valley talk about "fail fast," it doesn't make it any easier. We think about our users profoundly, and it can lull us into believing that because we have their best interest in mind as designers, then we don't have to validate our solutions with our users. This is false!

On the other hand, the role of user validation should occur early and often, as user feedback takes on different levels of severity to a software design team. No team wants to fail, but if you fail at the level of a cheap, quick paper prototype rather than a product launched on the market, you have much more to learn and much less at risk. Because user validation is essential across the entire software design process, let's discuss the three stages of user validation:

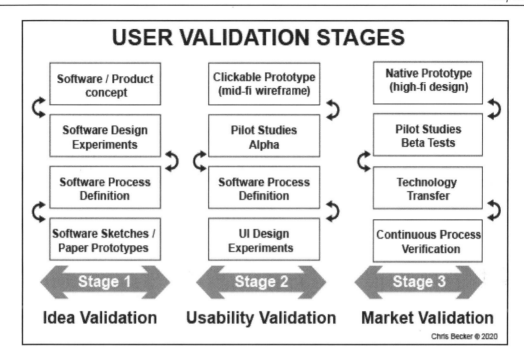

A software product team might create more than three validation stages; it would be up to the team, their project planning, and the business scope to determine the testing cycles. The goal is to test early and often, rather than later in the process.

Validation is critical at every stage of a software idea—from the early fledgling seed stage to the "our team thinks this will work" stage to the "this software is ready for market" stage. Software is not birthed perfectly formed; it requires iteration, and the best way to iterate is to test it on your users.

Stage 1 – idea validation

Validating ideas early during stage 1 allows software product teams to validate concepts under low pressure with low-fidelity paper prototypes. Concepts are part of the ideas that are cheap space. If you produce 100 quick paper ideas of what your software might do and test those quick and dirty paper sketches with a few users and only five come back that meet your users' needs, then the HCI designer's time has been greatly saved. 95 of these quick ideas are easily discarded for the 5 your users have validated through feedback. If you are new to software design, you might need to come up with 100 ideas to get the 5 that matter.

The pros of validating ideas are as follows:

- Ideas validated early on can keep a software design team on track and motivated that they are solving the right problems.
- Software design teams that generate a lot of concepts are more adept at creating innovative solutions.
- Validating concepts funnels solutions faster toward an end product as unvalidated concepts do not linger around the solution options.
- Teams are more motivated to solve the right problem.

The cons of validating ideas are as follows:

- No one wants to work hard for a product that fails. There are, of course, lots and lots of reasons why software can fail, but if a team is committed to identifying those failures early and often, then perhaps they can avoid failure in the end.
- Software design teams can spend too much time on concepts rather than choosing to move on.
- Ideas are precious and can move on regardless of being invalidated by users.

The reason paper prototyping becomes so valuable to a software team's process is intimately linked with its success. Validating that an idea is worth it leads to more software team members caring, and when you care, you make better products. Rest assured, with practice and building more software, your prototyping output-to-success rate with users will go up, and so will your ability to validate faster. When an idea is validated, that is not enough. Validation is like gasoline in a car. It runs out if you don't fill it up. We need to continue to validate our solutions continuously.

Stage 2 – usability validation

Now that an idea has been validated through stage 1 of testing, your validation process is just beginning. The paper prototype will need to be iterated through a usability perspective. This is where feedback from the user test for validation will help the software design team make iterations to the concept. An HCI designer will typically improve a paper prototype through digital means by creating the prototype in a wireframe and turning those wireframes into a clickable prototype. The reason this occurs is two-fold: one, to continue to think through the idea and two, to make it testable through another lens of creating great software—usability.

When validating a software prototype for usability, the are many ways to gather feedback, but what becomes paramount is asking a few questions:

- During the usability test, can your user quickly learn how to use the interface?
- Did you observe your user getting confused or selecting the wrong UI during a task?
- After your usability test, was your user able to articulate the perceived user-friendliness of the solution?

Of course, that is a deep, deep vein worth mining, which we will get to deeper in this book, but when it comes to usability testing, in the end, validating whether your software is useable is crucial. The reason usability validation is vital is as follows.

The pros of usability validation are as follows:

- Iterations can quickly be addressed through user testing on a clickable prototype.
- Usable software is a successful software, but not necessarily a loved software.
- Users can double-validate the idea and the execution of it being "easy to use."
- HCI practitioners spend lots of time considering what makes software useable, and when it works, it validates our skills and decisions throughout the software design process.

The cons of usability validation are as follows:

- Usability is not universal; every user will come to a computer with different understanding and experience.
- Software design teams can spend too much time noodling usability, rather than relying on the user to trust that it will get better.
- Usability is thought of as binary—it is either usable or it is not—but the reality is that it is much more nuanced.

The reason usability and clickable prototyping become so valuable is that software teams pride themselves on making usable software. By validating that a solution is usable, it helps build trust with your user. Usable software is excellent, but the reality is that usable is the baseline goal.

Stage 3 – market validation

Now that an idea has been validated through stage 2 usability testing, your validation process is starting to create some confidence in your software solution. The clickable prototype will need to be iterated through a market perspective. This is where feedback from the usability testing will help the software design team refine the concept. An HCI designer will typically improve a clickable prototype through visual design and code and make the prototype into a native prototype or a software version that can be released in beta. The reason this occurs is two-fold: one, to continue to build out the software and make it testable through multiple users and two, to allow the software prototype to grow up and become more like the final software product that you are trying to release to a broader audience.

Releasing a software product to the market is hard and can be very scary, but if a software team has validated with a market, as well as throughout the process, they should be more confident.

The pros of market validation are as follows:

- Successful beta launches lead to revenue and more users.
- Improving software early on leads to users loving the software.
- Users can triple-validate the idea and the execution of it being the right solution.
- HCI practitioners spend lots of time making a software solution worthy of their users. When tens, then hundreds, and then millions use the software, it proves the worthiness of validating along the way.

The cons of market validation are as follows:

- Users are aware of what a beta test equals and can be extra needy or critical.
- Software design teams can spend too much time looking for big numbers rather than growing their users slowly.
- Beta software is limited in its functionality and has more potential to crash or have user experience errors.

The reason market-tested prototypes become so valuable is that software teams pride themselves on making software that their users want. By validating a solution that is viable across the board, it helps build confidence in the team that solved the problem, as well as with the users to trust that the software has their best intentions in mind.

Challenge 17 – Prototype validation

Part 1: Complete your InVision dropdown prototype:

1. *Go to* `https://www.invisionapp.com/`.
2. *Open your dropdown mobile prototype.*
3. *Make sure your prototype is looping and does not have dead ends.*
4. *Add hotspots to every screen, allowing screen 3 to return to screen 1.*

Part 2: Validate your dropdown prototype with five users. (~15 mins):

1. *Using the* **Share** *tools for InVision, share your prototype with five friends.*
2. *Have them test your InVision prototyping in person.*
3. *Observe them using your dropdown prototype.*
4. *Ask questions from each stage of validation:*
   Idea validation
   Usability validation
   Market validation.
5. *Take notes on the success or failure of your dropdown prototype.*

Part 3: Evaluate your validation testing:

1. *Establish whether your prototype has been validated or not based on your five users.*

Use your friends and family as much as you can as prototype testers, but be wary that as an HCI designer, you can overtax those around you. Furthermore, they are probably not your target users. However, the ease of testing your early ideas on those around you is much better than not testing at all.

Congratulations, you are now quickly advancing your abilities to produce and validate a prototype. Applying this validation ethos to your process is super intertangled with prototyping in the first place. Testing your prototypes should not be too hard, but you should not try and validate an entire suite of functionality either. Being able to validate and test quick ideas will help you learn faster and improve your prototyping skills over time. The goal is thinking through ideas quickly and having feedback that pushes the solutions forward. HCI designers should always be advocating for getting their users using their prototypes and constantly iterating during the prototyping process.

Summary

Throughout this chapter, we started to get our hands into some skills and activities that an HCI designer can use to start designing software development. The skills and tools used by most HCI designers and are why HCI skills are such a vibrant and sought-after talent. The role of this chapter was to allow you to get some practice with them, and hopefully they will stick with you long after you have completed this book.

Because the skills and activities of an HCI designer are so vast, this chapter covered the potential roles that designers with HCI skills can occupy. The reality is that software is a team endeavor, and we covered why the HCI design process is related to interaction, and frontend and backend responsibilities that utilize an agile development ethos and cycles to create software solutions. Throughout this chapter, many challenges were thrown at you and hopefully, they got you to start practicing the HCI way with prototyping first and validating your ideas with users.

In the next chapter, we will focus on more skills in part 2 of the execution of software design through human-centered methods for user research.

Human-Centered Methods for User Research

5

Human-centered methods of user research consist of a combination of many user research methods, and we will focus on qualitative and quantitative methods that you will apply in your **human-computer interaction (HCI)** design process. We will frame the tangible steps taken while developing software and outline some of the methodologies for building human-centered software solutions.

As HCI designers, we should strive to make great software, which starts with focusing on what our users need and refusing to compromise the user's experience because other options are easier, cheaper, or faster to produce. Understanding your users at a deep level is essential to HCI, and this chapter is a practical guide to implement the human-centered design process. Design, development work, and research bring users together to build great software solutions, but they are only great if the software team is willing to put in the effort and work together to produce high-quality products rooted in user research.

Now that you are getting further along in your HCI journey, let's discuss why HCI gathers data. HCI focuses on the interaction between humans and computers, and we can understand the systems more completely through data.

The topics you will be learning about in this chapter are as follows:

- Gathering research data on our users
- The human side of data collection
- Exploring qualitative user research methods
- The numbers side of data collection
- Examining quantitative user research methods
- Using quantitative and qualitative data

Gathering research data on our users

Whether you like it or not, *data is king*. In the early 2000s, there was a saying that *content is king* because users were rapidly consuming content from the internet and to attract users that had shifted from other media: TV, magazines, newspapers, and so on. The only way to accomplish this was to offer better content. Content is still relevant – do not get me wrong – but as all that content moved online, along with it came the ability to gather data. Data gathering is everywhere. As the internet has woven its way into every aspect of our lives, what has come along with it is the collection of data. If you use Google, watch Netflix, find a restaurant to eat using Maps, or spend any time on Instagram, you are participating in data being collected on you, your experience, and your interactions. Though this might seem a bit creepy in the abstract, in reality, data is the mechanism that allows a user to receive any level of customization with an interface. Information data is the feedback loop of an interface.

Let's take Instagram, for example.

 I am not responsible for the Instagram algorithm; therefore, this example is based on interactions with the service along with knowledge of user-generated feeds.

Your feed as of 2020, is comprised of the following:

- Images from people you follow
- What you post yourself
- Sponsored advertisements
- Instagram Stories

Your feed is then tuned based on the photos from your followers that you double-tap to like. The content that you want then affects the types of advertisements you see in your feed and the type of content that you see from the people you follow. The ability for your feed to be individualized to you is only attainable through data. If you like a swimsuit from a sponsored advertisement, you will then receive more swimming-related content on your feed. The data gathered on you from Instagram allows brands, products, and services to tailor and customize content to user types based on their feed history.

Instagram is not the only company that is using data to impact users' content. Every major industry, from airlines to Amazon, is collecting, storing, and analyzing data to understand its users and change their business. Data is a way to gather the pulse of your users. Over time, a business, software product, or government can mine insights from the data or discover patterns in human behavior. Data boils down to the origins of the computer itself, and our ability to count more efficiently because a computer has allowed countless software solutions and services to be birthed from the need to evaluate data effectively. In the end, the information data we gather is a by-product of a system we are trying to understand.

For software development, the human part of the profession requires us to gather lots of data about people. The truth is people are hard to predict. Even with all the data that is collected on us, we still don't behave just as the data says we will. When we gather data on our users, we are doing so to try to help us understand their behavior even if we can't always predict it. Data analytics offers a broad field of value and adds clarity to complexity:

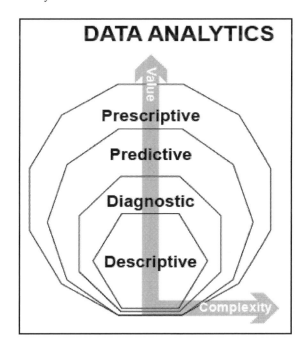

The data we collect can be used throughout the design and development cycles. Data gathering is essential to the human-centered approach as our user research helps a software team define who the users are, identify any existing problems, propose user insights, and influence a user feedback loop. The data intake process all supports the design and development of concrete solutions. Data analysis can then be categorized into four factors, and we will be moving from inside to out to evaluate how data analytics can be used in the software design process from descriptive to diagnostic to predictive to prescriptive:

1. **Descriptive: Data that helps us understand – what is happening?**
   Of all the forms of data, descriptive data is most abundant. For an HCI designer, this might look more like starting with understanding your user through their demographic and socio-economic and behavioral factors. Demographic data might be, for example, that 30% of your users are women between 25 and 30 years old. Socio-economic data might be that 80% of woman users between 25 and 30 earn and have a college degree. An example of behavioral data is that out of the 100 female users between the ages 25 and 30 who were surveyed, 65% are renters versus 35% who are homeowners. Descriptive analytics is made more effective through visualization tools that enhance the message of underlying data. For business, descriptive data provides an analyst with the ability to establish or track key metrics or **key performance indicators** (**KPIs**) and measures within the industry that could be a **profit and loss** (**P&L**) statement.

2. **Diagnostic: Data that helps us understand – why is it happening?**
   Diagnostic data is an interpretation of descriptive data, typically an assessment or analysis of descriptive data. Diagnostic analytical tools are used to explicitly expose the requirements of a software system and help identify what the users need or where the users are in trouble. Diagnostic data is about users' skills in both the application domain and in computer use. Diagnostic data analysis can also legitimize an HCI/**user experience** (**UX**) designer or user researcher's findings, as well as empower them to drill down deeper into the data. The goal is to use descriptive data in a diagnostic way to isolate the root cause of a problem. Diagnostic data for an HCI designer might look like software tools such as Google Analytics or user data from an application platform such as Apple iOS. The software can even be built on top of diagnostic data to create **business intelligence** (**BI**) dashboards. Data visualized into dashboards will incorporate data over time and features that help filter and drill down into the data capture.

3. **Predictive: Data that helps us understand – what will likely happen?**
   Predictive analytics is focused on forecasting. Predictive data models typically coalesce multiple data sources to make any prediction. Predictive data is about potential users' solutions where user requirements are anticipated and innovative recommendations can be proposed, such as new tasks or untapped audiences, or other unknown connections made available through predictive data. Predictive data attempts to forecast a quantifiable amount, through estimating the likelihood that something will happen or estimating a point in time at which something might happen. For example, a user over 65 who smokes is more susceptible to a heart attack. The predictive model would place the user's age and behavior in a linear correlation with heart-attack risk based on other users. The user data is then compiled together to establish a score or prediction. The ability to predict outcomes allows you to make better decisions. A user who is 20 and smokes can be shown a data drive prediction and the potential risks that smoking and heart-attacks create, allowing that user to modify their behavior to mitigate the risk. Predictive models are used across many fields, from health to finance to consumer confidence. Understanding your user is essential to UX and HCI and applying predictive data can help you address their needs.

4. **Prescriptive: Data that helps us understand – what do I need to do?**
   The prescriptive data model starts by understanding what has happened along with why it has happened and what is likely to happen in order to establish an analysis of what will happen. By combining these factors, prescriptive data informs its users and helps determine the best course of action. Prescriptive data is about what to do to create users' solutions. Take, for example, the Google Maps application. This is a location-based phone app that helps assist a user in establishing the best route to take to a destination. The predictive data takes into account the distance between the start and finish location, the average speed of travel by travel modality (that is, by foot, bike, car, train, boat, plane, and so on), the time of day, and the current traffic constraints, along with the travel history to prescribe optimal routes. This prescriptive data is useful both at the user level (micro) – getting one user from point A to point B faster – as well as at the parent level (macro), where all users in a city using Google Maps are moved around the location more efficiently.

As we get deeper into designing and developing software, the ability to track your user and test whether your software is working to solve your users' problem is essential to HCI. As HCI designers, we look to research and then evaluate that data. Data on its own is useless; it is just zeros and ones, but if we gather the data as a feedback loop to an existing hypothesis, then that data can help us understand whether a software solution is solving our user's problem. Let's start by discussing qualitative data.

The human side of data collection

Qualitative data is collected through methods of observations and gathers data that can be observed and recorded. Qualitative information data is non-numerical. HCI and UX tend to focus on qualitative research methods at first, especially if the software design team is designing something new. Qualitative data can help a group gather deep understandings of the motivations, problems, and past experiences of our users through observations and interviews.

Take the following example.

We are creating a high school band members' app:

- User data = 45 students in the user research group
- Version 1: Qualitative data set by band role:
    - 6 flutes
    - 7 trumpets
    - 12 drumlines
    - 3 tubas
    - 8 saxophones
    - 9 flag guards
- Version 2: Qualitative data set by student grade:
    - 12 seniors
    - 20 juniors
    - 7 sophomores
    - 6 freshman

The condition creates a quantity but can also associate a set of unique needs from that cross-section of the data. As an HCI designer or user researcher, a team could then dive into each cross-section with other qualitative methods to understand if, say, a flute user needs overlap with the flag guard user needs.

Qualitative research can get a bad rap as being time-consuming or all "warm and fuzzy" because the methods typically require interfacing directly with users. You can use qualitative data-gathering to validate startup ideas before you write a line of code, or you could use it to test significant company decisions. A qualitative user research study is typically trying to understand why and how a user performs a specific task. Qualitative research generates data around our users as we understand what their problem is and why it occurs for our users associated with any point of research interest. When understanding how a user interacts with a computer, qualitative research uses our human observation and user interviews and is a highly useful skill for HCI designers.

There's a bunch of qualitative research tools you can use to learn about a problem, user motivations, user feedback, and others. Let discuss a few methods, along with some challenges for you to do yourself as practice.

Exploring qualitative user research methods

As an HCI designer, you will spend a significant amount of time trying to understand your users, which is extremely hard. As we will discuss, your users are not a monolithic group; rather, they are a collection of individuals who are always in flux. Users are people, and people can be unpredictable. We are lucky that people are complex; otherwise, we would be able to program everyone to be the same and our software opportunities would be greatly diminished because all people would be like robots. Users are not robots; they are people who have human emotions, needs, and consciousness. The human considerations are what make designing software for humans so difficult. The reality is that people are like snowflakes: no two are alike, and because of this, an HCI designer needs to build a robust set of skills to try and understand people. We need to improve our abilities to gather data on our users. The role of qualitative user research is essential to understanding the human side of the equation in the HCI profession. Understanding humans and their relationship to technology and software is highly dynamic. As an HCI designer, we must be diligent with our curiosity as well and regularly pay attention to humans. In order to improve your qualitative user research skills, let's discuss four qualitative methods:

- Observation: Fly-on-the wall method
- Moderated observation method
- User interviews method
- User recording: A tracking analysis and interview method

Qualitative method 1 – observation – fly-on-the-wall method

The role of an HCI designer is to pay attention to be a "watcher." There is a ton to learn about how users experience the world, engage in a procedure, or use software just by watching them use it. One way to do this is through standard observation methods using your eyes, ears, and location to observe a scenario effectively. To observe effectively requires the observer to have anonymity. When observing, you don't want your users to know you are watching them. If human beings are aware they are being watched, they will modify their behavior, and your goal is to observe your users in their "natural" environment. Observing "natural" behavior might require long-form observation over time as the goal is to make users feel confident so that they can go about their daily life as usual. The concept of being a fly on the wall is that the observer occupies space without impacting the observed subjects. A software designer is always looking to understand their users and using the fly-on-the-wall observation tactic will help:

The art of being a fly on the wall has many strategies, including spying and sleuthing techniques. A popular spying technique is to blend into an environment through disguise to watch users who are unaware that you are observing them. It is not necessary to hide in a bush while observing your users, but if you think that helps you focus your observations and not impact users, then plan to use that strategy. If users are in an office or on an assembly line, it can be more difficult to be a fly on the wall as there are probably fewer places to hide, which will require scoping out and planning your observation strategy. Another strategy with observation is started by observing in public to semi-public places. Semi-public places, such as cafes or coffee shops, can be a great place to practice observing users without being too snoopy. Users in a cafe typically will spend a significant amount of time in the space and, if busy enough, will not be aware that they are being observed.

When practising observing in semi-public places, it is recommended to occupy the scenario and experience the space the same way that your observation subjects are as well. If in a coffee shop, this means following the procedure of ordering a coffee. If there is a line, you can look around and choose a subject to observe without being too obvious. Once you have selected a user to observe, attempt to sit near that user, somewhere you are in close enough proximity to observe but not where you will get called out on watching your subject.

Challenge 18 – Observation – fly on the wall

Part 1: Observation setup:

Go to a coffee shop or other public place where you can easily observe users.

Part 2: Observation:

1. *Observe one user throughout their experience at the coffee shop.*
2. *Watch and take notes every time they interact with technology (personal and coffee shop systems).*
3. *Take notes on your user's experience and your observations. Attempt to see what software they are using and whether they are successful or not based on their observed task.*

Part 3: Observation analysis and pattern recognition:

1. *Combine all your observations into a user observation summary document, capturing the following:*
   - Use your experience notes
   - Technology usage
   - Success and failures
   - Any images of your user throughout the process.

 Attempt to blend in and not be too obvious in your observations. Find a place to sit that is against a wall and gives you a good view of the people you are observing.

Qualitative method 1.1 – micro-observations

Observing users effectively without impacting their experience is a challenging skill and requires lots of practice. I recommend applying your observation skills throughout your day and engaging in a process I call "micro-observations":

- At the bank, micro-observe the line and how people occupy their time.
- When riding on public transport, observe how users interface with the ticketing kiosk.
- When out at a restaurant, observe how the table next to you uses their smartphones.
- At a park, observe social groups and how they interact with technology.

The list goes on and on.

Your ability to watch users throughout your day will collectively improve your observation skills and, over time, will develop your understanding of how users and technology are used "in the real world."

Qualitative method 2 – moderated observation

An extension of the "watcher" method is the moderated observation method. In this case, the HCI designer makes the user being observed aware of their presence. Typically, in this observation method, the observing researcher/HCI designer creates a scenario or some catalyst meant for observing. A user might be asked to go about a task to be observed for research, and then you evaluate the process. An HCI designer should get good at doing moderated interview sessions:

A moderated session, for the coffee shop example, might look like this.

Observer/researcher: "I am going to observe you, but don't mind me. Go about the process as "naturally" as you can as if I was not observing you at all. What I want you to do is order a coffee using your phone application and get your coffee. I am just going to follow along and watch you as you go about accomplishing this task."

User: Goes through the procedure of using their phone to order, submit, pick up the coffee, then complete the interaction.

Observer/researcher: Observes the user throughout the process, making notes, and capturing the process.

Challenge 19 – Moderated observation script

Setup:

Get out a sheet of paper/Google Doc/Word Doc.

Part 1: Observation script:

1. *Write a script for approaching a user for a moderated observation.*
2. *Choose a task that you would like to observe a user do.*
3. *Write an opening statement for gathering an observation participant.*
   - for example, "Good afternoon, my name is ___, I am an HCI user researcher looking for a few participants for my observations. It should take any more than X minutes. You seem like a really smart person and I was wondering whether you would be willing to help me out with a quick task? (Yes?...oh, great!)"
4. *Write out the established task for the user.*
5. *Define what a successful task completion looks like.*

Part 3: Participant thank-you script:

Write a thank-you script for any participants that agree to be observed.
Bonus: Go execute your moderated observation and practice your script on potential users.

 Practice your script on a friend or colleague. The goal is to make it feel natural and clear.

Moderated observation of users requires even more practice as creating your script and getting users to participate in your observations is no easy task. Be prepared to hear "NO" a lot. Moderated observation requires much more calculated experience as finding users who are able and willing is hard. I recommend applying an incentive structure to lure potential observation participants, such as a sign that says "let me observe you for one free coffee," or add the incentive into your script – for example, "Hi, I noticed you haven't ordered coffee yet? Can I buy you a coffee in exchange for letting me observe you?" (and then the remainder of the script).

Our ability to gather participants in our observations is just as important as observing users in the first place. If you can't get users to observe, you can't collect data. If you are using a moderated observation method, I recommend testing your script on your team and modifying it to be more successful at gaining participants. This process is very hard, especially if you are not comfortable speaking with strangers. This is where a great script can be handy for the user research team, along with substantial incentives, and you will see a dramatic improvement in the number of observation partners. With practice, your team will collectively improve your observation skills and your ability to attract users in the "in the real world" to participate.

Along the same lines as moderated observation is a user interview.

Qualitative method 3 – user interviews

User interviewing is an art, whether you are the person being interviewed or the interviewer. Great conversations do not happen just like that. They require lots of planning, lots of practice, and a touch of luck. An excellent interview feels more like a great conversation, rather than a series of questions that get asked. In culture, there are plenty of examples of those that make their living from interviewing, whether it be podcasts such as Without Fail with Alex Blumberg or WTF with Marc Maron, or on TV, Charlie Rose on PBS or Conan O'Brien on his late-night talk show, where at some point, they interview their guests. An HCI designer will need to practice interview sessions throughout their career:

Paying attention to those that are great at interviewing is worth your time, as there is a lot to learn from them. One thing they do out of the gate is make their interviewees feel comfortable and relaxed to set the interview tone and not pressure their interviewer with an agenda. Of course, they have some questions they want to get through, but as the interview goes on, the questions fit naturally into the conversation. Witnessing this is known as the "art of conversation" or the "gift of the gab." What makes interviewing very hard is that not everyone has this "gift of conversation." Furthermore, no two interviews are the same, even if you ask the same questions.

The most important part of interviewing is to ask a great opening question and then sit back and listen. If the interviewer is filling the conversation, they are damaging the interview results. During interviewing, listening is essential. Good interviewing is predicated on the types of questions the interviewee asks. To create a good conversation with your user, you need to start with questions that prompt your user to elaborate and tell a story.

Let's review some question types that elicit stories from your users during interviews.

Open question types

Open (-ended) question types are those that can be answered in-depth by your subject and allow original, unique responses that are hopefully filled with context, causation, and emotional qualities. Open questions help an interviewer see from the interviewee's perspective because you get feedback in their own words and experiences. The goal of open questions is to get your user to tell you a story about their experience that includes some emotional quality to describe the process. Great open questions prompt a user to respond with a meaningful story as a response.

Some open question examples are as follows:

- Can you share a time when you were amazed by technology?
- Walk me through your typical day.
- Why do you use your [product/service/software application]?
- When was that time you used [product/service/software application]? Can you tell me about your experience?

Probing questions types

Probing questions work together with other open questions and look to dig into detail on a particular matter. Good probing questions are typically used in response to something a user has shared while answering an open question. Considered follow-up questions are typically interjections by the interviewer with statements such as "Could you tell me more about that?" or "Please explain what you mean." The goal of probing questions is to clarify a point or help the interviewer understand the root of a problem. The challenge with probing questions is that they are contextually based on the conversation happening during an interview and are hard to write or plan. Good probing questions allow an interview to "flow" and move seamlessly along while digging deeper into a subject or drilling down into why a user has a problem. Improving probing questions requires lots of practice. Probing questions shouldn't interrupt your interviewee but can be brought back around to help dive deeper – for example, saying "You mentioned during your day you did X and Y didn't work; can you tell me why it didn't work?".

The ability to probe into aspects of a user's story during an interview to uncover any more profound emotional quality or get to the root of the problem is essential during interviewing. Using probing questions serves in understanding something deeper. If used ineffectively, they can quickly put an end to a great conversation, which is why listening during an interview is so critical.

Speaking of things we should not do during an interview, don't ask unhelpful questions. A couple of examples of unhelpful questions are multiple-choice questions – an in-person interview is not a survey, and asking multiple-choice questions can be somewhat awkward for the interviewer. Also, avoid closed questions or questions that can be answered with a "yes" or "no" answer. Third, steer clear of leading questions, which are questions that prompt or encourage the desired answer. An example of a leading question to avoid is "Do you like our software?". This is a leading question because it assumes the user has a positive relationship with the software solution when, in fact, they may not have a favorable response at all. A leading question encourages users to answer a certain way, and as an interviewer, you want replies to be as authentic as possible. Authenticity in an interview is the by-product of great interview questions. Closed and leading questions should be screened for during the interview planning process and removed from the set of potential questions that an interviewer can ask a subject.

Regardless of the challenge presented by interviewing, the ability to talk with your users and to hear directly from them is indispensable and the essence of qualitative research. Interviewing requires a lot of preparation. First, you have to prepare for the interview through planning. A good interview plan has three components:

1. **A user interview goal**:
   For example, the HCI research team will talk with N users for ~n minutes to determine whether our product is aligning with their needs.
2. **Great interview questions**:
   Questions that align with the interview goal and are useful for understanding your interviewee. All interview questions should be open or probing and be screened for closed or leading question types.
3. **Qualified interviewer**:
   A user researcher who is practiced in interviewing can capture the results through recording, notes, insights, and personal revelations from interview sessions.

Second, you have to acquire interview subjects. Soliciting users for interviews requires their skills. Finding interviewees requires gathering subjects either through email, social media, cold calling, or going out in the world and gaining subjects in public places. Getting interview subjects to agree to talk with a research team or to spend their time talking with you for an interview is hard. The interview "sales pitch" needs to be compelling.

A strategy for getting interview subjects is to put together a script first. An interview script should have three things:

1. A great introduction (who you are and why you are requestioning a person's time).
2. An interview time expectation (keep this under 20 minutes).
3. An incentive (butter up your interviewees with compliments and offer some compensation).

An interview script might look as follows:

Interviewer: *(Start with an icebreaker)* "Hello, sorry for the interruption, I want to tell you that I love your X (bag, shoes, shirt, and so on)."

Interview candidate: "Why thank you..."

Interviewer: "How rude of me, my name is X. I am doing user research on N, and you seem like you might be willing to help me out? My questions will only take a couple of minutes (insert an incentive – free coffee, ice cream, and so on). Do you have time?

Interview candidate: "Yeah, sure."

Interviewer: "Awesome. I appreciate this. I only have a couple of questions. Do you mind if I record this conversation? It will only be used by me later when I am done with my interviews."

Interview candidate: "I don't see a problem with that; let's do it."

Challenge 20 – Interview candidate script

Setup:

Get out a sheet of paper/Google Doc/Word Doc.

Part 1: Interview script:

1. *Prepare to write out a script for approaching a user for interviews.*
2. *Add an icebreaker.*
3. *Write an opening statement for gathering an interview candidate.*
4. *Establish a valid incentive.*

Part 2: Interview subject:

Define who your interview subject should be.

Part 3: Interview thank-you script:

1. *Write a thank-you script for any participants that agree to be interviewed.*
   Bonus: Go execute your moderated observation and practice your script on potential users.

Practice your script and consider a few options for incentives. Your interviews should not be too costly but will be time-consuming.

Your interview sessions are a by-product of planning and gaining great interview subjects. Be prepared to have a lot of people tell you "NO!" when asking them to be interviewed. It's OK, people are busy; however, don't give up! With practice and your script, you will find it easier to pitch, and you will also get better at choosing interview candidates that are willing to say yes.

Let's discuss two interviewing methods that will help you gather tons of qualitative data from your users.

One-to-one interview sessions

One-to-one interviews are where an HCI researcher recruits one interviewee and establishes a time, location, and sets of questions to ask during the interview. Any interview should be planned out with predetermined interview questions, and the interview subject should align with the interview goal. An HCI designer should not shy away from engaging in interview sessions starting with one-to-one interviews:

If you are new to interviewing, I recommend starting with one-to-one interviews because they are easier to record. When talking, make sure your interviewee is comfortable, is not distracted by recording technology, and is open to participating. By making your interviewee comfortable and paying attention to the interviewee's body language, you can assess how forthcoming or open they are to the interview. During an interview, make sure to remind the interviewee of the time expectation and start with a great open question. If your conversation starts to approach the time limit, make sure to respect your interviewee's time and say, "We are almost at the end of our time unless you would like to continue?...If not, perhaps we can continue our conversation in another session?". When the interview comes to a reasonable end, thank your interviewee and exchange contact info for any follow-up questions.

Individual interviews can be challenging to coordinate; however, they do not require hours and hours to carry out, and with video conferencing technology, they can be set up and recorded relatively quickly. I recommend practicing in-person interviewing before jumping into conversations that are mediated through software technology because in-person interviews are typically longer, have more room for probing questions, and are easier to pick up on non-verbal communications. Non-verbal communication is the sending and receiving of messages without using words, which includes body language, facial expressions, kinetic movements, eye contact, touch, and physical space or presence. During interviews, these non-verbal communications cues are ways to help an interviewer understand the success or failure of an interview. A goal of one-on-one meetings is to gain authentic responses from your users. Non-verbal cues can help the interviewer understand how reliable an interviewee is, as well as where to interject with probing questions or even finish and wrap up the interview.

Challenge 21 – One-on-one interview

Setup:

Get out a sheet of paper/Google Doc/Word Doc.

Part 1: Interview questions:

1. *Write out five open questions.*
2. *Use your interview script to obtain an interview subject.*
3. *Interview a user (~15 mins.) and record the interview.*

Part 3: Recording transcript:

1. *Send the recording to a transcript service.*
2. *Analyze the interview for user pain points, emotionally charged experiences, or interesting opportunities.*

Evaluate your interview after and refine your questions. Which questions worked best and which questions didn't lead to good answers? Practice will make your interviewing skills better.

One-to-many interview sessions

One-to-many interviews are where an HCI researcher recruits many interviewees and establishes a time and a location – typically round-table conference rooms. Sets of questions are asked during the group interview. An HCI designer should practice before executing a one-to-many interview session:

Like a one-on-one interview, the interview questions should be tailored to the group and start with a great open question that the group can answer together. As an interview moderator, you will need to direct traffic more meaningfully with your subjects. This might look like keeping group members from talking over each other or selecting members in the group to answer first. Group interviews are much harder to pull off effectively and should be executed by a team member with previous experience. They are also harder to record and to create transcripts. If you are new to interviewing, I recommend starting with one-on-one interviews because they are easier to record. When group interviewing, make sure your interviewees are comfortable, are not distracted by recording technology, and are on the same level within a company or social group. Don't mix groups that have a different organizational hierarchy.

For example, if you are working with a company that is looking to improve its internal software, you might do group interviews with the C-suite together, then the managers, but not together; the managers shouldn't be interviewed with their employees. Group dynamics can play a considerable part in group interviews. As an interviewer, you want participants to be free to speak their minds without fear of punishment or holding in comments because they fear for their job.

Group interviews are seen as a way to save money and simplify coordination during the interview process; however, the team doing group interviews will ultimately have to do more work to schedule effectively, process the interview data, and moderate the interview successfully. Although group interviews can be extremely tough to pull off, they can also result in conversations, data, and perspectives on a product that would be nearly impossible to reveal in a one-on-one interview. The very nature of group interviews means that the participants impact each other in their responses to questions. Group members can agree or disagree with each other, which can lead to really fruitful insights for the interviewer.

Regardless of the interview being individual or group in nature, it needs to be recorded so that it can be analyzed later in the process.

Qualitative method 4 – user recording, tracking analysis, and interview

The final qualitative method we will discuss is the user recording method. The previous qualitative methods all have some level of capture built into their process, from the observer/interviewer notes to interview audio recording and transcriptions. The user recording method can also be done independently or alongside any of the other qualitative methods. User recording is just increasing the level and amount of record. Like the fly-on-the-wall observation method, the user recording method substitutes technology in the place of an observer or, even better, enhances the observer's data collection abilities. An HCI designer should improve their ability to watch users through observations and recording users:

User recording can be misunderstood as surveillance and therefore needs to be communicated to your subject and set up with care so that the recording technology can capture what the observer is looking to capture. Like the fly-on-the-wall method, technology recording can impact how a user responds; therefore, the goal is to make the user recording method as least distracting as possible. A great thing about technology today is that it has gotten more reliable as well as smaller. It is relatively easy to record high-definition sound with a smartphone or set up a camera recording with a small tripod and a smartphone. The ubiquitous nature of smartphones has also allowed them to disappear and not be focused on during an observation session. Just go to a restaurant and notice how many people leave their smartphones out on the table as they dine. I am not saying that is a worthy habit; however, the nature of this phenomenon makes recording a user much more straightforward.

When using the user recording method, there are a few considerations for capturing a user. For obtaining a user, many films can deploy tricks, and if you have the resources, using the concept of coverage will help you gather more than one point of view as you observe a user. Coverage, often called camera coverage, is the amount and kinds of footage *shot* to capture an observation or scene. In film making, there is the luxury of actors repeating the same scene to gather coverage of a scene for editing purposes. For observation, your user will probably not want to do the same things over and over or answer the same questions after you move the camera position; therefore, if you want to gain more than one perspective, you should use multiple cameras recording at once.

When recording users, the recording technology should not be given any attention. It is just there to capture the process.

Challenge 22 – Observation recording

Setup:

Using your smartphone or another recording device, set up a way to capture both the video and audio of a user you are observing.

Part 1: Observation recording:

1. Capture an observation of the user using a piece of software.
2. Record enough of the experience that the user has clearly accomplished a task.

Part 2: Observation analysis:

1. Wait 1 day and then watch and listen to the recording you captured. See whether your video helps you see something you missed during the recording session.

 Evaluating your interview too soon will not give you a fresh perspective. Our memories are not that good, and using the recording of the interview will allow you to pick up on things you missed during the actual interview.

Qualitative data captured during user interviews can lead to deep user insights and knowledge about your users but requires a lot of practice over your HCI career. The reality is that no HCI designer is automatically good at gathering qualitative data. The user research methods are challenging for a reason, and if you want to call yourself an HCI designer, you should dedicate and commit yourself to practicing this over time.

The numbers side of data collection

Quantitative data is data that can be counted and is collected through methods of observation, calculating overtime, and applying statistics. Quantitative data is numerical. The collection of quantitative data provides the means for which observers can establish baseline averages.

HCI and UX tend to focus on quantitative research methods throughout the design and development process and become especially relevant during user testing. Quantitative data can help a team gather proof of whether that solution is working or not based on an established user need. For example, say you have a research group for an application for band members in a high school and it has 45 students.

Understand a way to apply quality to the following dataset:

- 6 flutes
- 7 trumpets
- 12 drumlines
- 3 tubas
- 8 saxophones
- 9 flag guards

Understanding that each member logs into the band application an average of 225 times a day or an average of 5 times per user per day is a quantitative result.

Through qualitative research, you might have understood that the user doesn't prefer to log in there, because it helps rationalize and justify the qualitative user issue through quantitative data.

Examining four quantitative research methods

Quantitative data methods are vast and used by many more professions than just HCI, which has allowed our methods to have value across the spectrum of an HCI team, as well as your clients, who should be familiar with consuming data.

In order to improve your quantitative user research skills, let's discuss four quantitative methods:

- Quantitative survey method
- A/B testing method
- Usability analytics method
- Accessibility compliance method

Quantitative survey method

The role of an HCI designer is to gather information for a number of sources. There is so much to learn from your users over time. Just as the HCI designer is the "watcher" for qualitative data, they should double down on that and also be the "collector." The collection of data is about using the tools available to understand more about a system. Qualitative observations and interviews, though incredibly useful, have the issue that they are hard to scale. If you have one UX/HCI designer doing interviews, they are constrained by time and space. This is where surveys come into play. A user research designer can gather lots of quantitative data through surveys:

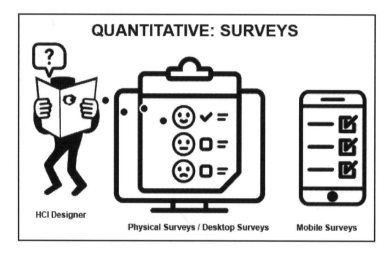

Surveys are a widely used method for gathering data. There are many, many ways to conduct a survey, and in 2020, the internet offers more opportunities than ever before to scale surveys to multiple users. There are so many survey tools available, including the following:

- **Google Forms**: www.google.com/forms/about/
- **Typeform**: www.typeform.com/
- **Survey Monkey**: www.surveymonkey.com/
- **Survey Gizmo**: www.surveygizmo.com/

Surveys tools are software suites for building interactive forms that can be distributed to users. The data gathered by surveys is captured and can then be analyzed to determine answers from the survey. Many survey software tools allow users to create surveys, distribute the survey, and then automate data reports on the survey results. The ease of this process has made using and deploying surveys more viable and meaningful for HCI design teams.

In UX, surveys are a prominent tool to gather feedback and measure human responses or software solutions. With the introduction of survey software tools, the cost to execute a survey is very low. Surveys can be quick and dirty – where they are put together on the fly to gather data – or more strategic, where the survey is given a proper business scope (timeline and budget), is planned (audience targets, survey hypothesis, and survey timeline), constructed (survey questions) and analyzed (review and assess survey data). Software design is connected to surveys through establishing goals for the sampling method, the use of survey design best practices, avoiding common survey biases, and improving survey evaluation.

To design a survey effectively is by no means simple. There are entire books on survey design, and I encourage you to read up on all the ways to improve your surveys. The quality of your user surveys will improve your ability to evaluate your users' satisfaction.

Challenge 23 – Quick-and-dirty survey

Setup:

Using Google Forms or Typeform, create a new survey (log in, create a new survey, and add a survey title).

Part 1: Create a survey:

1. *Create a 10-question survey for gathering quantitative data:*

    - *4 multiple-choice questions*
    - *4 linear scale (1 low–5 high) questions*
    - *2 short-answer questions*

Part 2: Share your survey

1. *Publish your survey.*

   - *Share with 10+ users via email.*
   - *Share on social media (Facebook, Twitter, Instagram)*

Part 3: Analyze survey results:

Wait 1–2 days and then gather the survey responses.

Surveys require some time to get applicants to complete them; don't close the survey too early as it can limit your data.

A/B testing (split testing)

In marketing and research, A/B testing is a method that implements comparing two versions of a product, marketing, web page, or software application to evaluate which version will perform better. The A and B versions are presented to a selected set of users at random. An A/B test should have equal testers of both A and B versions to create a discernable differentiation statistically between each version. A software designer should gather quantitative data through A/B testing:

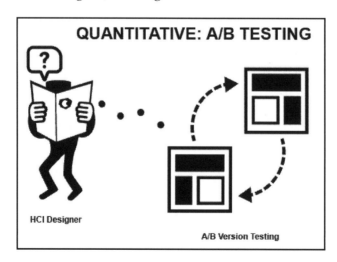

In an A/B test, a portion of your users will be shown version A, and the rest version B. Through A/B testing, an HCI research team can verify which version is getting more users and therefore should be applied to the software system. Similarly, A/B testing can be done on the same user, showing both A/B to them and evaluating which performs better. For web pages, A/B testing is used to optimize a page for conversions, and an A/B test can be used to understand the effectiveness of a solution in order from small to large:

- Small:
  - **Titles and headers**
    Content: Creating A/B titles of articles or content sections to evaluate what draws users in.
    Visual design: A/B versions of color or typography fonts can also make a testable difference.
  - **Call to action**
    Content: A/B for buttons. The types of UX language used (such as "purchase" versus "add to cart") can have a decisive impact on your conversion rate.
    Visual design: The design of the **call to action (CTA)** can quickly be A/B tested regarding color, the position, and the CTA shape.
  - **Images**
    Content: A/B testing the use of images can be equally as important as text. It is recommended to try different images.
    Visual design: An A/B test can evaluate the effectiveness of size (big versus small) or the aesthetic quality/image treatment of your photos (filter A versus filter B) as well as location (right versus left, up versus down).
- Medium:
  - **Forms**
    Content: An A/B test can evaluate how clear and concise a form is (labels on the top versus labels to the side) or how effective the form is for user completion (form A with an optional field versus form B, which removes the optional fields).
    Visual design: You can try modifying a form field title, changing the form placement, formatting the size, and so on.
  - **Navigation**
    Content: A/B test different page connections by offering multiple conversion funnels in one or several parts of navigation.
    Visual design: Navigation can have different colors, iconography usage, typography, and so on.

- **Page structure**
  Content: A/B test two unique page structures to evaluate which layout or page content is the most effective. You can A/B test the addition of a carousel or not, or whether to include a banner or include a featured product on the home page.
  Visual design: The page design can be light or dark, a layout can be inverted, and so on.

- **Pricing/sale conversion**
  Content: A/B testing on product pricing can be difficult because in many businesses, you cannot sell the same product or service for a different price. However, you can A/B test a Sale percentage or deals on the product or service.

- **Visual design**: If you sell products, offer different colors, shapes, or material, and so on.

- Large:

  - **Landing pages**
    Content: A/B testing lead generation landing pages is important to optimize your user experiences and test whether your user will take specific actions.
    Visual design: Landing pages can be designed differently with unique visual design treatment to test whether the visual elements impact user decisions.

  - **Algorithms**
    Content: A/B test an algorithm to transform your visitors into customers. This could be modifying the recommendation algorithm to compare similar articles versus the most-searched products.
    Visual design: Checking the way the algorithm displays content and where on the page can be tested.

  - **Business model**
    Content: Generate revenue models for business A and business B and create an action plan test and generate additional profits.

A/B testing is one method that can be used to evaluate the effectiveness of the software. How an HCI team chooses to deploy A/B tests is dependant upon their ability to design and evaluate the results of the test. A/B testing is widely used in the web world for marketing purposes and can be a valuable tool for considering both small and large aspects of a software solution.

Let's practice exploring how to use A/B testing for a small component of your UI prototype for ourselves.

Challenge 24 – A/B survey results

Setup:

Using Google Forms or Typeform, create a new survey (log in, create a new survey, and add a survey title).

Part 1: On a separate sheet of paper, write an A/B survey hypothesis for your A/B survey:

1. *Use the "If (variable), then (result) due to (rationale)" method.*
   For example, if we give 50 users $5 to test the UI form, then 90% will complete the steps due to incentivizing the completion of the task.

Part 2: Create a 10-question survey:

1. *Create a 10-question survey for gathering quantitative data:*

   - *Add a required question at the top of the survey to identify whether your user came from an email or from social media.*
   - *Add four multiple-choice questions.*
   - *Add four linear scale (1 low–5 high) questions.*
   - *Add two short-answer questions.*

Part 2: A/B survey results:

1. *Publish your survey:*

   - *A: Share with 10+ users via email.*
   - *B: Share on social media (Linkedin, Facebook, Twitter, Instagram, Snapchat, and so on).*

Part 3: Analyze the survey completion results:

1. *Wait 1 day and then gather the survey responses.*
2. *See which survey distribution had better results with the completion of your survey. Bonus: Work out the success rate for the method. For example, if 5 out of the 10 people you emailed completed the survey, you would have a 50% completion rate.*

Multiple surveys using different questions can help you evaluate a similar question through multiple lenses.

It is exciting to start to gather data around your design decisions. As you grow your A/B testing skills, you will find that your software solutions will improve over time and your ability to produce A/B tests will also improve. If an A/B test is taking your team too long to complete, you could be wasting time and energy. I recommend using A/B testing early on in your idea process to validate big ideas, such as the use of a feature, and then again later in the process to validate specific design decisions, such as color usage, typography, or software writing.

Along with gathering data on your software solution, your software itself should be gathering data on how it is being used. This system monitoring is known as analytics.

Usability analytics

Real-world websites and software generate data that we can then analyze through usability analytics. A software system can track where people arrive from and what they do once they are on a website if you build your software to communicate those actions. On the internet, this is managed by web analytics tools, which offer usability experts, business analysts, and designers the ability to identify and diagnose issues and track user interactions with a website or software. An HCI designer should gather quantitative data through usability analytics:

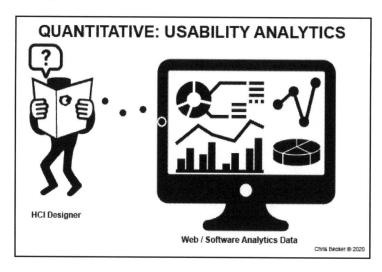

Web analytics is possible through the addition of adding an analytics tag to the source code of each web page, which allows the data to be monitored for incoming and outgoing traffic. The most popular analytics platform is Google Analytics, which has a robust set of tools and dashboards for understanding vast amounts of data.

As data gathering has become a big business, it has also created more scrutiny from users and government regulations. This has created policies such as the **General Data Protection Regulation (GDPR)** in the EU (and similar laws around the world). The analytics data gathered from users may be more complicated but becomes more transparent to your users.

The professions that makeup web analytics are continually evolving, but we should be aware of a few key aspects of a system that can be tracked:

- Conversions
- Pages per visit
- Time per visit
- Bounce rate
- Exit pages

Critical to developing a relevant and effective analysis of your software design is creating objectives and CTAs for your users based on their goals. It is possible to track everything, but as an HCI designer, you are trying to use analytics data to help you with what you are trying to solve. Along with tracking whether user goals are successful, you should work with your clients or businesses to identify KPIs to measure the success or failures for those objectives.

For example, a user's goal might be to find a product and add it to their cart. A business KPI might be to increase web sales by 5%. Understanding whether web software is encouraging a user to purchase can be tracked through counting how many users add items to their cart.

Challenge 25 – Analytics data gathering

Setup:

Log in to Google Analytics using a demo account: `https://support.google.com/analytics/answer/6367342?hl=en`.

Part 1: Explore Google Analytics:

1. *Explore the left-side column navigation to explore the analytics data:*

   - Realtime
   - Audience
   - Acquisition

- Behavior
- Conversions

2. *Review how data and insights change as you review by hour/day/week/month.*

Part 2: What did you learn from the data?

Make notes on the quantitative data that stands out.

Google Analytics has a number of great tutorials on how to use its platform. Explore them on your own.

Let's discuss how gathering analytics can help your websites be used by all your users. We design software systems to be used by all, which requires considering all aspects of accessibility.

Quantitative method 4 – accessibility compliance

For software, equal access is a way to ensure you are addressing the widest audience possible and not discriminating, but access is about complying with regional and global laws. An HCI designer should gather quantitative data on accessibility compliance:

The most universally accepted technical requirements for web accessibility is the **Web Content Accessibility Guidelines (WCAG)** 2.0, Level AA. If you are applying these best practices and testing your website and software systems against their guidelines, you can be confident that your solution will be in compliance.

As an HCI designer, the goal is design software that is not only useful to your user but also accessible and compliant with all government standards. You should be knowledgeable in the following standards:

- **WCAG 2.0** (`https://www.w3.org/TR/WCAG20/`)
- **Section 504**
- **Section 508**

To ensure that your websites meet the technical requirements of WCAG 2.0 or 2.1, let's practice testing our prototypes.

Challenge 26 – Accessibility for all via ANDI testing using WCAG 2.0

Setup:

Install and run ANDI: `https://www.ssa.gov/accessibility/andi/help/install.html`.

Part 1: Check accessibility:

Go to 10 web pages and evaluate their web page accessibility.

Part 2: Analyze the results:

Review which website had the highest scores and look into why.

 Experiment with other accessibility tools as well and consider why or why not accessibility is lacking on a web page.

Now that you have gathered some qualitative and quantitative data, let's find an opportunity to use it.

Using qualitative and quantitative data

It is worth repeating: software design is hard! There is no quick and easy way to jump into the end state where everything just works and your users are blissfully happy. To do it well, you have to get your hands dirty. The reality is that HCI designers get their hands dirty by gathering data from beginning to end. We establish user research and data as essential to the process. The research we do is fed back. Along the process, different qualitative and quantitative research methods are deployed to help us learn and address whether our user's needs are being met.

Not to over-complicate the process, but qualitative methods are more valuable toward the beginning of solving software problems and quantitive methods are more useful as solutions get created. HCI designers should understand where in the software process life cycle they are creating value through user research and data collection – for example, using qualitative methods of user interviews to establish whether a user insight has great value over time for a software team. The validation of that user insight will come down the road through quantitative methods of user testing. Without the user research that establishes a user insight, can you create a way to test whether that insight has been met?

Qualitative and quantitive methods are also not just used inside software design teams. Many times, the research data that is gathered is used to communicate outside a software team. Whether it be sharing progress with business stakeholders or adding content for marketing materials, the research an HCI software team gathers over time has value. The research we maintain as essential to building great software is also at the heart of building great businesses. If you can use data effectively to create software that solves your user's problems, then you can also use that data to communicate to your business, your competition, and even your users. Software is a highly dynamic process and the feedback loops and research methods we use can make the software design process explicit to your users and the teams who design them.

Summary

Throughout this chapter, we discussed how HCI applies to software development and building programs from computers over time. As we continue to get deeper and deeper into the HCI design process and the knowledge that makes HCI a vibrant community, the depth of your understanding should also grow, which is why we reviewed and practiced data gathering methods for both qualitative and quantitative measurements.

As we have discussed, software design is very hard, and without learning from your user, it is even harder – some would even say impossible. The value of data gathering for an HCI designer reaches far into your future and continues to be a set of skills that every software team is reliant upon. Mastering these skills through practice is essential to you growing as an HCI designer.

In the next chapter, we will focus on part 2 of the execution of software design through HCI design and development: human-centered thinking through cycles.

6
User Insights for Software Solutions

As you may be starting to pick up, **human-computer interaction** (HCI) is intimately connected to people through the research data we gather on them. A computer is good at gathering data, and we design computer software in order to capitalize not only on this collection of data but also on how this data feeds back into the software solution. Data on its own will not help an HCI designer create great software. A computer cannot create a software interface solution on its own, at least not yet; it is only an outcome of the work we as HCI designers create. User research becomes critical in the software design process, and we as HCI designers need to learn how to capitalize on our research data gathering skills, which includes observations, interviews, surveys, focus groups, and so on. Gathering user research data is only part of the challenge; next comes combining our user research data (data gathering, analysis, and interpretation), aligning software to users (data gathering, analysis, and interpretation), identifying user insights (data analysis and interpretation), and designing human-centered solutions (GUI, user interfaces, and data visualization).

The topics you will be learning about in this chapter are as follows:

- Synthesizing data into action
- Rooting action to a deeper user purpose
- Identifying and writing user insights
- Aligning solution to users

Synthesizing data into action

In the previous chapter, we covered eight methods for gathering both qualitative and quantitative data:

Qualitative methods:

- Observation: The fly-on-the-wall method
- The moderated observation method
- The user interviews method
- User recording: Tracking analysis and the interview method

Quantitative methods:

- The quantitative survey method
- The A/B testing method
- The usability analytics method
- The accessibility compliance method

Qualitative and quantitative research methods produce data on your user that an HCI designer can work with to synthesize and analyze. The role of synthesizing is essential in evaluating not just the data itself but also the lasting value any dataset can have on a product or the HCI designer's decision making. **Synthesis** is the opportunity for the HCI designer to be a detective with the data to find patterns, make correlations between ideas, reveal connections between different users and organized themes and trends, uncover holes or gaps, and ultimately highlight user insights.

The synthesis of data into actions is made up of two parts:

- Analysis of facts
- User insights

Part 1 – analysis of user research data

When working with qualitative and quantitative user research data, an HCI designer should start with an analysis of the facts. Data analysis comprises reviewing the user research data, and the synthesis of your data and facts into forms that can be analyzed.

For example, an HCI designer might have five interviews with their users, resulting in 8 hours or transcripts. Interview analysis is made up of reviewing the transcripts, while synthesis is comprised of combining all the interviews together and pulling out all similar comments, quotes, or issues shared between each interview session. Analysis of users' research data involves evaluating and formating data findings from both qualitative and quantitative datasets into a highly useable format. User insights are the highest value output of an HCI designer's research analysis, which we will practice creating in a challenge in this chapter.

Before we get to practicing analyzing our user research data, let's discuss three strategies for analyzing data:

- Collection and organization of user research data
- Mining user research data
- Sorting, clustering, and categorize the user research data

Collection and organization of user research data

The goal of this analysis is to make your user research data manageable. Data collected includes written notes, digital notes, sketches, photos, audio recordings, video recordings, and so on, and establishing a system for organizing this data will allow this raw information to be efficiently shared between team members. If you are working with remote teams, it is highly recommended to share source files through cloud storage through Dropbox or Google Drive. The data you collect during any user research should not be hidden, and the initial organization of data will help others who might happen to also want to access the information.

For example, if you have 10 interviews, they are not all going to be equal. Organize them by qualitative factors, such as how fruitful the interview was. The HCI researchers can quantify their opinion on how useful the interview was and rank the interview either through a folder structure of number or a color system or by including top-level note/cliff notes, such as a README in a GitHub development repository.

Mining the user research data

Identifying what you see in user research data involves lots of analysis. Mining user research data has a process that looks as follows:

1. **Define the goals and the desired output for your user research:** Identify whether the user research data gathered is relevant.
2. **Process the user research data**: Review each participant to identify findings and establish the quality of the user research data worth analyzing deeper.
3. **Gather useful findings**: Pull out user quotations, rephrased points, or unique facts that support your goals.
4. **Pay attention to key points**: Review user research data for behaviors and attitudes, as well as user needs and goals that can be pulled out of the data.
5. **Color-code, tag, or classify your participant user research data**: The types of findings, or whatever system supports your desired goals as a research team, should be categorized.
6. **Look for any patterns or correlations**: When reviewing your user research data classification, see whether there are any larger insights to be understood for the highlighted findings.

Visually organizing user research data is a common method for mining the data. Depending on your team, it is recommended to use a physical office space that will let you more clearly *see* what's there. Making your research visual can look a bit crazy, like your research team are conspiracy theorists with newspaper clippings and a string connecting patterns, but don't worry about the perception. Synthesizing data is a bit messy. As an HCI designer, one thing you should know is that human beings are much better than computers at finding patterns, especially when looking at multiple forms of user research data. The HCI research team should evaluate qualitative and quantitative data together, which makes making the data visual in an office even more essential.

Sorting, clustering, and categorizing the user research data

The ability to manipulate and repackage your user research data is a required step when trying to extract insights during analysis and synthesis. The HCI designer can apply their own experience and curiosity to the qualitative and quantitative data during this process. As you sort through the research data, you might find criteria to see whether any unique patterns exist.

For example, does age have any correlation to how positive or negative a response was that was given during a survey? (Is a 20-year-old 9 rating equal to a 50-year-old 7 rating?).

You might be able to reveal this pattern by analyzing the quantitive responses by age and cross-referencing against their qualitative interviews to see whether survey reporting is reflected in interview responses. There are countless correlations an HCI researcher can make with a dataset, but it is essential to look at both qualitative and quantitative user research data. Sorting and clustering techniques are used to reframe your data. If your data is in a physical office, you can use the walls, Post-it notes, and color tags to associate data and patterns that naturally occur during the process.

It is highly recommended to make your user research data as accessible and physical as possible during this analysis. Sorting and clustering user research data can be achieved quickly in an office workspace and should be done with a few team members. Combining multiple HCI designers will lead to sorting and clustering and data patterns that could never be achieved by one person alone. Executing user research as a team also has the potential of creating meaningful user insights from reviewing other team members' user research data, but also allows synthesis to occur as a group. User research should be shared and evangelized among a team and organization as there is so much to learn by working together and implementing a research feedback loop with your users.

Part 2 – user insights

User research comes in many forms, as we have discussed. As an HCI researcher analyzes and synthesizes their user research into knowledge about their users, the goal of both gathering all this data and analyzing it is to learn something deeper about your user, software, or society. The goal is to get past what is obvious and be able to see into the underlying motivations, underserved ideas, or new opportunities that can come from deeply understanding your users through research. Our user research is a feedback loop, and user insight becomes the center of that loop.

Identifying user insights

Once you have collected and organized your user research data, mined the resulting data, sorted and clustered it using physical space, and revealed patterns and correlations in the data, now you can deduce some bigger understandings about your users. User insights are about your users, gathered from your data, and can start with a small hunch and then be broken open through the synthesis of user patterns.

We can follow our small hunch and execute steps to identify and refine user insights:

1. **Use conversation and synthesis patterns as a team**: Discuss why you think each small hunch is important. Speak with the user research team and figure out what it means, and how you see that pattern in the user research. Recall qualitative data through referencing exact quotations or experiences (facial expressions, body language, feelings, and attitudes) from user interviews that reveal the pattern. Apply quantitative data to see whether there is a match in the user's sentiment. Patterns can be established as apples to apples – the qualitative and quantitative data correlates – or apples to bananas – there is a disconnect between qualitative reports and quantitative data. If a user says "I love using the feature" during an interview but then rates the user experience of the software a 5 out of 10, why does the discrepancy exist? This might be a hunch to track down or relate to a user insight if the pattern exists among multiple users.

2. **Write one simple user insight statement**: Draft each user insight on paper or large Post-it notes as a team. Each user insight can emerge out of patterns or points of synthesis; however, be sure to be flexible when you come back to them later and change them.

3. **Ruminate user insights**: Like allowing bread to rise, a user insight also needs some time to ruminate. Set your user insight aside for 24 to 48 hours. As a user research team, do some other work and remove yourself from the user insights. Return to the user insight statement after some time and see whether it is still as surprising as it was when you first created it. If the user insight is good, it will have grown your attraction to it just like bread. Now it is ready to bake and share with the rest of your team, stakeholders, or clients.

4. **Iterate the user insights with the team**: Your original user insight might be in the right direction but still needs some refinement during the baking period. With user research, the HCI team thinks of different ways to express or articulate the same user insight.

5. **Share, test, and socialize your refined user insights**: Show your user insight to other teams who were *not* involved in the user research. During user insight testing, give your tester some context, have them read the user insights, and capture their reactions. If a user insight resonates with your tester and beyond your research team, then you have confirmed a valid user insight. Ideally, you would also test your user insight on your users to see whether they get it. If all of these answers are yes, then you can solidify the user insight and share the result with your broader team, stakeholders, clients, and users. User insights should not be held secret once they are created; they are "truths" and can help drive value and meaning to those solving software problems.

The fruit of user research is user insights. As an HCI designer, if you gather compelling qualitative and quantitative research, it is like watering and feeding a fruit tree. A challenge with any research is that user insights are not quickly created: they take time, like allowing the fruit to ripen. The role of an HCI team is not only to advocate for the time to create meaningful user insights but also to be practiced enough with the qualitative and quantitative methods that they can quickly get the raw research materials to create juicy fruit in the first place.

User insights are really hard to come by, and design teams who focus on making sure their software design teams cultivate, generate, and socialize user insights will ultimately build better software that is rooted in solving deep user needs and responds to "key truths" from their research. User insights are about purpose, and it is purpose that can drive the mission of a software team.

The data we gather over time is ultimately linked to understanding our users at a deeper level. Let's discuss how our user research and analysis can help drive purpose into our HCI team and broader organizations.

Rooting action to deeper user purpose

Let's take a birds-eye view of why HCI should care about a user insight in the first place. We discussed how our user research, both qualitative and quantitative, gets analyzed and synthesized, but a broader question remains: does researching our user really create better software solutions?

User research for HCI designers is not an easy task. Not only are the skills we discussed nuanced and somewhat time-consuming, but the real challenge comes when trying to justify the need for user research in the first place. The skills of executing qualitative and quantitive research together have the opportunity to paint an accurate picture of your user and, if done thoroughly, they can have a lasting impact on software decisions and, ultimately, the success or failure of software solutions. For HCI designers, we need the research to understand our process, and some of you may focus solely on the research path. If you are so lucky, great for you. The rest of us have to fight and scrap to include user research into our projects.

As we discussed earlier, computers and software have changed rapidly over the past 40 years since the introduction of the internet. This rapid change has justified (incorrectly so) the squeezing of user research budgets in some scenarios. Software moves quickly and some software teams have taken to the *shoot first, then aim* mentality. Take Facebook, for example. Mark Zuckerberg once said, "Move fast and break things." This idea is rampant in entrepreneurs and start-up culture, where getting ideas to market first is valued over making sure the product is what a user actually needs. Move fast can be perceived as "ignore users" or "engineers know best." The lack of user research in these areas is only starting to unravel in our current culture.

User research is constantly on the chopping block of client budgets, software projects, and clients' expectations. There is the idea that deeply researching a subject or user is prohibitive to executing a solution quickly. This is where the skills we discussed earlier and the HCI designer's need to dispel that notion are essential. User research is not negotiable! Our user researching is not just done during a specific phase of a project is but rather an essential layer of the output. If you want a great HCI software solution, it comes with user research along the way. The better the research, the better the solution.

The purpose of designing HCI solutions in the first place is linked to understanding how humans and computers interact, which can only be understood through user research. They are symbiotic. It is one giant feedback loop. What is truly awesome about being an HCI designer is that during our research, we can uncover and validate the purpose of our users and thus the purpose of your software solution.

What can be helpful is to think big about the purpose of our users. Let's start and get a cosmic perspective and consider the deepest motivations that drive users with a challenge.

Challenge 27 – The deep purpose of people challenge

Setup:
Get out a sheet of paper.

Part 1: Users' purpose:
Write down the purpose of people/users:

> *A. What is the purpose of human beings? Start generally and consider motivations.*
> *B. Get user-specific: What is a teenager's purpose? Consider both external motivations (school, culture, and social status) and internal motivation (self-worth, curiosity, and knowledge).*
> *C. What is the role technology plays in the defined motivations?*

Part 2: Micro and macro motivations:
Write down both the micro (short-term) and macro (long-term) motivations.

Part 3: Analyze the motivations:
Review your motivations for correlations – for example, if a short-term motivation is to save money, a long-term motivation might be to retire.

 Don't just consider your needs. Go back to your data and consider what you observed, heard, and experienced from your users during qualitative and quantitative research.

Aligning to deeper motivations within our users that were only discovered during user research and the creation of user insights is nothing short of profound. This is not just in us believing that computers can help our users but rather that we have changed our users' existence and helped them evolve. Through linking our computer to a deeper purpose, we can validate our role and reasons for solving our users' problems. The back and forth between understanding user research and relating that research to the purpose our users create is why we analyze and synthesize our findings. Relating the deeper role and value user research plays in the role of HCI design is executed through the creation of user insights. A great user insight is the embodiment of the rationale and effort put into caring about our user and doing a human-centered design research process from the get-go.

Identifying and writing user insights

As HCI gains popularity, one thing seems to separate the quality of designers: the foresight and knowhow to articulate deep user insights. User insights are a catalyst for executing human-centered software solutions. A great user insight is the by-product of the analysis and synthesis of your qualitative and quantitative research data. To gain a deep perspective on your users is no walk in the park. Conceptually grasping the idea of understanding your user deeply is like recognizing water is wet. Insights hold value when they can help a research team understand a "deep truth" about their users. User insights are necessary when solving problems, but the challenge comes in understanding why.

User insights are hard! As an HCI designer, you will be called upon to assemble a solid user insight, but it takes practice to get deep meaningful outcomes. People are generally able to articulate something obvious, but the role of an HCI designer is to drive beyond what is right in front of your face and dig deep below the surface, which becomes a challenge.

Let's use IDEO's mad lib challenge to break down the user insight problem. Try to write one for yourself.

Challenge 28 – IDEO's POV mad lib

Setup:
Get out a sheet of paper.

Part 1: Write a POV mad lib:
Write a sentence using the following POV mad lib:

{User/persona} needs to {user needs} because of {surprising insight}.

Part 2: Read your POV out loud:
Read your sentence out loud. If it sounds obvious, iterate your surprising insight.

You will not write a good POV mad lib on your first try. This will require multiple rounds of iteration.

The exercise is a great starting place for growing your ability to start creating a user insight from your research findings. Like I said, writing great user insights is very hard. The true challenge comes when trying to generate something genuinely "surprising" when it comes to your users. There is no cheat code for getting user insights: you just have to put in the work and research and keep pushing at them and iterating them until they resonate with you, your team, and your clients. Let's explore an example.

To help our user insight writing, we will use an IDEO POV statement, which might be something like this:

> *POV version 1:*
>
> *A teenage boy needs to eat more fruits and vegetables because vitamins are good for your health.*

Iteration is essential to improving a surprising user insight as the initial user insight typically lacks this value. The goal is to dive deeply into the user insight to find that elusive surprising factor.

The original idea is still kept in the insight but the outcome is improving three key components:

- Increase the emotional quality of your user needs.
- Establish a broader context for your user.
- Push the insight past an obvious insight into a surprising insight.

As a way to iterate your user insight, try to write a more surprising insight.

Challenge 29 – IDEO's POV mad lib iteration

Setup:
You will be using your POV insight from Challenge 28.

Part 1: Iterate insight:

1. *Iterate your insight, improving the following:*

    1. *The emotion of the needs of your user.*
    2. *Add context to your user/persona.*
    3. *Push the insight to not be obvious but rather surprising.*

2. *Rewrite using the same POV mad lib from Challenge 28:*

{User/persona} needs to {user needs} because of {suprising insight}.

Part 2: Share your insight with another person:

1. *Test/read your POV insight to a friend, colleague, or significant other, and see whether the insight is surprising.*
2. *If not, keep iterating. Some user insights need to be rewritten multiple times until they resonate as surprising and meaningful user insights.*

Part 3: Save your POV insight:
You should be able to speak about why your POV insight is "surprising" and record how many iterations your insight went through.

Feedback here is essential. You might think you have a deep insight but once someone else reads it, they might not see it or worse, they might disagree. Share early and often.

POV version 2:

A growing teenage boy with many factors pulling at his attention needs to be more socially supported by his peers when eating healthy food because, in his environment, his social circle has more impact on his health habits than his doctor or parents.

An iteration of the IDEO POV might look something as follows:

1. Increases the emotional quality of the user needs so that it is noting not just a teenager but a teenager with a bleak outlook.
2. Establishes a broader context for the user by adding that the teenager is growing.
3. Pushes insight past an obvious insight into a surprising insight by saying that food decisions for a teenager are socially impacted, which is more surprising than the obvious fact that vitamins are good for your health.

As you can see, generating a unique user insight is no simple task and requires synthesizing research, observations, interviews, and life experience into every aspect of the user insight. The mad lib will not magically produce a surprising truth, but with hard work and practice, you can write a number of them until you get it right.

The role of an HCI designer/researcher is to go below the surface and find deep insightful meaning from their research. With deep user insights, an HCI designer can drive a number of solutions. User insights should not have a solution tied to them but rather influence the team that uses the user insights to create a variety of solutions. When user insights are deep, they can be used by an HCI design team for long periods of time as they reveal a key "truth" that remains relevant, regardless of whether an HCI team creates a solution based on the insight or not. Aligning user insights as the engines of potential solutions is the greatest value they offer to your team.

Aligning a solution to users

An HCI designer must work very hard to refine their user insights into sharable deliverables that can be used by their team, clients, and stakeholders. A great user insight is like catching a big fish: you want to be able to mount and display it for all to see.

User insights have a paradox as they are essential in helping design teams create solutions but should not contain a solution on their own. Rather, user insights should align an HCI design team toward multiple solutions. The user insight can be valued by the number of possible solutions it helps create. A great user insight will not have just one solution but rather will allow an HCI team to devise multiple solutions. User insights drive an innovation cycle for software teams:

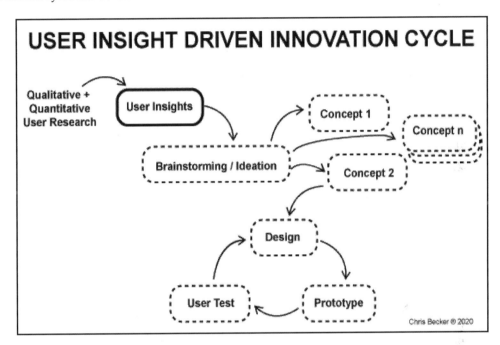

Our user insight:

> *A growing teenage boy with many factors pulling at his attention needs to be more socially supported by his peers when eating healthy food because, in his environment, his social circle has more impact on his health habits than his doctor or parents.*

Take the user insight I provided as an example. The user insight does not have a solution attached to it. There are many, many ways to impact the social acceptance and education of teenagers, as well as many, many ways to identify and impact social and environmental risks associated with health.

One way to orient a user insight to help an HCI design team align with potential solutions is to reframe the user insight as a *how might we* question.

A "how might we" user insight statement:

How might we help a growing teenage boy with many factors pulling at his attention that needs to be more socially supported by his peers when eating healthy food because, in his environment, his social circle has more impact on his health habits than his doctor or parents?

The user insight is framed as a question that might spark a number of ideas and potential concepts to be generated. A good user insight will produce lots and lots of ideas (hopefully). One thing you might notice about our user insight is that is doesn't indicate how a solution will be created and includes no technology references or problem causes. The relative openness of the *how might we* statement from our user insight allows an HCI designer to consider how software, applications, or technology might help solve the issues targeted in the user insight.

If your user insight does not create a useful *how might we* question, then it might point at two things. One, your user insight is not deep enough and you need to iterate or rewrite it, or two, your user insight is too complicated and needs to be reframed so that ideas have more opportunity to be produced from the user insight. An HCI designer wants their user insights to be readily available and easily communicated to their clients.

Summary

Congratulations, you are officially halfway through the book and there is still a bunch to learn and explore! Throughout this chapter, we started to get our hands on some skills and activities that an HCI designer can use to start designing software. A unique factor for any HCI designer is that a majority of the skills that we learn and the activities that we use are addictive. How we think and learn impacts future versions and iterations, and this is why we covered how to start learning and understanding from qualitative and quantitative research data. Great software solutions are rooted in solving a deep user insight, which is why we focused on and practiced formulating user insights of our own throughout this chapter. As discussed in this chapter, user insights are not surface-level; they require lots of digging and, hopefully, your insight is also a launching-off point that can be improved over time with practice. I will continue to bolster the point that practice is what makes an HCI designer better and, hopefully, the skills and challenges up to this point are methodologies that you will repeat in your journey toward mastery.

In the next chapter, we will focus on more skills in part 2 of the execution of software design through human-centered methods for user research.

7
Storytelling and Rapid Prototyping

As you continue to grow your **human-computer interaction (HCI)** skills, it is essential to practice these skills over time. Up to this point, we have learned how to combine our research data from our new qualitative and quantitative methods, as well as to align our software analysis to our users through data gathering, analysis, and interpretation. All of the HCI user research has allowed us to understand something true and hopefully produce a deep and meaningful user insight. The user insight is the kernel of a solution or multiple solutions, and our role now is to unpack how we move from user insight to a software solution. An HCI designer's job gets very tactical as we move from user research to creating human-centered solutions. Based on the user insight, the HCI designer can start employing human-centered storytelling methods that help to align software solutions to their users.

Now that you have a solid grasp of HCI user research, both qualitative and quantitative, and how that research helps an HCI designer generate user insights, let's discuss what to do with this valuable user research data. An HCI designer's success is ultimately measured by the software they create and because HCI methods have produced more useable, accessible, and useful software products for users, this chapter will cover how we take user research and start to generate a software solution. This chapter will converge and focus your research data into making a software solution via software prototyping. Software solutions are at the heart of HCI design and the skills of prototyping will show you how to go about taking your user research and building software solutions.

In this chapter, we will be capitalizing on data through the following topics:

- Prototyping first
- Systems diagramming
- HCI interface best practices
- Software prototyping tools

Prototyping first

As a growing HCI designer, you will start to see a lot of conversation in the community about prototyping. The role prototyping plays in the creation of great software is hard to overstate.

Prototyping, as we have discussed, is the creation of an early model of a software solution that is built to test the success or failure of the solution with our users. In the HCI design workflow, creating a prototype is essential to flushing out software ideas. The origins of the word come from the Greek word *prototypon* (πρωτότυπον). When you first start to create software solutions, they are never fully baked; they are early ideas and are supposed to be primitive. Ideas should be plentiful and the research you do as an HCI designer should uncover a lot of opportunity from a few useful insights.

Out of your user insights come ideas, concepts, or potential solutions. Many software opportunities can be generated from a user insight by using an ideation method known as a **How Might We (HMW)** statement.

For example, I created 15 ideas quickly from the HMW user insight statement presented in the previous chapter:

> *HMW statement:*
>
> *How might we **help a growing teenage boy** with many factors pulling at his attention that needs **to be more socially supported** by his peers when **eating healthy food** because, **in his environment, his social circle** has more **impact on his health habits than his doctor or parents**?*

The HWM statement is a jumping-off point from our user insight and a catalyst for creating ideas.

 I hope the HMW statement sparks ideas of your own. Before moving on to reading my ideas, I recommend you write down some possible solutions you thought of to the provided statement as practice.

Here are some ideas that I generated from the HMW statement:

- Design and integrate health tips into the teenager's social media.
- Create a social group for teenagers with a bleak outlook.
- Incentivize healthy eating through a partnership with a celebrity.

- Create a teenager-based social networking site centered around improving behaviors including health.
- Design a health education platform that is socially accepted by his peers.
- Create a peer-to-peer network for sharing social taboos that are supported by health tips.
- Create a teenage persona that allows the teen to identify where his social decisions impact his health factors.
- Design a cookbook app for teenagers.
- Create a messaging bot that shares health tips for teens.
- Design an ad campaign targeted at the biggest health risk caused by a social risk.
- Help teenagers track their health decisions with their friends.
- Design a social app that rewards teenagers in groups for accomplishing healthy-eating goals.
- Create a teenager-based education platform that decreases the social risk of healthy decisions.
- Create a teenage robot companion that shares healthy tips among teenage gossip.
- Design an email and text message communication platform that shares teenager-relevant health tips.

None of these ideas are worth anything in the form of written concepts, although having a lot of potential ideas from one user insight is incredibly helpful for the HCI team. Not only can an HCI design evaluate many ideas against each other but it can also start to reveal patterns and themes in the ideas created before moving onto the execution of the idea through a prototype. Among my 15 quick ideas, there are some similar concepts:

- **Ideas 1, 2, 4, 6, 11, and 12**: A social networking theme as part of the solution, which is logical based on our audience as well as the subject. Plus, many social application software solutions are available and suited to create something new.

- **Ideas 5, 8, 13, and 15:** An education theme for improving and solving user insight. The education theme is included because teenagers' brains are still growing and improving behaviors is a goal achieved over time through practice and education.

These themes are important and may directly influence the direction of a chosen solution. Along with idea themes, you can also combine ideas into one stronger idea. For example, there are six ideas on social networking, and three of those ideas –**ideas 2, 4, and 11** – all deal with a social app of some kind.

What would it be like to combine the ideas? Let's take **ideas 2, 4, and 11** – to make a social health application.

For example, say we want to make a social health application targeted at teenagers that focuses on health behavior-based content that includes incentives and rewards for completing health challenges with their friends.

When generating ideas, make sure you don't jump into the combining stage too quickly. Ideally, you are also combining your ideas with others on your team. The value offered by many potential solutions and then reviewing them as a group will reveal more themes and potentially more ideas that can be combined between group members. If many team members generate ideas with a similar theme, it might point to a particularly deep idea that is worth pursuing. Identifying the potential of ideas is the reason HCI designers generate lots of ideas in the first place. If you generate a lot of ideas on a similar theme as a team, it shows that those ideas may be more appropriate for addressing the user insight with a solution.

Now it is your turn to try and create some ideas.

Challenge 30 – Idea/concept generation

Setup:

Get out Post-it notes, paper, and pens/pencils. This challenge will be based on your HMW statement from `Chapter 6`, *User Insights for Software Solutions*.

Part 1: Post-it ideation:

Take 20 minutes to write down as many possible ideas, concepts, or solutions for your user insight. (Do not self-edit during this process; any idea is worth writing down.)

Part 2: Capture your process:

Take a picture of your raw ideas.

Part 3: Idea patterns and categorization:

1. *Categorize your ideas into themes.*
2. *Take another picture.*

Part 4: Analyze your ideas category themes:

1. *Reflect on the themes and combine any ideas/concepts/solutions that are similar.*

Do not edit yourself during ideation. Any ideas should be written down, even if it has already been created or seems outlandish. DO NOT EDIT DURING IDEATION!

Of course, there are many other potential ideas for solving our user insight, but if the HCI team continues to generate ideas that revolve around these themes, then you will know that you have some potential. Every user insight will generate unique ideas and therefore have unique idea themes. The goal is to generate a lot of ideas to give the HCI team options, as well as to make sure the user is being the most served by the chosen idea. Hopefully, you have created a bunch of ideas and continued to grow your ability to generate ideas from your HMW user insight statement.

The number of ideas generated during the ideation of your user insight can be evaluated through Laseau's funnel.

Laseau's funnel

In Laseau's funnel, Funnel one is the exploration of ideas – a funnel that is widening over time and starts with user research and is fueled by user insights. Laseau's funnel is the combination of the divergent elaboration of ideas and the convergent reduction of ideas through prototyping:

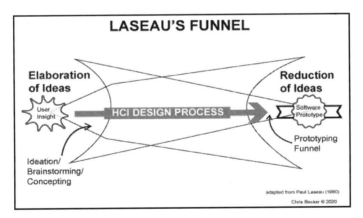

Over time, the ideas produced increases as the HCI designer learns more about their users, creates deeper user insights, and generally improves with creating ideas through practice. The second funnel is an inverted funnel that focuses on ideas. This funnel can be characterized through prototyping.

Ideas can only be understood if they solve the problem, not through testing. A prototype makes an idea tangible and, in terms of software, it allows users to interact with the solution and reduces the idea down to something that can be validated.

Once you have a number of idea themes going as a team from your user insight, the next stage is to select a few ideas to move forward with and establish a hierarchy. If you have lots of ideas to choose from, this is a better position as an HCI team. Ideas and their potential are only evaluated against another idea. If you only generate one idea, then that is the solution you have to pursue. This is a risky position. If your user insight is only generating one solution as well, it is either a weak user insight or your ideas are also lacking quality. Having only a few ideas are a clear warning sign that a deep user insight has not been discovered yet. On the other hand, if you have lots of ideas, this allows the HCI team to quickly pit ideas against each other and allow the best idea to win out. Choosing ideas is not purely about the survival of the fittest, however; it is about establishing a hierarchy of ideas. Let's discuss a few methods for determining how a team can choose the best ideas.

Dot voting

During dot voting, participants choose from a set of options – in our case, ideas – and apply their vote. Dot voting allows team members or stakeholders to voice and visualize their opinion:

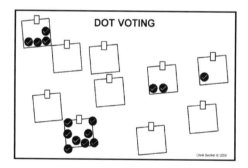

The dot votes should have enough votes per member to create a way for voting ties to not occur – for example, if you have a team of 5 and you have 2 ideas that are being voted for, each member should be given one vote. In the case where 2 ideas are voted for, the voting tally can never result in a deadlock with an uneven set of votes. Avoiding voting deadlock is a good thing. For the same reason, the supreme court in the USA has 9 justices; dot voting should attempt to allow ideas to clearly be established via a vote.

2x2 opportunity matrix

Furthermore, the matrix can be made with any two factors that might help plot your idea, but typically, it will include looking at value (idea originality/innovation) versus financial stake (cost/implementation). When evaluating ideas that are worth pursuing first, look for ideas that live in the highly innovative, low-cost space first. Plotting ideas on a 2x2 matrix can also be helpful when done alongside the first dot voting method as the team may vote for a highly innovative idea without considering the high cost associated with implementation:

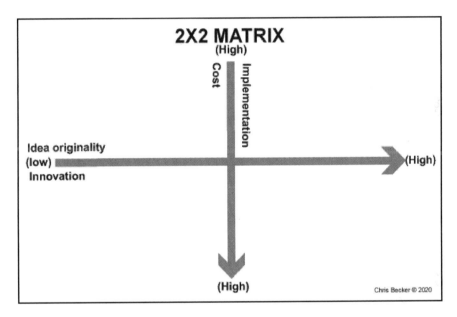

The goal in choosing an idea is not to create just one solution to rule them all, but rather having lots of ideas, which is challenging, and evaluating the ideas before your team commits more energy and cost to the solutions is essential. Many times, the best outcomes of dot voting and plotting ideas on a 2x2 matrix are it allows you to move forward with a few ideas in an established hierarchy. This idea hierarchy is where we lean on the need for prototyping. Starting off with a number of opportunities also allows an HCI team to practice the art of "prototyping first." Prototyping is making an idea tangible and ideas can quickly be validated by your user through making a solution. Prototyping allows the HCI designer to funnel the chosen ideas into possible solutions. Prototyping is an essential process for any HCI designer. Let's discuss the types of prototyping options.

Paper prototyping (low fidelity)

For instance, paper prototyping is a process by which cheap paper models are used to simulate a computer or web applications for building software quickly and cheaply. The goal of paper prototyping is to act as the quickest method for simulating software and getting your ideas into the hands of your users. Paper prototyping relies on tangible objects (paper) for usability and functions under the assumption that the user will interact with the paper object as they would with a real software application or technology. Paper prototypes are a form of idea sketching that allows an HCI designer to think through a software experience. Typically, paper prototypes are early models and are rendered through low-fidelity visuals known as (sketched) wireframes. Sketched wireframes are a representation of a user interface of a software product or website that is drawn by hand rather than rendered via a software application.

A wireframe is higher fidelity than a paper prototype, which is typically sketched or hand-drawn. A paper prototype is far from the final product and won't look like or feel like the final product. If you put multiple wireframes together as a way to test an interaction or software feature, where each paper screen mimics the possible design, the wireframes/sketches are no longer static, elevating the sequence to a paper prototype.

In usability testing, a test participant is shown the paper prototype. The prototype moderator has to get the tester to use their imagination as the paper version of the software is not actually interactive but rather controlled by the tester. Paper prototype user testing attempts to validate the initial interface ideas and can quickly uncover whether a software feature or user interface design is working or not with the user testers. The prototyping stage is when HCI teams should be looking to catch software design flaws, and the flexibility and ephemeral quality of paper encourage experimentation and speedy iteration, or even allows a radical change in direction if ideas are not validated with users through prototype tests.

Paper is cheap and you can write notes right on the paper prototype or on the back of each paper sheet or index card. The value of creating a solution though cheap materials is essential when thinking through a software solution. Paper allows the ideas captured to not be treated with too much reverence. This is really key when coming up with lots of ideas. Your paper prototype is not precious; it is a sketch and should be batted around, poked at for holes, and generally be run through the wringer. Among a software design team, paper prototypes can represent lots and lots of options that are being explored. Through making and having tangible outcomes as paper prototypes, a team can quickly move solutions forward. Many paper prototypes operate as failures as a way to eliminate options, rather than making only the "right" decision.

Making decisions about what not to do is just as important as what will work. If you create a paper prototype in 30 minutes and test it with your users to discover your potential solution is too hard to use, this method has now saved the software team countless hours of work that would include polishing the design, developing code, and testing with users. That idea just dies at the paper prototyping stage right then and there, but it only took up a short amount of time to eliminate that option. A design team should be able to eliminate lots of paper prototypes. It can be hard at times to kill ideas, but if you build prototypes using cheap materials and are not laboring too long over the early solutions, then what you end up moving forward with is ultimately stronger because it is the by-product of all the failures that came before.

Paper prototyping is a great place to experiment and take a risk. During paper prototyping, solutions are not yet truly invested in and have not been developed and scaled to all your users. The experimentation with a paper prototype is contained and allows the HCI designer to quickly validate their ideas. An HCI designer might ask, "Will X work with our users?". A paper prototype can determine whether it will work or not. Trust me, there are a lot of ideas where X just won't work, but you will never know until you test it. Paper prototyping can also help improve the final product through making decisions, and this includes what not to do.

I was once working for a large university client on redesigning their website. One big problem they were trying to fix was helping undergraduate and graduate students choose a major and a minor. They had 88+ majors and 60+ minors to choose from. This resulted in quite a challenge for how students would be able to search and filter these many options. During the process, the client wanted to shorthand the major/minor distinction as MAJ/MIN. Luckily, we had done a quick paper prototype with this major/minor labeling system and found students did not know what those labels meant, especially undergraduate students. The ability for our team to anticipate our client and have a paper prototype ready for them to experiment with, as well as some initial testing results with students, allowed us to quickly move past this small but important usability issue that our client was pushing for. Paper prototypes build accountability into the design process and allow client and user tests to constantly tune a software experience.

There are three dominant accountability opportunities with paper prototypes:

1. **Presenting a solution to your HCI team**: Your team has a vested interest in a software product being built correctly and wants to see how a solution might work before committing time, money, resources, and marketing to a solution. Paper prototypes allow an HCI designer to show thinking through a solution and make the idea tangible for other team members to play with themselves. Many times, it can be evaluated by other team members who will be involved in implementing the solution through code. If the paper prototype is approved by design and developers, then moving the solution forward will be more coherent among team members who are all on the same page.

2. **Validating the solution with users**: Paper prototypes can be shared with users that run through a set of existing paper mock-ups and give feedback based on their experience with a given software solution. Similar to getting your team members on board, validating a solution with users will also double the value that a paper prototype holds. Team members and stakeholders can be reassured that the solution is moving in the right direction through user testing.

3. **Acquiring buy-in from your stakeholders (clients)**: Paper prototypes can be equally shared with stakeholders who can also play with tangible solutions. Similar to getting your team members on board, acquiring buy-in from your stakeholders will also go a long way in delivering the value of design. Stakeholders can be reassured that the solution is moving in the right direction through data on paper prototype user testing as well as experiencing the solutions for themselves.

Your stakeholders are most likely not your users, however, building a rapport as well as a design rationale with your stakeholders and clients will go a long way in communicating the value of human-centered design throughout the process.

Paper prototyping is also a clever way to get stakeholders involved in the design process early on. Not everyone needs to be able to build the final product, and many people, including stakeholders, can have good ideas but not know how to execute them. Paper prototyping can help democratize design, development, and rapid interaction design and allow innovation to not be the responsibility of a small group of people in any organization. As simple as it sounds, paper prototyping can bring more people into the design and development process early on, which can lead to better products. Let's practice ourselves.

Challenge 31 – Paper prototype sketching

Setup:

1. *Get out three sheets of paper (Letter or A4 paper).*
2. *Start by tracing your smartphone on your paper.*
3. *Trace 2^two screens per sheet – trace the screen size to scale.*

Part 1: Idea selection:

1. *Choose an idea from the ideation session challenge. Choose an idea that can be put into a mobile app. This does not have to be your most innovative idea.*
2. *Start by determining the task your user will accomplish.*

   For example, a social health application targeted at teenagers that focuses on health behavior-based content and includes incentives and rewards for users completing health challenges with their friends (such as sharing a health incentive with five friends).

Part 2: Paper sketching:

1. *Start sketching the software interface wireframe onto the screens.*
2. *Include as many paper prototype screens as needed to accomplish the task.*
3. *Take a picture of your sketched wireframes.*

Part 3: Paper prototyping:

1. *Cut out each screen and place it in the order of the task.*
2. *Flip through the screen to make sure your sketch wireframes have enough information, context, and visual design so that a user, if asked, could accomplish the task you just built as a paper prototype.*
3. *Record you moving through the paper prototype interacting with the model just like it was a computer screen.*

It is highly recommended that you explore a number of software tools for quickly creating software prototypes.

An overview of tools can be found here: `https://www.prototypr.io/tools`.

I recommend signing up for accounts with the following sites:

- `www.InVisionapp.com`
- `https://proto.io/`

Also, it is recommended to get access to the following creative software:

- Figma
- Sketch App (Apple only)
- Abobe XD

Now that you have an early paper prototype, a very important aspect is to document your process. A paper prototype operates like a tree in the forest: "If no one is around to hear a tree fall, did it make a sound?". Similarly, if a paper prototype has no record, did it help a design team make a decision? Documentation of the design process for an HCI designer is really important not only for the HCI designer's own education but also as a way to involve your clients and stakeholders without requiring them to make the sausage with you.

With the preceding example I described of the university, I was grateful to have documented the paper prototype and when the major/minor suggestion was made, I had the paper prototype images and user tests locked and loaded not just as justification for our solution but also as a way to bring our client into the way we work. HCI design is not a mystery and using methods such as paper prototyping allows us to make the process visual and fold others that are not HCI designers into our way of working.

Paper prototypes can and should be fun to make and test. If your team is spending large amounts of time building "perfect" paper prototypes, then the process is working against you. Remember, paper prototypes are meant to be as follows:

- Fast and cheap (low-fidelity)
- Built for quick user testing and idea validation
- Made with materials that can be manipulated (drawn on, folded, cut or torn, or crumpled up and thrown away)
- The first step in prototyping (a form of sketching)
- Shared and made tangible for your team and users

Once you have completed a few paper prototypes, the process will speed up and become second nature to thinking through a software solution. Paper prototypes are really useful for an HCI designer but can be more challenging to use for testing with users or even your clients and stakeholders. This is where paper prototypes can quickly be turned into clickable prototypes.

Clickable prototyping (mid-fidelity)

Similarly, clickable prototypes are just as they sound. They are a software simulation that adds interactive mock-ups that can take users through product features and software user flows. Clickable prototypes are built in order to test a user flow more efficiently than a paper prototype. Clickable prototypes can be built through many different types of software; I have seen clickable prototypes executed with PowerPoint through to more complex clickable prototypes executed through user interface software such as Adobe XD, Sketch, and Figma.

The goal of a clickable prototype is to allow a user to journey through a product and be able to test how smooth, consistent, and easy to navigate the steps of interaction are. Like paper prototyping, clickable prototypes should be quick to produce and be used to evaluate and validate the design process. Clickable prototypes do a better job of mimicking the software context and are typically facilitated by software themselves.

A possibility is also to make "empty shell" UI clickable prototypes using pure HTML / CSS or XML. Empty means without functionality, just the UI. With some UI editors / interface builders (`https://bootstrapstudio.io/`), making a clickable mock-up can be quick even if the generated code may not be reusable at scale. Such clickable mock-ups are also usable for motion prototyping (see below). It is not in contradiction with "Front-End Prototyping", because there is no functionality, just an idea of the UI. It allows us to see whether the prototype mock-up is ultimately "codable".

Designing and developing a software product is complex and requires a lot of iteration, and none of it would be possible without prototyping and user testing. Clickable prototypes are built so that software design teams can test their solutions. If you are building clickable prototypes only for yourself, your team, or your stakeholders, you are doing it wrong. Although these team members are important, they are not your users. Therefore, your clickable prototypes should be tested with your users first. Clickable prototypes are invaluable from an HCI perspective for their ability to generate user feedback and they often lead to discoveries that influence product development. At their best, clickable prototypes allow features to emerge as a result of early-stage prototype testing.

Let's practice creating a clickable prototype out of our paper prototype.

Challenge 32 – Clickable paper prototype

Setup:

1. *Get out your materials: paper prototype screens, camera/smartphone, and the InVision app (or another prototyping application).*
2. *Start by iterating any paper screens from paper prototyping challenge 29. Redraw any screens based on feedback. All screen sketches should have enough content and context to be understood by your user.*
3. *Take photos of each screen in your paper prototype sequence. Lay the screens flat and do not take photos at an angle.*

Part 1: Prepare paper sketched images:

1. *Crop each photo to just the screen size and relabel each photo with* `#-app-screen-title-type-version`, *for example,* `01-SocialHeathApp-SignIn-pp-v1`.
2. *Download images to your computer in a folder called* `App-paper-prototype`.

Part 2: Use InVision to create a clickable paper prototype:

1. *Log in to* `invisionapp.com`.
2. *If you don't have an account, register for a free account (allows you to create one prototype for free).*
3. *Create a mobile prototype and add a label.*
4. *Upload/drag and drop your paper prototype screen photos.*
5. *Using the build tool, add hotspots to your paper prototype and connect the screens together.*

Part 3: Test your clickable paper prototype:

1. *Select the preview mode (eye icon); you can click through your paper screens.*
2. *From the upper-right corner, select the SMS-to-mobile button and share your clickable app to your phone for mobile testing.*

Part 4: Share your clickable paper prototype with users:

Share your clickable paper prototype with a friend for some feedback.

 Use social media (Twitter, Facebook, or LinkedIn) to get people to use your prototype. You would be surprised at who will interact and give feedback.

Now that you have made your paper prototype into a clickable prototype. you have a faster way to validate your idea. If you test it with users, you can quickly make iterations to your idea by moving your paper sketches into user interface software for building digital wireframes and eventually user interface design compositions. There are many tools for creating digital wireframes, but software solutions should iterate quickly based on user tests. I recommend exploring a number of digital wireframing and UI tools but personally, I use the combo of the Sketch app and InVision App with the Craft plugins to speed up my prototyping process. Sketch and InVision together can manage prototypes through the Sketch application and keep your prototypes synced online for quick updating and user testing. Use user interface software that speeds up your team's ability to produce clickable prototypes as a team over time. Getting everyone working with similar tools will speed up the ability to share the prototyping load and produce solutions and software systems that can iterate and scale.

Challenge 33 – Clickable wireframe prototype

Setup:

1. *Log in to the InVision App.*
2. *Open digital user interface software (I recommend using Sketch, Adobe XD, or Figma).*
3. *Recreate your paper prototype sketches with digital software.*

Part 1: Import paper sketches into a digital tool:

1. *Create artboard screens and label artboards for your screens.*
2. *Import images of your screens to your digital artboards.*

Part 2: Digital wireframing:

1. *Recreate your paper sketches digitally as wireframes.*
2. *Export your digital screens.*

Part 3: Wireframe clickable prototyping:

1. *Log in to invisionapp.com and select your paper prototype.*
2. *Upload/drag and drop your digital screens.*
3. *Using the build tool, add hotspots to your digital screens and connect the screens together.*
4. *Select the preview mode (eye icon) to click through your digital clickable screens.*

Part 4: Share your clickable wireframe prototype with users:

1. *From the upper-right corner, select the SMS-to-mobile button and share your clickable app to your phone for mobile testing.*
2. *Share your digital clickable prototype with a friend for some feedback.*

Make sure your images are cropped to the aspect ratio of the device. Do not import a screen at 900 px x 900 px that is designed for an iPhone X, which has a screen size of 1,125 px x 2,436 px.

Practicing with user interface software is essential to growing your software design skills. Using tools such as Sketch, Adobe XD, or Figma should be done in the service of building prototypes that can be tested by users. If you are new to software design, your prototypes may not be very good, so build a lot of them and practice executing a lot of different solutions through sketching testing iterating digitizing wireframes testing iterating digitizing high-fidelity comps testing iterating, and so on. As with any craft, software design requires time to get better and faster. If you and your team practice with the tools that build prototypes together, then, in turn, your prototypes will improve and your software solutions will get better as well.

Clickable prototype tools such as Sketch and InVision are great for creating and sharing mostly static prototypes, and they work well for the majority of day-to-day design tasks. But there are limitations, and clickable prototypes can only address certain aspects of an interactive system. Clickable prototypes often look, behave, and feel a bit different than the intention of the final coded product. The gap between the prototype and the product exists throughout the prototyping process. The goal is to close the gap from paper to high-fidelity prototype versions and work with your team to faithfully represent what you can build in your prototyping process. At each prototyping stage and iteration, the gap gets smaller. This is where motion prototypes come into play.

Motion prototyping (high fidelity)

Likewise, motion prototyping uses software to add motion and interaction to user interface elements in an interface prototype. Typically, motion prototypes are applied to the prototyping process when clickable prototypes become limited. Motion can be achieved through code but requires more time and therefore should be figured out via a prototype first before committing to the effort during the production of the software.

For example, suppose I want a drag and drop feature for a list. A static prototype would have a hard time approximating this behavior for a user. A motion prototype, on the other hand, would allow users to seeing the object animate during a drag and drop behavior, as well as see how the element might move and animate from position to position.

Motion is essential to prototype for user interface elements as the addition of dynamic movement within a user interface can help train your users and improve not only their usability but also their overall software experience. Through building motion prototypes, an HCI team can add nuance and polish to a software solution.

Motion prototypes attempt to figure out three main questions about an interface's behavior:

1. **The behavior of a user interface motion**: How does a user interface element respond during an interaction? For example, if you hold down an item to drag and drop it, does it shake, pop, or glow? Animation can help define this behavior.
2. **The behavior of a user interface feature**: How does a user interface feature respond during the execution of a feature? For example, when swiping to the left to delete, as you drag a card to delete it, does it slide off the screen, fold, detach, or crumple up?
3. **The behavior of a transition**: As a user moves between screens, features, or content, how does the software transition present itself based on the feature? For example, when you load a new page on a website, does the content transition from top to bottom to mimic a scroll? Do images slide in from the left to indicate a sliding motion?

Motion prototypes are typically more sophisticated and can require more specialized software to help execute animations, such as that of Adobe After Effects. Because of the added sophistication and nuance of motion design, motion prototypes are typically not where an HCI designer will start with prototyping. Motion prototypes will inherit a high-fidelity quality as testing motions or transitions is not helpful in design decisions that might be invalidated through an easier and faster clickable prototype.

One value that motion prototyping has is that your prototypes start to get really close to the desired end product. Adding motion allows your user to participate in this experience and can be very helpful, especially as you get closer to finalizing the software design.

A point of caution!

Make sure your motion prototyping team and your development team are aligned on their capabilities during motion prototyping. Some motion prototyping tools are very robust and can make a screen experience do lots of things that, during the coding of the final product, might take your development team weeks to produce. This could be problematic as your client or user has been shown a prototype that does more than what your team can faithfully execute. Prototypes are meant to design what your team can develop within the software design budget and should be used to help set expectations with clients.

Frontend prototyping (low to high fidelity)

As a result, frontend prototyping uses code to quickly produce interactive software solutions and typically focus on the visuals of the screen interfaces. *Frontend* refers to frontend technologies used in coding web interfaces, typically HTML/CSS and JavaScript. Many frontend prototypes will utilize a code framework to speed up the development process and allow the frontend team to focus on producing a working prototype, rather than writing all the code from scratch. Popular frameworks are Bootstrap, Angular, React, and Vue.js.

Many HCI designers and developers think coding prototypes first is the most powerful way to test them. The end product is code anyway, so why not prototype in code along the way? There are many ways to harness HTML/CSS and JavaScript and make good use of it for building web prototypes.

Depending on your software design team's skillset, the role that frontend prototyping plays is a by-product of how familiar the team is with coding. Frontend prototypes typically break down into two categories:

1. **Low-fidelity, high-functionality frontend prototypes**: A version of frontend prototypes that are used by developers. Typically, the visual elements are not to spec or are missing altogether, but the functionality of the code is high.
   For example, a carousel prototype, where the coded prototype allows the user to actually swipe through boxes, move left to right, and zoom in/make a selection but does not offer the design elements for text areas, call-to-action-buttons, and so on. Such prototypes are generally lacking in robust CSS or customized JavaScript.

2. **High-fidelity, high-functionality frontend prototypes**: A type of frontend prototype that offers a high level of visual detail along with a robust set of functionality. Typically, these frontend prototypes are nearly final versions of the actual project.

The role frontend prototypes play in the production of software can have huge implications when it comes to producing production-ready scalable software solutions. A frontend prototype has code that can be refactored or used directly in a software solution.

Challenge 34 – Frontend clickable prototype

Setup:

1. *Log in to GitHub.*
2. *Create a GitHub repository.*
3. *Open your text editor (I recommend VS Code).*
4. *Recreate/code your digital wireframes using HTML/CSS/JavaScript with Bootstrap.*

Part 1: Code HTML and CSS:

1. *Create an* index.html *page.*
2. *Link Bootstrap (CSS and JavaScript) through the **CDN (Content Delivery Network)**.*
3. *Code and recreate your sketched wireframes digitally as wireframes in code.*
4. *Add interactivity via Bootstrap and custom CSS.*

Part 2: Test in the web browser:

Display your screen in a browser.

Part 3: GitHub repository:

1. *Log in to GitHub and create a frontend prototype repository.*
2. *Clone your repo to your computer.*
3. *Push your frontend prototype screen to GitHub.*

Part 4: Host your web page using GitHub Pages:

Using GitHub Pages, host the web page.

Part 5: Share your web page coded prototype:

Share your frontend prototype URL with a friend for some feedback.

 GitHub is highly shareable and has a large community of developers and open source users who are interested in providing feedback.

The prototyper (developer)

Being able to develop a design-oriented frontend prototype brings huge value as an HCI designer. The reality is that our world is built out of code and creating products from this code is what we do for a living. As HCI designers, our role is to know more about code, not only so that we can determine the possibilities and limitations of current technologies but also so that we can code more demanding prototypes much faster for our users.

However, jumping directly into code is not a quick fix. There is no substitute for following the prototyping process and validating solutions through the quickest means possible. Frontend prototypes should not be where an HCI team starts. However, if a paper prototype is enough to validate an idea and the frontend prototyping team is clear about the software intentions from the sketches, then there is no reason why a frontend prototype can't get started directly from a sketch. With practice, frontend developers can quickly approximate solutions and use open source code frameworks such as Bootstrap 4 or Foundation to improve their prototyping speed.

In reality, a robust prototype should be executed by a skilled frontend developer. Along with skill in writing code comes the ability to apply shortcuts, all while executing coding best practices, the proper code architecture, and efficient data models. Once you have skills in the frontend, you can then apply that knowledge to frontend frameworks that use component-based, view-layer-oriented concepts, such as Bootstrap, Vue.js, or React. The frontend framework will speed up your prototyping process. Designing and coding frontend prototypes have become faster than ever before but must be executed and tested with users, rather than skipping those steps because it is easier or faster to market.

Now that we have an understanding of the prototyping process, let's relate how we start building out complex systems that need multiple aspects or features to be prototyped over time.

System diagramming

Another point to consider is system diagrams – a visual model of a system, its components, and their interactions. With supporting documentation, it can capture all the essential information of a system's design. There are many variations of diagramming styles, but all attempt to articulate the interaction between humans and computer systems. System diagrams can be used as thinking tools. By studying a system diagram, you can discover problems and shortcomings of the design it represents, and at the same time, construct a final document that will capture the entire design. Thus, system diagrams should be constructed during the design process, and used as the basis for refining and specifying various aspects of the system:

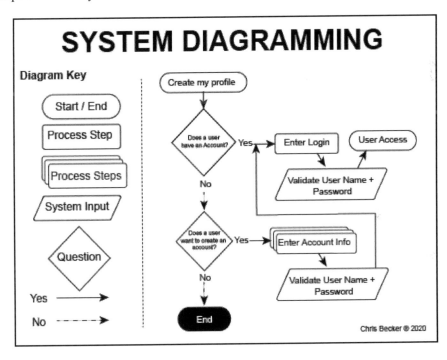

There are many methods for developing a system diagram, but I recommend starting with a pencil and paper or a whiteboard before jumping into the software to build a system diagram. The reason is that thinking about systems at first can be messy. There are a lot of moving parts to identify, which requires a looser method at first to capture all the parts. Pencil and paper can be quickly manipulated and part of the system can be quickly erased, moved, or relabeled on paper easier than in software. Recommend starting with the more simple oval, rectangle, diamond method before utilizing more complex systems like Unified Modeling Language (UML: https://www.uml-diagrams.org/).

Software-based diagrams are easier to maintain and to produce in a neat and concise form. The final decision is, however, up to each design team.

Challenge 35 – System diagram

Setup:

1. *Get out the required materials: paper and pencil/pen and a system diagram key.*
2. *Think of your prototype as a system of parts. Make a list of all the parts that make up your application (the system can include app features, technology requirements, business functions, user platforms, data systems, and so on).*

Part 1: System diagram:

1. *Identify the primary system or your prototype.*
2. *Add your primary system to the middle of your diagram.*
3. *Organize relationships with your other systems, drawing lines and adding labels.*
4. *Apply the system diagram key.*
5. *Add flow or direction to show how your system works.*

Part 2: Share your diagram:

Share your diagram with a friend for feedback.

Part 3: Iterate your diagram:

Iterate your system diagram based on feedback.

 Diagrams are hard and get complex very quickly. Start on paper and make sure your logic and sequence are sound before moving on to a digital tool.

Now that we can consider a larger software product through system diagramming and the prototyping of individual features or interactive parts, let's cover how we maintain and dictate quality throughout our process.

HCI interface best practices

HCI can be used in all disciplines wherever there is a possibility of using a computer, and because of the widespread use of computers, HCI practitioners should strive to apply their craft meaningfully together as a collective group. Best practices are a set of guidelines, ethics, or ideas that represent the most efficient or prudent course of action. Best practices are often set forth by an authority, such as a governing body or management; from an HCI perspective, they have been set out by thought leaders and pioneers in this field. Best practices come into play as a process for improving quality and creating standards that are used across products. Best practices are always evolving and adapt to new technologies, modalities, and audiences over time.

The prototyping methods we just discussed should do their best to apply some or all of these best practices. There are a number of best practices and we will cover them here.

Challenge 36 – Researching HCI user interface best practices

Setup:

Create a new Google Doc to document research and user interface best practice notes.

Part 1: Shneiderman's 8 golden rules:

1. *Research Ben Shneiderman.*
2. *Write down each guideline and why it is useful to a user interface.*

Part 2: Don Norman's 7 principles:

1. *Research Donald Norman's book* The Design of Everyday Things.
2. *Document the 7 stages that can be used to transform a difficult task.*

Part 3: Jakob Nielsen's 10 usability heuristics:

1. *Research Jakob Nielsen.*
2. *Research his 10 usability heuristics.*
3. *Document each heuristic.*
4. *Research and find a sample of heuristic evaluation.*

Part 4: General interaction best practice guidelines:

1. *Research interaction best practices.*
2. *Document the list.*

There are many resources, and I recommend using some heuristics Chrome extensions.

Now that you have familiarized yourself with some user interface best practices for HCI, you might see that there are a few overlaps. The reality is that each of the HCI designers/**user experience (UX)** designers/computer scientists who have contributed to these lists has been influenced by each other and they all concentrate on the same problem: humans using computers.

Challenge 37 – Researching software tips and tricks

Setup:

Create a new Google Doc to document research and software tips and tricks.

Part 1: Information display tips and tricks:

1. *Research information display for HCI and software.*
2. *Write down each recommendation and why it is useful to a user interface.*

Part 2: Data entry tips and tricks:

1. *Research data entry for HCI and software.*
2. *Write down each recommendation and why it might help your user.*

There are lots of recommendations, so make sure to bookmark useful websites or resources.

All of these best practices are internalized by an HCI team and executed into software over time. Software design teams will also go through the effort of producing documentation about their software known as interface design guidelines.

Interface design guidelines

From your research, you will start to see three categories of HCI design guidelines: general interaction, information display, and data entry, which hopefully you found to be great best practices during your challenge. Interface design guidelines are designed and maintained to build an understanding of the user interface best practices and components, along with user interface behavior, through supplying real examples for a design and software development community.

Interface design guidelines are software documentation that is helpful in outlining a user interface system. The values of user interface guidelines are as follows:

- A collaboration between multiple team members.
- Define user interface component specifications (UI specs).
- Help a team keep a consistent experience throughout a software product.
- Describe best practices.
- An educational document.
- Developers can refer to guidelines and prebuilt code components to quickly assemble user interfaces.
- Relatively easy to update guidelines based on new technology, new standards, and changing trends.
- Versionable and iterated on overtime.

The guidelines typically include the following (if you are not familiar with these terms, use Google to look them up):

- Style guidelines
- Layout guidelines
- User interface component guidelines
- Typography guidelines
- Interaction and behavior guidelines
- Platform guidelines
- Accessibility guidelines/WCAG 2.1 (`https://www.w3.org/TR/WCAG21/`)
- Reusable design pattern guidelines

Interestingly enough, design guidelines are no longer internal documentation and have been opened up to the broader software design community in order to increase the education of those products. They are also being used as a marketing component for expressing the rigor and value design holds for a software team. We will cover some prominent design guidelines in the following challenge.

Challenge 38 – Researching popular user interface guidelines

Setup:

Create a new Google Doc to document research and popular user interface guidelines.

Part 1: Information display tips and tricks:

1. *Research information display for HCI and software:*

   - **Apple user interface guidelines**: `https://developer.apple.com/`
   - **Microsoft Design guidelines**: `https://docs.microsoft.com/en-us/windows/uwp/design/`
   - **Google's Material Design guidelines**: `https://material.io/design/`
   - **Airbnb design methodology**: `https://airbnb.design/the-way-we-build/`
   - **Dropbox design guidelines**: `https://www.dropbox.com/branding`
   - **IBM user interface guidelines**: `https://www.carbondesignsystem.com`
   - **Oracle Alta guidelines**: `https://www.oracle.com/webfolder/ux/middleware/alta/index.html`
   - **US government websites guidelines**: `https://designsystem.digital.gov/`

Part 2: Data entry tips and tricks:

Document what is similar and what is different about each guideline documentation.

 You will be an expert at reviewing software documentation. Start with the system you are already familiar with.

Now, you might think these best practices feel like a lot to consider, and you would be right! The role of an HCI designer is not to be taken lightly; we need to care deeply about our products and our users, which not only includes how we execute best practices but also how we maintain a quality software product over time.

Software prototyping tools

More specifically, my personal choice for a clickable prototype application is the InVision App as its speed, communication features, deep hooks into the Sketch app, and sharing features make building clickable prototypes really fast and easy to iterate. Just like paper prototyping, clickable prototypes should not be too time-consuming and should encourage iterations and updates. The HCI/UX and frontend design communities have created many prototyping software tools. I recommend checking out `https://uxtools.io/` and `https://www.prototypr.io/home/` as a way to survey the tools used to create clickable prototypes as well as experimenting with a number of tools.

Your ability to integrate clickable prototypes into your HCI software design process will make your software solutions improve faster and your ability to use a diverse set of tools will help you be more employable as an HCI team member.

Motion and interactive prototyping tools include Adobe XD, Figma, Flinto, Framer, InVision Studio, Marvel, Origami, Principle, Proto.io, and Famous.co. Each of these is like a crayon in a crayon box. Each software is designed to help in the creation of software but they all go about it slightly different. It's great to explore multiple tools for quickly building clickable/motion prototypes with complex logic-based interaction and buttery-smooth animations, and each tool also comes with a learning curve. Start with prototyping tools that don't have too steep of an entry.

Summary

In summary, to reflect on this chapter, we started to extend and dive deeper into the software design ethos. The skills and tools used by small and large teams are rooted in doing work overtime and start with software teams applying a prototype. The ability to generate solutions from our previous research and user insights is not an arbitrary feat but rather a by-product of a design team that recognizes that they don't know the answer and need to understand their user to figure out a solution. We applied these practices throughout this chapter to allow you to practice your own ability to prototype, design a system diagram, and apply industry best practices through tools that produce prototypes first.

In the next chapter, we will focus on more skills in part 2 of the execution of software design through human-centered methods for user research.

Validating Software Solutions 8

As you may be starting to understand, HCI is intimately connected to people through the data we gather on them. A computer is an awesome tool for gathering user research data, and we design computer software in order to capitalize not only on this collection of data but on how this data feeds back into the software itself. User research data on its own will not help an HCI designer create great software as it is just ones and zeros, but when used alongside an HCI designer's intuition, curiosity, and understanding of their users, data can give us an in-focus picture. The computer cannot create on its own (at least, not yet); it is only a reflection of the solutions we as HCI designers create and code. Software solutions are fundamentally better when we can incorporate the data we have on our users, the data we gather along the way about our users, and the feedback we receive from our prototyped solutions over time. Because we are constantly tuning our experiences through data, it becomes critical to bake data collection into the process.

We capitalize on our data from observations, interviews, surveys, focus groups, and all the other user research methods available. Our ability to actualize solutions from our user research makes the software more human-centered and thus more useful to its users. However, there is no guarantee, which is why as HCI designers we need to work extra hard to build the best software we can. In the real world, this means not taking too big a risk, and not making huge assumptions about what will work for our users. As HCI designers, we can only know so much, which is why we continue to learn and grow our skills. This chapter is all about putting our user research knowledge into action and building software solutions through prototyping, a process that allows us to fail quickly and learn as much as we can along the way about our users and about what makes software successful.

All of our hard work is in service of solving our user's problems, and when new problems arise, we know the HCI design process can quickly and effectively address any changes in any system. The HCI design process is not perfect, but it is flexible enough to be able to address feedback.

Let's keep adding to our skills by creating a software hypothesis.

In this chapter, we will align on how to capitalize on data throughout the software design process:

- Establishing a software hypothesis
- Prototyping and iteration require feedback
- Validating prototyping solutions
- Executing usability tests
- Iterating software solutions

Establishing a software hypothesis

Software is a risk because you are solving human problems and, as we have discussed, humans are hard to understand. If you believe you are solving problems correctly, it requires you establishing a question to ask to know whether you have solved the problem. A software hypothesis works like any other hypothesis and becomes a starting place for understanding whether your idea, built into computer software, works. Prototyping, as we have been discussing, is a way to test your hypothesis. As an HCI designer, setting a good hypothesis allows you and your team to focus on what they believe they can achieve.

A hypothesis states the HCI team's predictions about what your software will do for your user, and is a preliminary answer to either a research question or a business problem that a piece of software is hoping to solve but that has not yet been tested. Some software teams will write multiple hypotheses that address different features or assumptions about your user's needs.

A hypothesis should be based on existing software understanding and knowledge about what your users can and cannot do with the technology. An important factor in any hypothesis is that it must be testable. Any software can be tested through experiments, observations, and analysis of data, but what you measure is rooted in what your team is trying to solve.

How can we write a software hypothesis in four steps? The following list shows you:

1. **Start with a question**: Writing a software hypothesis starts by considering a researchable, focused, specific software project, which begins through a question that you want to answer via user research.
2. **Engage in some preliminary user research**: Consider a research framework to identify which software variables your user research team will gather user data on. As a user research team, it is recommended to gather other user studies, published software papers, and inspiration from existing software in order to produce some educated assumptions about what your software could be.
3. **Generate a hypothesis**: Write your initial answer to the question from step 1, being as clear and concise as possible, and make sure to include measurable criteria so that your hypothesis is specific and testable.
   For example: Being able to save personal preferences in a grocery app will increase my user's frequency of use.
4. **Iterate and refine your hypothesis**: A hypothesis can be phrased in many different ways. Iterating your hypothesis will allow the predicted outcome of the experiment or analysis to come through with clear and relevant results.
   For example: Being able to save personal preferences for a woman in her 20s will increase the number of saved items they log and how frequently they use the application to buy groceries.

Here are some sample hypotheses:

1. **Research Question**: What are the health and behavioral benefits of tracking your nutrition through a mobile app?
   Hypothesis: Increasing calorie consumption tracking will result in a decrease in the number of doctor's visits.
2. **Research Question**: Which travel modalities (airplane, train, boats) have the most delays?
   Hypothesis: Low-cost travel industries are more likely to have delays than premium travel.
3. **Research Question**: Does a remote work arrangement improve job satisfaction?
   Hypothesis: Employees who have remote working hours will report greater job satisfaction than employees who work in an office with defined hours.

Any research question or hypothesis requires feedback and iteration from all those in a team that will engage in solving a problem.

Challenge 39 – Software hypothesis

Setup

1. Get out *a sheet of paper.*

Part 1: Write a software hypothesis question

1. *Using the first of the four steps listed previously, write three to five questions you want to test with your software.*
2. *Review your questions with step 2: do some light research to see if any of your questions have been answered already. Choose a question that is either under-researched or that you think has research potential for your software.*

Part 2: Write a software hypothesis

1. *Follow step 3: Write an initial software hypothesis statement.*

Part 3: Iterate your software hypothesis

1. *Follow step 4: Iterate and refine your software hypothesis.*

Part 4: Share your software hypothesis

1. *Share your software hypothesis with a colleague or fellow HCI designer for feedback.*

 Research some hypothesis statements before writing your own.

In the previous chapter, we covered why prototyping first allows software to be better. There are many ways to prototype, but at its core, prototyping is a process of thinking through and making a software solution tangible. The prototyping process from low-fidelity to high-fidelity allows the HCI designer and software team to solicit feedback. If you are not getting feedback from your users with your prototypes you are doing it wrong!

Your users are the people who you are solving problems for; therefore, getting their feedback on your prototypes allows you to validate and tune your software experience. Plus, it is nice to know you solved a problem through the data. User feedback is not just for validation, although that is super helpful, especially early in the design process. Feedback from your users can take a number of forms. Each has its place in enhancing and improving a piece of software, but can also vary based on the feedback types.

Let's review some types of user feedback.

Informal user feedback

Informal user feedback is something that emerges automatically from being in the moment and talking with your users about your software solutions or prototypes. Informal user feedback can happen during an action by your user or during other qualitative feedback sessions. For example, during a user interview, a user might be made comfortable enough to tell you why they don't use your software feature even though you never asked them a direct question about it.

Informal user feedback requires building a rapport with your users to effectively encourage them to respond and articulate their decision-making process behind using or not using the tested software. Feedback might occur during live interview sessions, over the phone, in an online forum, or in a virtual space. Informal user feedback is a byproduct of wanting to hear from your users and having them play with and use your software prototypes.

Typically, informal feedback sessions happen organically as part of the prototyping process. The very nature of building prototypes is begging for them to be played with, which is why we create them in the first place. When a prototype is completed and made tangible, it is ready to be tested. Guerrilla usability testing is a popular informal user feedback method that utilizes rapid, low-cost capturing and recording processes to gather feedback. Typically, it involves an HCI consultant or a UX professional asking questions about specific areas of a website or software application prototype. Guerrilla usability testing sessions can be done at coffee shops, libraries, bars, or any other place a user tester can quickly place their software prototype in the hands of potential users.

If you are not the most gregarious person on your HCI team, I recommend adding a person to your team who loves doing this type of work. The reality is you have to be open to getting a lot of feedback and this requires putting yourself out there. The feedback is not about you as a person, but it is essential to improving your software product.

Luckily, modern prototyping tools such as Adobe XD, Sketch + InVision, or Figma and maze.design have made executing guerrilla user testing easier than ever. An HCI software team no longer has an excuse that executing prototyping testing is too hard or too time-consuming because the process of designing the software should be intimately linked with creating a prototype. An HCI team needs to embrace all forms of feedback and make it part of the prototyping process. A prototype is not complete until it has been tested with users, otherwise, it is a fruitless endeavor.

Let's practice gathering some informal user feedback by engaging in a quick guerilla user test.

Challenge 40 – Informal feedback guerilla user testing

Setup

1. *Use any of your prototypes (Challenges 29-31 from* Chapter 7, *Storytelling and Rapid Prototyping).*

Part 1: Share your prototype for guerrilla user testing

1. *Share your work either in person (at a coffee shop, round a dinner table, or whatever) or digitally (via a conference call, email, social media, and so on).*
2. *Get some informal feedback from your user.*
3. *Capture unsolicited feedback through notes, photos, and a recording of what your participant had to share about your prototype.*
4. *Thank your participant (tip: offer to buy them a coffee/beer/snack for their time).*

Part 2: Iterate your prototype based on feedback

1. Based on feedback, choose one or two issues to focus on and iterate your prototype to address your user's feedback.

Testing and feedback are essential to making great software. Smile and be friendly.

Formal user feedback

Formal user feedback has similar goals to our guerilla user testing, but rather than happening spontaneously, it is planned and scheduled by a software design team into the software design process. Typically, they are given a budget and dedicated resources for gathering user feedback throughout the software design and prototyping process, which includes prototype usability testing, marketing criteria, user achievement, and assessment tasks. All formal user feedback is typically recorded for both the software team and for the organization as evidence of the users' success or failure when using a prototype. Since resources and a budget are dedicated to gathering formal feedback, the record is also crucial for refining and evaluating the success of your user tests along with the investment, and an HCI team has to be consistent to improve the software product.

Formal user feedback comes in many forms, from remote online task-based studies to formal in-person lab testing. Typically, the feedback can also be assisted through user testing software that tracks and records a user testing session and helps a software team keep track of the feedback data.

Most formal feedback sessions are made up of these five phases:

1. **Prepare your prototype to test**: This requires building out all prototyped features and making sure the prototype works in multiple locations.
2. **Recruit your participants**: This includes sourcing, scheduling, and preparing users for a feedback session or usability test.
3. **Write a feedback/user testing plan**: This is made up of a participant script, a prototype task flow, a user testing hypothesis, feature assumptions to gain feedback, and feedback procedures.
4. **Moderate the feedback session**: This requires executing the feedback/testing plan with the number of recruited users for feedback, recording the feedback sessions, and taking notes on the users' feedback.
5. **Present your findings and feedback highlights**: This concludes with transcribing recordings, combining notes, analyzing the user feedback, identifying any similar patterns between users, and flagging feedback responses that are really good and really bad.

A prototype feedback test can be basic, with participants in live sessions, or more involved, such as an online study with participants responding through screen capture and conferencing technology. The goal is to get users to use your prototype so you can see what they do with your solution and hear what they have to say. Feedback from your users at every phase of software design is so crucial. As HCI designers, we load our software prototypes with assumptions because we have no other choice. However, this is where an HCI team needs to iron out those leaps of faith in our product solutions as quickly as possible. The feedback tools we deploy in our design process should assist us in making better and more meaningful product iterations, iterations that are rooted in user testing, and applied through the prototyping process.

Of course, every HCI designer would love to have an endless amount of time and a huge user testing budget for their software problems. The reality is that this is hard to find. The HCI design team must value user feedback and make sure the user-centered iterative process is being applied regardless of the budget. It is our role to articulate the value of talking with and spending time with our users throughout the process. Some software design teams and some clients are less receptive to this kind of investment. The reality is you may find this to be true, but I recommend trying to build feedback into your process and joining teams that value it as well.

A note of caution

Joining a software design team that is hostile to feedback, user testing, or even prototyping should be avoided.

Do not perpetuate poorly built software by burying your head in the sand. However, bringing these skills to a team that is underserved with user testing can make you a valuable asset to any software team quickly.

There are many user testing services and a wide variety of costs. Like any software-assisted process, the features and opportunities should be defined by the software team, along with the types of feedback they are hoping to achieve.

Here are some recommendations:

- https://maze.design/
- https://www.hotjar.com/
- https://www.usertesting.com/

Formal user feedback is a process that needs to be practiced with your team, and the more you do it, the easier it gets. Formal feedback can also be improved through five categories of feedback:

1. Formative assessment and user feedback
2. Expert feedback
3. Self-feedback and reflection
4. Critique/feedback
5. Summary of user feedback

Formative assessment and user feedback

Importantly, the goal of formative feedback, sometimes called formative assessment, is to monitor and evaluate a user during multiple ongoing feedback sessions that can be used by an HCI team to improve their product or software over time. Formative user feedback is best when the same user can give feedback on multiple versions of the same prototype. Formative user feedback is best given early in the prototyping process, as it helps an HCI team iterate a solution and hopefully prevent the team from making similar mistakes.

For example, say the same users who had feedback or issues during the testing of a paper prototype are used when testing the clickable prototype. If the updated clickable prototype does not receive the same issues or feedback as the paper prototype had, it can be assumed the iterations have addressed the user's needs and improved through software iteration and through testing and feedback. Prototype feedback is required before a solution can progress to the next stage of the design process, which should then rinse and repeat the testing process. All prototype feedback is formative because it helps inform the iterations a software design team can and should make to their solutions over time. The formative process should be documented to indicate the learning and build upon where other prototypes failed.

Expert feedback

There is a need for experts within software development. Building great software is very hard, and there is a lot to learn from doing it, but we can't know it all. Sometimes, HCI software teams are also too close to their ideas. This can create bias and encourage a team to overlook or even outright ignore user feedback. User testing feedback can be ignored for many reasons, but typically it points back to the fact that the feedback is either inconvenient or it challenges the position of the HCI designer or the software team's assumptions.

Prototypes should be put through the wringer. Using an outside usability expert can highlight feedback and improve a software product quickly because an expert brings their experience and previous software knowledge to the table. Experts should be able to apply actionable feedback to prototype solutions and apply deep insight into the feedback loop for the design and development teams. An expert should be able to "tell it how it is" and should not shy away from poignant and salient feedback points about the failures or shortcomings of a software solution. Experts should not just tear down a solution either, and if they have nothing good to say, the expert may themselves be biased or hoping to exaggerate the severity of a perceived issue to enhance their own position. The success of an expert opinion is predicated on their ability to learn about the process a software team went through to execute a solution. Many times, outside expertise can highlight the flaws in software product decision making. When done effectively, outside experts are not just pointing out usability issues but are getting to the root of "why" those decisions were implemented in order to make recommendations, moving a software product forward.

In many cases, flawed software decisions or broken user experiences are the by-product of too little time and too little understanding of the value a feature or process has to its user. Many times, this can be attributed to the product owner, or to business stakeholders demanding features outside the scope or realm of the actual users' needs. One of the hardest things to do as a human-centered designer is communicating with business owners or software product teams that they are not in fact the user. Experts operate in relatively short turnaround times or provide ongoing support and can give valuable feedback, which is useful to a software design team, but only if the team trusts the expert's advice. Besides being a fresh pair of eyes, an expert can also enrich software teams' own internal learning experiences and help develop their own feedback and user testing skill set.

Some experts in feedback are as follows:

- `https://www.nngroup.com/`**Nielsen Norman Group (NN/G)**: Founded by Don Norman and Jakob Nielsen
- `UIE.com`: Founded by Jared Spool
- `http://sensible.com/`: Founded by Steve Krug
- `https://jaimelevy.com/`: Founded by Jamie Levy

There are many others.

Self-feedback and reflection

The ultimate goal of feedback is to allow a software team to learn if their assumption and user insights that drive solutions are correct. In education, feedback is an essential tool for helping students learn. The software design process is one big educational process, and helping software teams reach solutions and learning how to build great software requires feedback. Feedback is a learning loop that is essential to identify, share, and clarify the learning goals and success criteria of a software solution. Self-feedback and reflection are ways for software teams to understand the success or failures of their design process and be honest with themselves for how they solved or didn't solve a defined problem.

Critique feedback

The goal of a critique is to gather feedback on a solution. Because an HCI designer is always trying to improve their software solutions for their users, they should get good at receiving and giving constructive critique feedback. On the one hand, critique in design culture has a dubious reputation because many confuse critique for complaints. On the other hand, an HCI designer should seek out critique from your peers and fellow teammates. The role of Critique should be a constructive process.

There are four types of critique:

- **Negative critique/feedback**: Typically, a corrective comment that focuses on design decisions or research behavior that wasn't successful and should not be repeated, and it should be corrected during an iteration. For example, *You clearly designed this feature for yourself and not your user. This feature is flawed and should be removed or redesigned.*
- **Positive critique/feedback**: Typically, an affirming comment that focuses on design decisions or research behavior that was successful and should be continued or highlighted as useful. For example, *Your feature is clearly user-focused as the needs are validated through user interviews and Google Analytics data.*
- **Negative critique-forward/feedback-forward**: Typically, a restorative comment about future performance that centers on design decisions or research behavior that should be avoided in the future. For example, *Your user need was only confirmed by one interview. How do you know that multiple users are experiencing the same issue? The validation of product needs should be acquired through multiple users.*

- **Positive critique-forward/feedback-forward**: Typically, confident comments about future design decisions and research behavior that should be maintained and will improve performance in the future. For example, *Your user needs were validated through multiple interviews and correlated through your surveys and Google Analytics data. Keep this up because your software team will have more confidence in solving these user needs first.*

Summary of user feedback

Summative feedback is the collection of multiple user reports and reviews that are related to the specific aspects of the software solution. Summative feedback is the summary of all the feedback plus a record of all the iterations accomplished for a prototype as it works its way through the process. A prototype is a dynamic living outcome of an HCI designer's work and is very likely the product of a number of team members. Creating a summative record of what worked well through feedback and user testing is helpful both for your team and also for your clients if you are building software for an external partner.

In UX and HCI circles, summative feedback might take the form of expert usability assessments, heuristic evaluations, or best practice recommendations. Summative feedback may include an assessment of other types of feedback from the informal guerrilla tests to formal feedback sessions and take into account the software systems and user types used to gather feedback.

Summative assessments almost always take place at the end of a prototype design phase. If your HCI software team decides to break a software prototype into more manageable chunks, you can use summative feedback reviews to be a record before moving on to the next stage of prototyping. They are cumulative, and they're used to evaluate the success or failure of how user feedback and product iterations have improved a software solution.

Feedback and iteration are essential to any prototype, and helping you and your HCI team learn over time is how you will grow as not only a software designer, but also as a team.

Challenge 41 – Formal user feedback

Setup

1. *Use any of your prototype challenges.*

Part 1: Write a formal feedback testing plan

1. *Create a formal feedback plan:*
   - Establish the user task.
   - Write a user flow script and task request for your user to complete. For example, create a new post and share it with 5 friends.
2. *Establish 5 to 10 questions to ask your user after the user task is completed.*

Part 2: Recruit users

1. *Recruit a user for a formal feedback session (minimum 15 min).*
2. *Share your work either in person (at a coffee shop or diner, or wherever) or digitally (such as in a conference call or a screen capture scenario).*
3. *Gather formal feedback from your user.*
4. *Computer solicited feedback through notes, photos, or recording of what your participant had to share about your prototype.*

Part 3: Analyze feedback

1. *Look for patterns and similar usability issues between user feedback and testing sessions.*

Use social media to recruit users.

If your prototyping is coming along, it may help you answer some questions and assumptions you have about your user. To help the process along, it can be helpful to establish if your prototype is completing your initial hypothesis that you and your team believe will be achieved with your prototype.

Validating prototyping solutions

Accordingly, designing and testing software is connected to the idea that we are addressing a human need.

If you are not testing with your users, you are not validating your solutions:

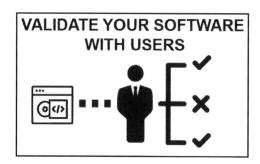

Screaming this is sometimes necessary because there are some involved in the software design business that sees user testing as a nice thing to have rather than an essential requirement for designing and creating great software. In life, validation is one of the hardest things to come across. We look to external sources for validation, whether from coaches telling us "good job" or teachers giving us grades, or friends accepting us into their group.

Validation is not only important to individuals, but also to the products and services they work on. The software can be improved over time through the validation of ideas, just as humans are improved by validation through their peers and those that understand what behaviors to validate. The question is, when do you validate a software solution? Validation is really hard to qualify, but every idea has a point at which it either lives or dies. Validation is the process of identifying whether an idea should continue to live. It sounds brutal, but the role of an HCI designer is deciding if ideas live or die. At first, you are going to kill a lot of ideas. You should if they are not worth it, even if they have made it to prototype. The reality is that they are ideas that you think work, but only through testing did you realize they should be killed. Though it's difficult to solve a problem and have your users invalidate and kill your idea, this is not a bad thing. Learning what ideas work or don't work only happens through validation with your users.

Prototyping as a process is essentially a process of validation. If you validate your idea with your users, you can establish success over time. Success is not guaranteed, but I can promise you if you don't validate your ideas with your users, you will definitely fail. Validating early allows a failure to not be so costly, both in terms of time and in terms of solving your user's problems.

Challenge 42 – Prototype validation

Setup

1. *Use any of your prototype challenges (Challenges 29-31 from Chapter 7)*

Part 1: Write a validation question

1. *Establish a validation question. What do you assume will work on our user? What task is your prototype accomplishing?*

Part 2: Recruit validation users

1. *Recruit a small group of users to validate your prototype solution (start with five user tests).*
2. *Run a formal user testing with the five users to see if they successfully use your prototype to accomplish the task it's designed for.*
3. *Compile solicited feedback through notes, photos, or recordings of what your participants had to share about your prototype.*

Part 3: Evaluate your prototype tests

1. *If each user has agreed that your prototype has worked or is valuable for their needs, record the validation data both in terms of qualitative interviews and quantitative interaction data.*

 Don't be discouraged if your early ideas are not validated.

Now that you have validated your idea through a prototype, you are on the right track, but it doesn't mean your software solution is perfect. Rather, it is just a starting point for improving the prototype and making it usable. Many validated ideas are not great in terms of user experience and require huge improvements to their usability.

Executing usability tests

If you are not user testing to improve the usability of your solutions, you are underserving your users:

Designing and testing software is connected to the idea that we are designing software that needs to be usable. I know I am doing a lot of screaming at you in this chapter. I don't mean to be demonstrative, but I think it is important to get this across. Usability testing your prototypes is part and parcel of user validation. If your idea works for your user, you want to make sure it is also usable. Many before me have established software usability best practices, and they have been established through rigorous user testing outcomes. We discussed usability heuristics and other methods that help a software product be useable. The only way to truly understand if your software is usable is to test it with your users.

Like other forms of user feedback, usability testing is focused on the user's ability to use a UI effectively throughout the execution of a software task. Sometimes, usability is glaringly obvious in a prototype. If a user is trying to accomplish a software task using a prototype and they get stuck or cannot complete the task, then there is a high probability there is a usability issue. The software team hopefully has validated the idea with a user before testing the prototype of usability issues. It is important as an HCI team to distinguish if a user fails at a prototype because they don't think the idea is valuable or if the prototype execution is unusable. User testing for usability issues is not validating an idea; rather, it is attempting to improve the effectiveness and users' ability to execute a validated user task.

Usability can be thought of as black and white: it is either usable or it is not usable. In reality, usability is a scale, and every software product has a range of usability factors. This is why usability testing prototypes with your users is so important. Usability issues that arise during usability testing that block users from completing their tasks are critical usability issues. These are usability failures. An HCI team wants to identify any usability failure during a prototype and not have that failure make its way into a software product.

For example, a software team may have validated the idea that creating a login is essential to an application. A critical usability error might be not being able to recover a password due to a missing link under the password UI input form.

After identifying any usability failures and iterating the software prototype to address these blockers, an HCI team can repeat the usability testing process to help nuance and improve the evolving usability of a prototype. Ultimately, the final software solution will be the result of lots of user tests and the solution will be as usable as possible. Continuous usability testing of prototypes will allow an HCI team to make refinements to their user's experience. When applying HCI interface best practices, an HCI team can quickly learn what to do and what not to do when solving a software problem, but this only comes from learning through testing.

An HCI team should get good at taking notes during usability tests. Look for these scenarios, which might signal there is a usability issue:

- Any areas of user pause.
- A look of confusion on the face of a user during task execution.
- The user selects the wrong UI element.
- The user goes back and forth in the UI.
- The user asks the usability tester questions.
- The user strains to read or moves the UI closer to their faces.
- The user makes an error, and this gets caught by logs.
- The user tries to jump ahead in the process.
- The user opens and closes other UI elements looking for their options.
- The user asks a question or looks surprised it worked.

There are many other things to look out for during usability testing, but it's important to evaluate and understand if your user feels that the prototype is usable. Start by observing them use the prototype and then ask them what they thought of the experience. Some of your users will not be shy in letting you know a prototype isn't usable if it is not. Others will not be as forthcoming, and you will need to rely on your observations of their behavior during the usability test. Typically, a user's ability to accomplish a task in a convenient fashion and how they talk about it later will match up. If your user's behavior and response don't match, this should be taken into account and might be an indicator of a usability issue.

Let's give a usability test on our validated prototype a spin to see if we can find any usability issues.

Challenge 42 – Prototype usability testing challenge

Setup

1. *Use your validated prototype from the previous challenge.*

Part 1: A usability task

1. *Establish a usability task and question for your user to accomplish.*

   User: *Can my user move from point A to B of a task?*
   Usability tester: *Can a user execute the prototype task smoothly without any confusion or pauses?*

Part 2: Recruit testers

1. *Recruit a small group of users to do a usability user test on your prototype solution (start with five usability testers).*

Part 3: Execute the usability test

1. *Run a formal usability test with the five users and see whether they successfully accomplish your prototype task.*
2. *Capture usability feedback through notes, photos, or recordings of what your participants had to share about your prototype.*

Part 4: Evaluate usability issues

1. *Identify any critical usability issues.*
2. *If there are no usability blockers, take notes about any areas of pause, confusion, selecting the wrong UI element, or going back and forth in the UI because these are indicators of a problem area in a user's task.*

Users will ultimately let you know if your solutions are usable or not.

Awesome! Now you have some usability data to evaluate and make some iterations to your prototype! The role of usability testing is to help make iterations to your prototype over time. Usability testing is a continuous process and should continue to happen even as the software is put in front of all your users. At this point, if you have been keeping up with the prototyping challenges, we have a prototype that has been validated and run through a usability test. The next part of any amount of user testing is to fold that feedback into the prototype through design iterations.

Iterating software solutions

As we discussed, HCI is an iterative practice and the prototypes we have built up to this point are a reflection of the idea that design can be altered over time for the better. Fundamentally, this is why we do user testing. If we thought our ideas and software solutions were perfect and solved all our user's problems with no issues, we would skip all this work. However, that is not how the real world works. Software is very risky, as we have already discussed, and therefore we take all the precautions we can throughout the process to decrease the risk. HCI software prototypes are not risk-averse, but rather they are risk sponges. Every validation user test is sucking up a set of business risks. As a prototype moves past validation, it needs to be usable and the prototype evolves through iteration. It is then tested for usability and iterated again, and the process repeats itself until the end of time. The HCI design process is then improved by the practice of iterative design to a multitude of software problems that we solve.

At first, your software prototypes will require a lot more iteration as you are a new HCI designer and you are not considering all the scenarios, but rest assured, with more practice the amount of iteration and the number of usability issues will decrease as your software knowledge and usability best practices increases. That improvement in skill should not come at the expense of user testing. The acronym **ABTI** means **Always Be Testing + Iterating**:

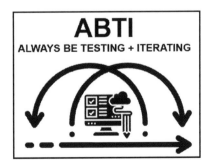

Regardless of your experience or the number of prototypes you have built, if you are not putting your work in the hands of your user you are doing it wrong and you will fail.

Let's practice iterating our prototype challenge based on our user feedback.

Challenge 43 – Iterate your prototype challenge

Setup

1. *Use your usability prototype from the previous challenge.*

Part 1: Review usability issues

1. *Review your usability feedback from your tests.*
2. *If you identified any critical usability issues, document and flag them for future iterations.*

Part 2: Iterate prototype to correct issues

1. *Iterate your prototype to fix those errors.*
2. *If there are no usability blockers, identify any other improvements that could be made to the prototype.*
3. *Iterate your prototype to anticipate usability problems down the road and stay ahead of your user.*

Iteration does not have to be a radical change. Start small if that is necessary.

I hope your prototype is starting to show some massive improvements and that you are starting along the path of an HCI designer who understands the value of incorporating their users into the software design process.

As you have been practicing and testing your prototyping skills, I hope you are learning by doing. There is so much we can learn by creating a solution and putting it in front of our users. Through practice, you will continue to grow your prototyping knowledge and speed as well as avoiding mistakes that were made in the past. At first, you will make lots of mistakes, which is totally acceptable, especially if that mistake happens on a prototype.

As you grow your HCI skills, know that there are many others besides myself who are engaging in, writing about, and thinking about the design of the software. I highly recommend researching way beyond this text, and I hope your curiosity will continue to grow.

Summary

In summary, the ground we are covering is getting larger. Throughout this chapter, we got our hands dirty by taking the prototypes developed in the previous chapters and allowed those ideas to be pressure tested with users. User testing is risky because failure is always around the corner; however, as we discussed in this chapter, when failing their users an HCI designer has actually learned something. Failure is part of the learning process but nevertheless it is learning and improving a software solution. The sting of failure shouldn't last long because the ability to practice the iteration of a prototype solution is the basis of covering idea validation and usability refinement. The skills and practice of user testing prototypes will last long after this book because every HCI team should ABTI —always be testing and iterating.

In the next chapter, we will focus on more skills in part 3 of the execution of improving software solutions through data.

HCI resources

Here are some of the HCI references that I highly recommend you read alongside this book:

- *Designing the user interface* by Schneiderman, B. (1998). Third edition. Addison-Wesley. (First edition published 1987).
- *Heuristic evaluation: Usability inspection methods by Jakob Nielsen* (1994). Nielsen, J., and Mack, R.L. (Eds.). John Wiley & Sons.
- *Software for use*, by Constantine, L. and Lockwood, L. (1999). Addison-Wesley.

- *About face 2.0: The essentials of interaction design* by Alan Cooper. and Reimann, R. (2003). John Wiley & Sons.
- Cognitive engineering principles for enhancing human-computer performance. International Journal of Human-Computer Interaction by Gerhardt-Powals, J. (1996).
- *Universal principles of design* by Lidwell, W., Holden, K., and Butler, J. (2003). Rockport Publishers.
- *Ten usability heuristics* by Jakob Nielsen (1994). `http://www.useit.com/papers/heuristic/heuristic_list.html`
- *First Principles of Interaction Design* by Tognazzini, B. (2003): `http://www.asktog.com/basics/firstPrinciples.html`
- *Principles for usable design* by Multiple Authors: `https://www.usabilitybok.org/principles-for-usable-design`

Section 3 - When to Improve Software Systems

These chapters are a view into how HCI implements the ideas, principles, and coding concepts reviewed in *Section 1* and *Section 2*. When to improve software systems will frame the practical steps taken while improving software and outline some of the methodologies used for evolving Human-centered software solutions.

We will dig deeper into the pillars of *Learn HCI* by covering the following chapters:

- Chapter 9, *Improving Software Systems with Data*
- Chapter 10, *Human-Centered Solutions*
- Chapter 11, *Extending HCI*
- Chapter 12, *The Future of HCI*

As you complete this book, you will learn why human-centered methodologies are timeless, and how to consider the fast-approaching future.

Improving Software Systems with Data

9

Design and development together can build great software solutions but the software is only as good as the team's ability to continue to improve over time for its users. Throughout this chapter, we will extend our skills with improving software over time. The role HCI designers play has a huge range, from inventing new software ideas to maintaining and iterating existing software. We participate in a highly dynamic field where technology, coding languages, and software tools are constantly changing. These changes are good as they are an example of the HCI community continually improving their profession and, along with it, the software they create. The ability of HCI designers to add value to their software teams is essential to helping our users and scaling software solutions around the globe. Let's take the opportunity to understand how user data and user feedback are the fuel with which we improve the software over time.

Just as user research data is essential to address a user's needs with a software solution, so is the need to continually improve those solutions. Software is not etched in stone, but rather is like painting the Golden Gate bridge. By the time you complete one coat of paint, you have to start over again. Not all software requires starting from scratch, but any piece of software can be improved through data. Now that you are growing your HCI skills, let's discuss why HCI gathers data on software solutions, and why HCI targets the interactions that happen between humans and computers. Throughout this chapter, we will understand how software systems become more complete through data.

We will be covering the following topics in this chapter:

- Designing software for all user with universal design principles
- Applying usability for all users
- Valuing accessibility
- Designing useful interfaces, period!

Designing software for all users with universal design principles

Software design is executed at a fast pace in our world due to the demand of our users; however, this speed has outpaced our ability to make sure the best software is available for all users. The importance of going beyond the **Minimum Viable Product** (**MVP**) and evolving your software systems to adapt to the changes in culture and technology rather than the other way around is a big reason why software teams and HCI/ UX designers exist in the first place.

Software is indispensable in our society, and building solutions that address our users' needs is a bigger responsibility when those users are more diverse and have different abilities than the teams designing them and creating them. Full disclosure: I am a English-speaking male who is able-bodied, writes with his right hand, has 20/20 vision, and an average mental focus. Having self-awareness when thinking about a problem or devising solutions is really important. As an HCI designer, **I am not the user**! The solutions I create are not for me. Many users are in fact very different than me.

As we discussed earlier, this is where having empathy for your users is essential as an HCI designer. The reality is all the empathy in the world will not be enough to make your design for everyone. That takes real effort and moves beyond your own empathy for designing solutions and requires digging deeper and getting your entire organization to care about the widest range of users possible. Empathy matters, but an HCI team should collectively combine all their approaches and all their individual empathy to consider the broadest set of users. Empathy for your users helps focus on one user, while the universal design is the inverse of that, allowing your empathy for one user to be distributed to all users. The goal of HCI becomes a virtuous cycle that allows considering and focusing on one user to scale outward to all users. The empathy cycle created by HCI designers allows software solutions to be designed with universal appeal. Empathy is essential to universal design:

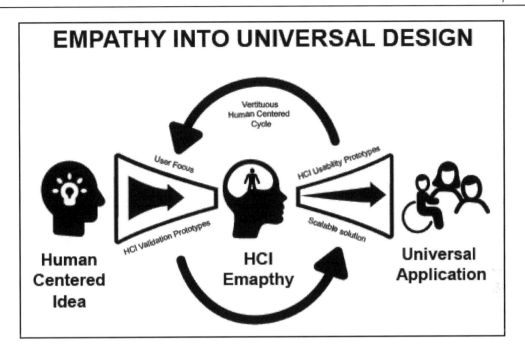

HCI software solutions are designed for the widest set of users possible, which aligns its creation inside the values of universal design. The concept of designing an object or product to suit a person's needs is not new and dates back to when Cro-Magnon man used materials such as rocks and bones to create tools. However, the articulation of universal design was established in 1997 by a community of architects, engineers, environmental design researchers, and product designers. The late Ronald Mace at North Carolina State University led this group and created the Center for Universal Design. Ronald Mace was himself wheelchair-bound and led a movement to grow the consideration of design for all users. The universal design movement and universal design principles push all designers, from architecture to graphic design to HCI design, to consider a much broader responsibility.

Challenge 44 – Research universal design principles

Setup:

1. *Create a new Google Doc to document universal design.*

Part 1: Research and document the seven universal design principles:

1. *Use Google to look up* The Principles of Universal Design, Version 2.0. Raleigh, NC: North Carolina State University.
2. *Copy each principle into your Google Doc (there are seven principles).*
3. *Reflect on and write why each principle is universal.*

Part 2: Review a website to see if it applies the seven principles:

1. *Go to a web page of your choice.*
2. *Take a screenshot of the home page.*
3. *Place the screenshot into a tool to add annotations (such as Adobe XD, Sketch, Figma, or Adobe Illustration).*
4. *Add notes where the web page is representing any universal design principles.*

Part 3: Return to your Google doc and score each universal principle:

1. *Based on your home page review, add a score next to the seven principles for how hard or easy the principle is to recognize.*
2. *Reflect on and write why universal design is valuable to software design.*

 Universal design also applies to architecture and other forms of design, so they can apply to the use of a computer.

More recently user-centered design has been applied to describe design solutions and design process that focuses on the user first as it identifies and addresses the needs, abilities, and limitations of its users in the process of creating solutions. Much of user-centered design has adapted and applied universal design concepts throughout the process, along with other disciplines, including human factors, ergonomics, and other functional design approaches.

Universal design is not just a concept that HCI teams should pay lip service to. Decisions throughout the HCI process that build thinking about the broadest range of users possible in your software products are attained by collecting and utilizing data and testing your software prototypes with a wide range of users. Feedback and user testing data, as we have been discussing, are ways to validate and confirm your software is indeed being designed toward universal acceptance. Universal design solutions are attained by checking that software does the following:

- Applies usability
- Values accessibility

These factors are both data-driven and a result of HCI teams valuing these factors and designing them into the software process.

Let's continue to discuss how usability is something an HCI team should value.

Applying usability for all users

Usability is a software design approach by which HCI designers determine how difficult a user task is to learn and accomplish when accessing an application. HCI software designers take into consideration many users when solving software problems and take into account that some may already be familiar with some **Graphical User Interface** (GUI) patterns. Usability is a goal for all your users, not just those that you focused on during the empathy phase. Usability is only attained through user testing but is affected by many factors. As we have discussed, humans are complicated creatures, and the ability of our users to learn and be trained over time affects how we evaluate and judge how usable a product is.

The essence of usability is that a user should not have to be forced to think like a computer to accomplish a software task; it should be the other way around. A computer should be designed to fulfill human potential by folding naturally into their everyday processes as well as enhancing their existing problem-solving apparatuses. The goals of usability are both general, such as "Make a piece of software as usable as possible," and specific to discreet interactions, such as "A user should be able to access the software through a login." Usability is a continuum of valuing your users and designing all the user interface features to work together. All of this requires designing software with these factors in mind but also relentlessly testing your software solutions throughout the prototyping process. Usability is not just a one-factor consideration, but rather requires an HCI designer to consider many usability goals when designing software:

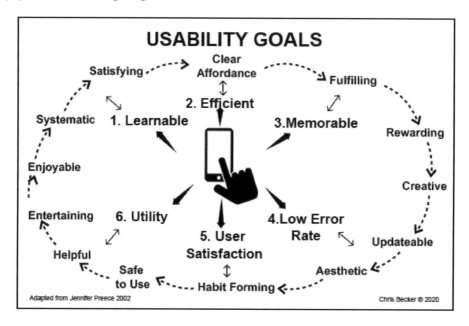

Through usability testing, an HCI designer can explore the six main components of usability:

- Learnability
- Efficiency
- Memorability
- Low error rate
- User satisfaction
- Utility

Learnability

Importantly, learnability is how easy is it to perform basic software tasks. Learnability is particularly relevant to new users of a software interface because experiencing a solution for the first time requires the largest amount of learning from your user. Learnability allows users to quickly become familiar with a product or software interface. If users can easily make good use of software features and capabilities, we can say the software is highly learnable or the software has a shallow learning curve. Software with a shallow learning curve tends to be called "intuitive," when in fact it is has a quality of highly "learnable design." If a software product is quickly learned and has clear and obvious affordance (thank you Donald Norman), this is how we determine how learnable it is. The extent of learnable design represents how easy a software feature is remembered and repeated by your users.

Usability testing a software solution for learnability requires testing your user as they explore and navigate a software interface for the first time. It is recommended to record your users' faces in these types of usability tests because facial expressions and monitoring how quickly they recognize UI elements is key to if a user can navigate a task just through the cues given by the software design.

Efficiency

Likewise, software efficiency is how much time it takes for users to find what they came for. Efficiency in a software solution is a question of what the tasks are and what the user is expected to accomplish. Some tasks take longer to accomplish but are very effective. Time-on-task in software is connected to what a user is accomplishing with a software feature.

Take writing a three-paragraph email to your boss. The process of writing the email might take anywhere from 15 minutes to multiple hours depending on the content of the email. However, the process of using the QWERTY keyboard to type the words into the email is very efficient and can be made more efficient by the user learning the location of the A-Z letters in the QWERTY keyboard interface or using other type-assist features such as a spellchecker or Grammarly.

Usability testing a software solution for efficiency requires testing your user as they explore and navigate a software interface. It is recommended to record and time your users in these types of usability tests because you need a baseline time expectation for completing the software task. If multiple users successfully accomplished your task in 1.3 seconds and then, during another test, a user takes 3.5 seconds, you can use the baseline time expectation to identify the success or failure of an efficient UI.

Keep in mind the type of interface you are designing for your software solutions. Generally, users will spend more time using computer desktop software than mobile phone software. Smartphones are small and handheld and meant to be used quickly, so the task expectation for a smartphone is therefore different than a laptop computer.

Memorability

Can a user repeatedly perform their tasks? Software solutions are not luck. We don't design them hoping our users will just happen upon our feature like coins on the beach. Instead, the HCI designer strives to make software memorable, which is accomplishable through a combination of usability factors. Designing software to help your users remember the tasks and recall your features is essential to making a usable software solution.

Take Venmo, which is a mobile application that allows users to quickly pay friends and family via the application that links to your bank account or debit card:

Venmo has made its software memorable through a quickly learnable UI that allows users to request payment or pay another user. It has made the exchange of money efficient and quickly communicates the value that is being shared through emojis, which makes the task of sending or receiving money more memorable.

Usability testing a software solution for memorability requires testing your user over time. It is recommended to record and repeat these types of usability tests as you need to understand if a user can retain the knowledge of how to use your interface over time rather than having to relearn the software tasks each time. Keep in mind the memorability of software is also affected by other factors of a software business, including advertising (such as movies, TV, and radio), branding and visual design (such as logo, colors, iconography, and typography), and other factors (such as whether it is on the PC or Mac platform).

Low error rate

Can a user perform their tasks without making an error? Software solutions are designed so that (hopefully) your users don't make mistakes. However, when multiple steps are involved in a task or a UI gets more complicated, the potential for your user to make a false step or not complete all the required steps increases. An HCI designer should have empathy for their users during the prototyping and design process and attempt to anticipate or even prevent your user from making errors. Decreasing errors and anticipating where your users will ask questions or get stuck will improve your usability.

Usability testing a software solution for errors requires testing your user over time. It is recommended to record and repeat these types of usability tests as you need to understand if a user can repeat a software task without making an error. I recommended recording your user's face for these types of usability tests because facial expressions can help you determine how severe the error is, as well as where it occurs in your user task.

User satisfaction

As a result of the preceding tests, you will be able to gauge the level of comfort users feel when using software solutions. The HCI designer strives for user satisfaction, which is again a combination of multiple usability factors. A piece of software could be easily learnable and efficient, with memorable tasks and low numbers of errors, but still fails to help your user accomplish a meaningful task – this would fail at user satisfaction. User satisfaction is not only the ability for software to accomplish a task but also reinforces the value the software provides to a user. Allowing users to feedback on how satisfied they are with your software solutions is connected with user testing and usability.

Usability testing a software solution for user satisfaction requires executing all the usability tests and then gathering qualitative data from your users. It is recommended to record and repeat these types of usability tests because you need to understand if a user gains user satisfaction over time. User satisfaction typically is not determined by one feature or one software task but rather is the culmination of the entire software's usability combined with the value added to a user. Typically, if a software solution is highly learnable, efficient, and memorable, with a low error rate, a user will continue to use the solution, which in turn will grow the user's satisfaction with the solution. Keep in mind the user satisfaction of software is also impacted by other factors of a software business, as mentioned in the *Memorability* section.

Utility

Does the user rely on the software? Do they repeat tasks over time? The HCI designer has made an impact on a software solution when a user relies on a solution like a utility. When software is designed and executed in a way that allows a user to repeat its use and make it part of their daily, weekly, or monthly habits, that software solution has reached the value of utility for users. Only through creating a software solution that creates value over time can you get to the status of a software utility. Software utilities are leaned on by our users to accomplish tasks through software.

For example, Google is a search engine. Their success at making software that is learnable, efficient, and memorable, with a low error rate, and that is satisfying for its billions of users has made "google" a verb. Nothing says software utility like allowing users to say "google it" and without a computer or interface in front of them and they understand the task as well as the value it provides.

Usability testing a software solution for utility requires executing all the usability tests and gathering qualitative data plus building other usable software solutions so that your users come to trust your brand. It is recommended to understand your users through research so you can address their needs with software solutions that are worthy of attaining the status of a utility to your users. It is highly recommended to study other software solutions that have risen to that status, including the likes of Apple, Microsoft, Adobe, and Google.

None of these software companies made their software valuable as a utility to their users overnight. It requires a long hard process, but if you continue to value usability at the core of your software solutions and continually test your software prototypes for usability, then you might make your users delighted over time as well.

Usability is a lofty goal for software, and our users are demanding at a minimum that their software is usable. If you fail to make your software usable, that leaves an opportunity for other software to come along and supply that need to your users. In other words, usability becomes a **Unique Selling Proposition** (**USP**) for your software. There is lots and lot of competition in the software landscape, and a software design team cannot afford to just be first to market. They must continually improve their software to keep their users and maintain the values we have been discussing. As we have been discussing, usability involves more than just one factor to consider; it is also linked with making your products accessible.

Valuing accessibility

Accessibility makes your software products, including websites, as usable as possible by as many people as possible. It is the practice of thinking about all your users, including those with disabilities. Accessibility is thought of as treating all users equally, regardless of their ability or circumstances. Many in the design world and the software design community confuse accessibility for simply helping the disabled. Unfortunately, such a narrow understanding of the role of accessibility diminishes the role designers can play when they solve software problems by considering all their users. This is equivalent to adding a wheelchair ramp for a building after it has been built: although it makes the building more accessible, it is not accessibly designed from the beginning. Adding an accessibility ramp on the surface is not altogether bad; however, including the consideration for all users, including those with limited access, in the heart of solutions from the beginning when making software is the right thing to do. Besides the benefit that accessibility alters the HCI designers' perspective, it also prevents solutions that limit accessibility and allows ideas such as ramps in buildings to be integrated as part of the solution rather than a barnacled afterthought. Assessability is also a larger umbrella than purely considering user's disabilities.

Disability impairments

As an HCI designer, you will be expected to care about all users. This responsibility will not reside only on your shoulders, but being aware of primary disabilities is helpful as an HCI professional when considering accessibility.

Cognitive impairment

Cognitive impairment is in reference to a large set of disabilities, from users that have intellectual disabilities through to users of advanced age and those who have difficulty with their memory:

Considering your users' mental capacity is not just relevant to the usability of your software solutions (such as memorability), but is also relevant to the fact that users can only hold so many pieces of information in their short-term memory.

Challenge 45 – Research Miller's law

Setup:

1. *Create a new Google Doc to document Miller's law.*

Part 1: Research Miller's law:

1. *Use Google to look up George Miller and Miller's law in psychology.*
2. *Abstract the learning from cognitive science and write about how it can apply to software design.*

Part 2: Review a website to see if it applies to Miller's law:

1. *Go to a web page of your choice.*
2. *Take a screenshot of the home page.*
3. *Place the screenshot into a tool to add annotations (such as Adobe XD, Sketch, Figma, or Adobe Illustration)*
4. *Add notes where the web page is representing the use of Miller's law.*

Annotations are essential to being an HCI designer. Practice with screenshot tools such as the awesome screenshot Chrome extension: `https://chrome.google.com/webstore/detail/awesome-scre enshot-screen`.

Using your memory and making your solutions consumable is also about accessibility. Beyond cognitive memory, cognitive impairment encompasses a wide range of mental illnesses, as well as users with learning disabilities, which includes attention disabilities such as **attention deficit hyperactivity disorder (ADHD)** and reading disabilities such as dyslexia or aphasia. Cognitive impairment has a disputed medical definition but from a software perspective, it refers to any issue your users might have, ranging from difficulties with content (understanding or consuming it), recalling how to complete software tasks, and general confusion caused by software solutions.

Your user's brain should not be taken for granted and, as we have been discussing, should be constantly tested against during the software design prototyping process.

Mobility impairment

Mobility impairment includes any disabilities concerning movement and could be physical, neurological, or caused by genetics. Mobility impairment has a wide range of use cases. Users with slight mobility impairment might struggle with the precise hand movements required to use a computer:

This could be a user in the early stages of Parkinson's disease or anyone with a broken arm/wrist/hand in a cast. Those more severely affected may require the use of eye-tracking software or a head pointing device to interact with computer software. This could be users who are paralyzed or suffer from debilitating diseases such as Amyotrophic lateral sclerosis (ALS or Lou Gehrig's disease). Addressing mobility impairment during web development work typically requires software teams to build controls that are accessible via the keyboard.

Hearing/auditory impairment

Hearing/auditory impairment is a user group that has low hearing levels or no hearing at all, which is a wide range of users. Hearing-impaired people might use technology to assist in their hearing. Known as **Assistive Devices (ATs)**, these devices are great but often are not designed specifically for computer use:

When it comes to supporting the hearing-impaired, there are software solutions and alternatives that provide textual or audio content. These usability solutions include **Closed Captions (CC)**, which can be displayed along with a video or content article, as well as screen readers, which use the textual coded information used to make a web page or software solution. A screen reader is only as good as the team designing the software oorf the web page, and those teams need to make sure the user experience for the hearing-impaired is just as good.

Visual impairments

Visual impairments include any users with any range of eye issues, from low-level vision to color blindness to complete blindness. Users with a wide range of visual impairments rely on screen magnifiers that are either physical magnifiers or software zoom capabilities. In 2020, modern web browsers and computer operating systems have built-in zoom capabilities:

Users with more severe visual challenges will utilize screen reader technology, software that turns web page code into digital text that is read aloud. Just as a screen reader is useful for visualizing a UI for the hearing impaired, it also is used for those with visual impairment. A screen reader's output is only as good as the team designing the software of the web page, and those teams need to make sure the user experience for the visually impaired is just as viable through auditory cues. I recommend that you familiarize yourself with a few screen reader tools as well as best practices for creating web pages that are accessible.

Challenge 46 – Screen reader tool

Setup:

    1. *Install a screen reader extension to your web browser.*

Part 1: Test a web page with your ears

    1. *Navigate to a website of your choice and launch the screen reader software.*
    2. *Place a blindfold on over your eyes.*
    3. *Using the tab or arrows on your keyboard, navigate around your web page.*
    4. *Take notes on what is being communicated to you through the screen reader.*

Part 2: Remove the blindfold and see if you can locate what you interacted with

    1. *See if you can recognize with your eyes the UI elements you explored through the screen reader.*
    2. *Take notes on what was easy and hard to experience through a screen reader.*

Use the Chrome screen reader for
Google: `https://chrome.google.com/webstore/detail/screen-reader-for-google/`.

Although disability greatly impacts accessibility, there are considerations with accessibility that benefit both groups. Making websites accessible also benefits any user on a mobile device, as well any user with a lagging network connection. Accessibility is caring about all your users, which is the right thing to do for your software. Designing and developing accessible software products is also part of the law in some regions, including the USA and the European Union.

Now that usability plus accessibility are at the front of your mind, what do you get out of it from a software perspective? What you get is loyal customers and your software is treated as a utility.

Designing useful interfaces

Many of the greatest inventions in the world are useful. Take the wheel, for example. It is quite possibly the most useful invention for man. The value that the idea of a wheel has spawned endless iterations, all on the back of the idea that a wheel is useful because it can spin, carry things, and makes moving from point A to point B faster. In 2020, computer software is as dominant as the wheel, and the idea of computer software has become as useful to us as the wheel is remarkable.

Quick question: If you have to go to a party across town without your smartphone, how would you do it?

For many, this might would be a daunting task because we as users have become so reliant on software such as Google Maps, Waze, and Apple Maps. Your method of using a piece of software is very useful, and not using it properly would then be useless. Navigating a city is potentially complicated, and the usefulness of directional software has made it so widely adopted.

The value this type of software brings to our user's world has risen to the level of being useful, and some software even operates as a utility. Utilities are typically thought of as any organization supplying a community with electricity, gas, water, and garbage and sewerage disposal. Utilities are essential for living in a city or participating in a community. When software is useful to the point where communities rely on the software to supply them with life-saving information, or as essential as getting water to people, the software had better be usable, accessible, and useful.

"Useful" is a human value because humans can be useful to each other. Useful software is used over and over again, which makes it all the more important to make your software usable and accessible by the broadest user base possible.

Summary

In summary, as we move into the last third of *Learn Human-Computer Interaction*, this chapter started to cover considerations that every HCI designer should know and that software should apply, but sadly does not. Our prototype practice from previous chapters was preparation for executing the HCI design process but was missing specifications regarding what makes great software, which is the role of reviewing universal design, usability, accessibility, and useful products as a basic human need that all software should satisfy. As an HCI designer, your role will be to build better software, which means considering all your users, not just the ones who validate your solution. As we have discussed, HCI is hard for a reason, and great software can and will impact the world, so take it seriously and apply the ideas in this chapter to all your solutions.

In the next chapter, we will focus on more skills in *part 3* of the execution of software design through human-centered solutions.

10
Human-Centered Solutions

Now that we are getting deep into HCI in this book and you are starting to realize how software is meant to be designed for the widest set of users possible through usability, accessibility, and caring about your user's needs, let's consolidate our knowledge and discuss what makes software successful.

As you continue to grow your HCI skills, it is essential to allow not only your skills to radiate into all your solutions, but also to allow the value and importance of your decisions to reflect the broader community of HCI and human-centered design practitioners. Software design does not exist in a vacuum; it is part of the culture and an HCI designer's ability to anchor their solutions deep in the communities they serve allows us to earn that right and also the right to not accept or tolerate bad software. We now know how to fix it, so let's do it.

In this chapter, we will discuss how to capitalize on success from the past:

- Exploring open-source software culture
- MVC, not MVP
- Iterative loops for improving software, which improves culture

Exploring open source software culture

Open source refers to anything a group of people can modify and share because its design is publicly accessible. HCI designers and software developers have championed the 'open source' concept and it lies at the heart of the internet itself. Tim Berners-Lee, in all his glorious wisdom, understood that to make the internet possible, you would need everyone using the same tools and accessing the network through the same technology. The internet is an open source idea in that sharing the code along with the delivery system makes others want to use it. Because of this shared technology, it creates a network of a global scale that drives the standardization of code (HTML/CSS/JS) itself.

Open source software is a product of public and open systems, supported by a community, and made up of shared and distributed materials and documentation:

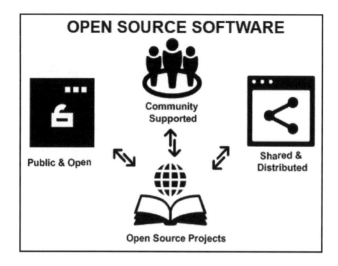

In reality, the internet and all the software that is created around it is more complicated than this simple idea, but without open source, we would have multiple internets all using different standards, different code bases, and different interfaces. Frankly, it would be a nightmare. Fortunately, we have a system that maintains itself, and an HCI designer in the USA, in Japan, or anywhere else will be executing HTML/CSS/JS to make web-based software. If you think about it, it is pretty remarkable and the world has been fundamentally restructured because of the scale and wide use of these internet technologies. Not only can we communicate around the world; we have a method for delivering software that can solve problems around the globe as well. The communities around the globe that access and utilize the internet to run their business, interact with customers, or just create a place for information – they all commit to keeping the internet open.

Offering software at scale is very hard and requires lots of work, which is why open source ideas have been supported by the HCI and developer communities. We get to stand on the shoulder of giants and can prototype software much faster because the HCI designers and developers are not required to reinvent the wheel and code everything from scratch. Using open source is like using a cheat code in a video game but in this case, you still have to know how to use and/or code using the open source materials as a starting place.

Besides the fact that open source code bases reduce the barriers to entry for a software solution, they also allow code bases to be maintained and supported by a global community of designers and developers. As we discussed, the web coding languages of HTML/CSS/JS are open source code bases that anyone can use or modify using the inspect features on their web browsers. There are many other 'open source' coding ideas but what makes 'open source' so valuable is the notion that its authors make the source code available to others who would like to view that code, copy it, learn from it, alter it, or share it.

Open source software projects can require users to accept some terms of a license but many open source licenses allow users to copy, modify, study, and distribute software built using the source code. In general, open source licenses grant computer users permission to use the code for any purpose they wish, which makes them entirely unique in our world. 'Open source' is a concept that represents a broader set of values inside the development community. These values are predicated on the idea that you get farther by working together rather than walling off your garden. Open source projects, products, and initiatives embrace and celebrate principles of open exchange, transparency, collaborative participation, meritocracy, rapid prototyping, and community-oriented development. There are many open source software projects. I recommend getting starting by creating an account with GitHub.com. GitHub contains a version control software system and open source community software creation hub that allows teams from all over the world to collaborate on software.

In GitHub, you can create repositories and join code **repository** (**repo**) projects to make contributions. Although some repos have selected access to make sure those designers and developers adding to the open source code are qualified and won't create problems with the code base. Joining a community code project can be a rewarding process, a great way to practice what you preach, and a way to learn how to create open source projects as part of a community.

Now, let's examine some well-known open source initiatives.

Open source projects

It is also important to highlight there are thousands of open source projects with very different levels of support. That being said, we will explore some of them here.

Bootstrap (Twitter)

A free frontend web framework centered around responsive, mobile-first web development. Bootstrap is a collection of CSS and JavaScript/jQuery-based UI design elements for typography, forms, buttons, navigation, and other web UI components. Bootstrap is a very popular frontend web design framework that is used to produce many websites on the internet:

Web: https://getbootstrap.com/
GitHub: https://github.com/twbs/bootstrap

Angular

An open source JavaScript framework that can be added to an HTML page that extends HTML attributes with directives and binds data to HTML with expressions. Angular is a toolset for building the framework most suited to your application's development:

Web: https://angular.io/
GitHub: https://github.com/angular/angular

Node.JS

An open source server environment that runs on various platforms and uses JavaScript on the server to allow developers to manipulate data from the backend to the frontend:
Web: https://nodejs.org/en/
GitHub: https://github.com/nodejs/node

NPM (Node Package Manager)

NPM is a package manager for Node.js that is used as an online repository for open source Node.js projects, as well as being a command-line utility used to install Node.js packages. So basically, it is used for managing various server-side dependencies. This tool is used by over 11,000,000 JavaScript developers around the world:

Web: https://www.npmjs.com/
GitHub: https://github.com/npm/npm

React Native (Facebook)

React Native is a declarative UI framework for iOS and Android, developed by Facebook. Using React Native, you can apply native UI controls and have full access to the native platform functionality. React Native is similar to React, but it uses native components instead of web-specific components as building blocks:

Web: https://reactjs.org/
GitHub: https://github.com/facebook/react-native

VS Code (Microsoft)

VS Code is a popular text editor tool that combines the simplicity of a code editor with what developers need for their core edit-build-debug cycle:

Web: https://code.visualstudio.com/
Github: https://github.com/microsoft/vscode

You might notice that many of these open source projects are associated with an established software company, whether it be Twitter, Facebook, Google, or Microsoft. The reason this occurs is that many such projects were launched at these companies initially as private software, but got to a place where their scale and value were so great to the designer and developer communities that it created a need to transition them to open source.

Take Bootstrap for example. It was started at Twitter in 2010 by the following developers:

- **Mark Otto** (https://twitter.com/mdo, https://github.com/mdo)
- **Jacob Thornton** (https://twitter.com/fat, https://github.com/fat)

The development of the framework was aimed to encourage consistency across internal tools at Twitter, but as a code base, its usefulness for building responsive websites had far more potential than just to be used internally at Twitter. After teams at Twitter started contributing to the code base, it was released as an open source project on August 19, 2011, and is still on of the most popular frontend frameworks for RWD web design, and is now on its fourth version (v4.4.1).

Challenge 47 – Research an open source project and contribute

Setup:

1. *Install Git.*

Part 1: Research an open source coding project:

1. *Navigate to a code base and read the contribution rules.*
2. *Make a request to join the open source community of your choice.*
3. *Add to the documentation and code to help solve problems in the open source way.*

Part 2: Share your contributions to the community and recruit your friends to join.

1. *Share how you are involved with an open source product.*
2. *Working on projects is more fun with friends, so see if you can get your friends to help.*

 Do some basic research on version control systems along with the language and features associated with Git terminology: branches, pull requests, merging, merge conflicts, and so on.

For designers and developers who were looking to update their web platform, they recognized the framework of code was being created to be scalable to the entire web, especially as mobile devices started to dominate internet traffic around 2009-2010. Bootstrap inside Twitter was only somewhat viable as a project but as an open source frontend code framework, maintained and extended by a community of designers and coders, it has become well supported and maintained. Currently, the frontend framework is used in education, frontend prototyping, and to help developers speed up their web software development process.

There are many more projects, and equally as many more that are build on top of these open source code foundations. As an HCI designer, developing an understanding of how you can contribute to a software development team will be easier if you're familiar with how the software is being coded. As we have discussed previously, knowledge of what is possible is a collaboration between design and development. If you know an application is being coded with AngularJS, you should learn how to prototype with those open source code tools that speed up the development process but also make sure that you, as an HCI designer, won't suggest solutions or UI elements that are not in the AngularJS code elements.

Besides having lots of designers and developers knowledgeably working with a code base, using open source methodology allows teams to share the same values. The code that is being used is not a secret; it is out in the open, which changes how a team looks at solutions and thinks about creativity. The best ideas can be explored more freely in open source because it is all about solving a user's problem and not about creating proprietary intellectual property that cannot be shared, copied, or modified by anyone else. Rather, open source allows an HCI designer to focus on the most scalable and supportable solution for a problem that hopefully then gets used but countless others without the risk of being hounded by lawyers for stealing a software idea.

As an HCI designer, you may not always work on open source software, but I can guarantee you will use open source code inside proprietary software because it will speed up your work. Getting software off the work studio floor is hard and open source helps in speeding up your software prototyping process, as not a designer or developer wants to write every line of code from scratch. Being faster and working better together is why open source has been so pervasive in software design communities. Join the conversation and use the skills we have been discussing in this book in the service of sharing and contributing to the greater good. If you have a say in the matter, attempt to push your projects to be open source themselves and you will be astounded by the level of community support and contributions.

MVC, not MVP

Furthermore, as an HCI designer, you will work on solving problems for your users. In Silicon Valley and on the mouths of those involved in business start-ups is the term **Minimum Viable Product**, or **MVP**:

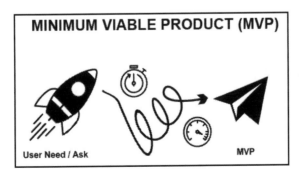

An MVP is the idea that a production team should produce the simplest version of a software product that offers only the highest value to its users in order to be first to market. An MVP focuses on the impact of learning in new product development. If you are not familiar with Eric Ries, he wrote a book called *The Lean Startup*, which has impacted the way many software companies, entrepreneurs, and start-ups have oriented their software development teams and in turn, developed software solutions. The MVP helps in the validation of ideas upfront and holds that learning comes in the form of whether your customers will actually purchase your product.

As we have been discussing, human-centered software has the ability to address the requirements of an MVP. A key premise behind the MVP concept is that an HCI team will produce a product that you can offer to customers and observe their actual interactions with that product or service. I hope this feels familiar with the idea of prototyping we have been discussing up to this point. However, an MVP is the finished product, where a prototype is used to be learned from before completing a final launchable solution. HCI can use their skills to see what people actually do with respect to a product, which is why we can get pulled into creating MVPs. The thinking behind an MVP is that testing products on actual users is a more reliable approach than asking people what they *might* do.

The challenge with an MVP is that it rests on the assumption that a fast-moving HCI design team can address their users' needs quickly – an approach that values speed and being first to market over solving the user's problem the right way. An issue is that an MVP places an undue burden on selling the MVP solution as the correct answer rather than validating multiple solutions through prototyping. The MVP becomes a de facto foundation for a solution and will only be abandoned if it doesn't prove to capture the desired users. Many MVPs fall subject to "pivots" or changes in direction from the business if the developers don't get the solution right first time.

The high-pressure MVP existence has helped some start-ups address their users faster. However, it involves tons of risk. In order to minimize this risk, I think building prototypes that are validated through a **Minimum Viable Culture (MVC)** is more successful:

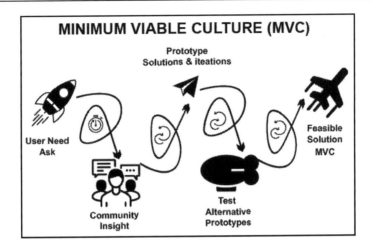

MVC refers to the set of shared values and purpose needed to deliver a company's value proposition to customers. In other words, users don't just use software because it solves their problem, they rely on and trust the brands' ability to create solutions over time. If your product or your company values do not resonate with your users, then you face a risk in convincing them that using your software will solve their problems. Culture goes both ways and software solutions are a response to your users' culture. The two-way street is why I have been discussing user research and driving human-centered values throughout this book.

In many ways, software solutions are wrapped in their own form of culture. For example, look at the number of users who call themselves "a Mac person," suggesting that somehow using Apple software has altered their personality and fundamentally changed their approach to learning and using the software. The reality, however, is that this is true, and if you look deeper at this sentiment, you might see how it is connected to the idea of MVC. Learning and using Apple software and a computer OS is participating in the computer culture of Apple, which then establishes a set of software values that then get applied to other software solutions. The user than participates in software that is connected (or at minimum, related) to the user experience expectations set by Apple. The software doesn't exist in a vacuum; it is all related, which makes it important to pay attention to the communities that use software and create the culture around it.

The reason considering and building software through an MVC lens is that it allows the HCI designer, along with their research in building rapid prototypes, to narrow in on what makes their software prototype successful. An MVC is not just about validation but rather a method to see if the software solutions are aligned with the cultures of the users they are ultimately serving. An HCI designer can be much more confident in a software solution when they know their solutions have not only been vetted by their users, but also valued by them as well. A software solution has many possibilities but if an HCI designer can establish a strong culture that will support their solution, then it is less likely to be changed, pivoted, or abandoned as a viable solution.

The idea of MVC has been deeply understood by software brands, and if you end up working on a software product that is designed for a particular operating system, such as iOS, you too will be required not only to use the software patterns of their platform, but also, iOS has some criterias for allowing your software to exist on their platforms. As an HCI designer, your ability to be well versed in multiple software communities will allow you not only to research them more effectively, but also makes you more valuable as a team member as you can switch between platforms, all while folding human-centered ideas and values into all of your software solutions.

Iterative loops for improving software, which improves culture

As we have been discussing, an HCI designer creates software solutions over time with the goal of producing human-centered solutions to continually improve our users' experiences. The iterative design process is fundamental to how we think about, design, prototype, iterate, and ultimately launch software for our users. The idea is quite profound as an HCI designer is not just solving problems for users through software; they are impacting culture. Because an HCI software designer has the ability to impact culture, we should take that responsibility very seriously and make sure our solutions are what that culture needs. Iterative design is valuable for culture:

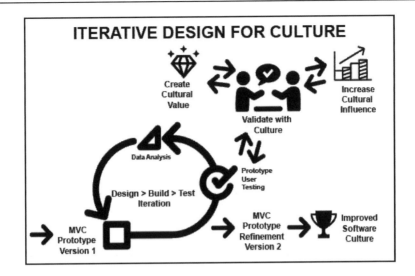

Culture is malleable and we don't want to create software that can break the cultures we are attempting to impact with our solutions. As HCI designers, we must look long and hard at whether the software we design is doing what it was intended for, while also improving the culture, or whether it is morphing that culture in ways that are unintended. For example, Twitter is a form of software that has modified culture in ways I don't think they intended. However, when politicians or other users can use it to spread misinformation without any recourse, the culture it is fostering needs to be checked and the software needs to be iterated in order to not destroy the culture it is trying to serve. The cycles of software iteration, then, are not just for the HCI teams solving problems, but should be as far-reaching as possible into the communities they serve. At the heart of HCI is the human, and we need to iterate our software within the cultures that those users exist, and not the culture we hope or wish would exist.

If you are addressing a culture with your software solutions, you are also considering the widest set of users possible through usability and accessibility, while caring about your user's needs. As we discussed, what makes software development hard is that users are always changing and so is the culture. By building software that can be iterated on, an HCI designer can keep up with the changes in culture. Some cultural changes occur very slowly, while other aspects move very fast.

The technology we as HCI designers are attempting to support is a part of the technology culture that we need and have willingly joined. Don't get me wrong – I highly encourage you to dive into your HCI community and culture, but I also highly recommend finding opportunities to stand back from it. Being able to look into a culture from the outside has value and you do not want to participate in too much confirmation bias. If you are too close to your HCI software technology culture, you might miss something that is not net positive for that given culture. Culture is a *big picture*, and if your view of that culture is too narrow, you can quickly start only considering an increasingly narrow set of solutions that are acceptable to that culture. This type of cultural iteration is dangerous. As an HCI designer, I highly recommend you find opportunities to validate your solutions with cultures that are not your own. The reality of software solution development is that we have to make assumptions, and these assumptions need to be validated not only with our users but potentially with those that are not our users, especially if the goal of the software is to serve everyone, everywhere.

I hope you have gotten the gist. All I am just trying to get across is that, as an HCI designer, you need to care about the users If we don't hold our solutions to a higher cultural standard, we will continue to prop up and produce software that is not only bad for our own community but can have negative implications for the wider culture as well. Take the skills we have been talking about up to this point and deliver them meaningfully in your interaction with your culture(s), making sure to continually validate and iterate them over time.

Summary

To summarize, we started with discussing how software design thrives within the vast community of designers and developers. We covered software as a culture and discussed how collaboration on open source problems creates opportunities for HCI designers to scale their contributions around the globe. We also considered how software design is difficult and time-consuming, and therefore, sharing has become essential to speeding up solution times. The community and team environment in which software solutions are produced also lends itself to maintaining and building for culture of that environment and community. The open source ethos has birthed ideas like the internet, and therefore, we reviewed why iteration and software development aimed at the betterment of mankind is not just a pie-in-the-sky idea but rather something that we as HCI designers can continue to hang our hats on at the end of the day.

In the next chapter, we will focus on more skills in *Part 3* as we discuss methods for extending HCI throughout your careers.

11
Extending HCI

Now that we have reviewed some ways to produce human-centered solutions at scale, let's discuss how the ideas and skills covered up to this point can be extended and maintained over your careers. As a budding HCI designer, you are well on your way to impacting your users in a positive way. The roles we play in culture are linked to our ability to design, test, and iterate software solutions for our users, but we also have the opportunity to improve ourselves. Extending our own skills will ultimately improve the speed, attention, and value that our solutions bring to our businesses and our users.

Now that you are progressing in your HCI journey, let's discuss how HCI skills can create value over time. Software design and development careers are in high demand. The US News and World Report lists the top jobs each year. In 2020, the #1 best job in the US was that of software developer, at 241,500 projected jobs with a median salary of $103,620. (`https://money.usnews.com/careers/best-jobs/rankings/the-100-best-jobs`). The reality is that with demand comes high levels of skill requirements as well as high levels of competition. The skills we have been reviewing are just a starting place for getting you up to speed and into a new HCI role. One thing that should be a comfort is that software design is not a one-person show and HCI is best executed and scaled across a team.

The purpose of focusing on software development as a team endeavor is because, to be a good HCI designer, you should be curious about humans. Being surrounded by other equally curious team members will amplify your skills. We have discussed how designing great software is difficult, but working with team members who do not see the true value in caring about their users can make it downright painful. If you wish to extend the HCI skills we have been practicing throughout this book, look for software teams that emulate the skills and values associated with HCI. Let's discuss how we scale HCI skills and evangelize the value of human-centered design to every team member.

The upcoming chapters are meant to highlight the long-term value that an HCI designer can bring to solutions when they use their skills consistently over time.

In this chapter, we will be learning how to extend our HCI skills through the following:

- Contributing to software development as a collective team
- Exploring how great solutions are shared and scaled
- Evangelizing to your team and sharing common goals
- Demonstrating how you care

Contributing to software development as a collective community

As we have already discussed, HCI and designing software are a team endeavor. The reality is it is more like a league of teams all competing but working toward similar goals. All the companies and individual HCI designers, software developers, project managers, and so on are all part of a collective community. One big family. We might occupy our own little specific space of expertise or software knowledge but when it comes down to it, we all make software and we all work on the same teams.

In the past, and in some instances today, our communities created walls between the design (art) and the code (technical) aspects of solving software problems. Unfortunately in some cases, it has gone so far inside the industry that designers and developers don't actually work together on solving problems, but rather lob solutions back and forth from department to department. We as an industry created management ideas, such as the Waterfall development methodology, that kept the artistic, creative thinking and the technical thinking quarantined from each other, as if somehow these communities were incapable of communication and didn't share similar goals. Hopefully, it's not surprising to you that this was and is false, and is where HCI and the UX/UI professions have found a unique shared footing. As these community walls get demolished, the ideas and considerations flowing in from each side allow us to collectively focus on common ideas.

We learn from each other and rely on the community to prototype together, support standards, share code, and apply solutions that can scale across the globe. We are all stronger and better at solving software solutions because we don't keep it to ourselves or hide behind proprietary closed systems or ways of thinking. Software design is not magic; it is hard work, but it is knowable for and achievable by all parties. We extend our knowledge and share how we go about solving difficult problems so that others can follow in our footsteps, and all users are better for it.

As an HCI designer, you should look out for the bridges between the design, development, and business communities. Software communities should be rhizomatic with connections built between community nodes. If they don't exist, then find ways to create them.

Throughout this book, you have learned HCI skills that span a wide spectrum of the software design process and this is why we are particularly focused on seeking out and codifying our community connections. As you continue to build your network and engage in different aspects of the software design and development community, look to align with others on common goals.

Here are ten goals that you as an individual can hopefully look for in your software teams as well as in the software league (community):

- Software design is human-centered and designed for people, by people.
- Software design is iterative and can be improved over time.
- Software design is usable and accessible to all users.
- Software design creates a net positive impact on its users.
- Software design gives humans more time.
- Software design is not biased and should not push an agenda outside its own value.
- Software design is better as open source.
- Software design is agile.
- Software design is accomplishable only as a team.
- Software design is interconnected.

Over your career as an HCI designer, you will probably not work on one piece of software or for one company. According to Indeed.com, the average tenure of a software developer is around 3 years (`http://blog.indeed.com/2017/04/03/silicon-valley-tech-job-migration/`). Regardless of where you work or what software you help build, the products you design will still be used by people. Because there is a lot of switching teams, your ability to be a good teammate and quickly help your organization build and maintain software is essential to you being able to move around in the first place.

Although there is a lot of competition in the software world, another interesting thing we have is coexistence. For example, Apple and Microsoft coexist and are both widely successful. If you know some of Apple's history, you would know that in 1997, upon Steve Job's return, they took significant investment (150 million USD) from Bill Gates and Microsoft. Until that point, the software industry was fighting like cats and dogs, but they realized that with the competition, you also get a larger global reach for technology, even if it isn't your brand.

UX, UI, frontend dev, backend dev, PM, business, and ops

Furthermore, there are a lot of roles in the software design community. We have covered a number of them by this point but applying your HCI knowledge of the software design process is applicable inside any role. By gaining skills in HCI you will be able to span between many of these roles and hopefully move up throughout your career. Moving up in the software design process typically equals moving into management and overseeing the production of a software team rather than the individual execution of design or code. Moving up in the ranks will require an overall view of the process and if you experience each role directly, rather than just jumping to managing all of the roles, you will have a better idea of how all the parts work together. A good way to consider the whole system as a manager is to use the project management V model:

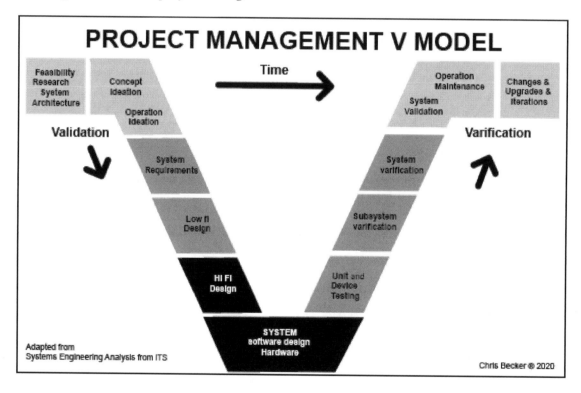

A process that applies validation that can use the design thinking process to solve the problem and then employs verification to find if the solution is useful, usable, deployable, and scalable to your users through system testing. Managing software over time will require the whole team. Many roles in this software design process start out as junior roles, as there is a lot to learn about how a software team functions. As you start to look for work or join a software team, applying HCI skills is more effective when others on your team are also either familiar with your expertise or share in your knowledge and passion for building human-centered software. The opportunity to work with software teams that understand what an HCI designer can bring to the table makes executing your role that much smoother and allows you to step in and help the team right away. By gaining an overview of how HCI applies to each of these roles you can also be a better teammate and hopefully then take these skills up the chain as you work with more designers. Ideally, you will learn along the way, both from this book and other sources, and that education will be transferred to those that you work with or that you yourself help to train.

Not every software team has all the aforementioned roles. If you are new to HCI and need some practice, I recommend not joining a team that is too small too early in your career. The reason is there will be lots of overlap between the UX, UI, and frontend dev roles, and maybe even backend responsibilities that might be too much to handle without the additional experience that comes from working on a bigger team. Besides the fact that you don't want to do the roles of four separate people, smaller teams typically run into capability issues as software either grows in size (that is, features and functionality) or scale (the number of users of the software) and small teams can struggle to keep up with the complexity, especially if they have never experienced it before. Big companies such as Google employ thousands of software developers with HCI skills in teams that include all these roles and more with multiple team members per role, which is why they can support globally scaled software solutions. Google is not the only company that has this type of organization. There are lots of different companies all solving very different problems through software. This is both a blessing and a curse, as where to go apply your HCI skills is hard to discover.

The challenge is to uncover the heart of a software team, which should be displayed in their human-centered actions:

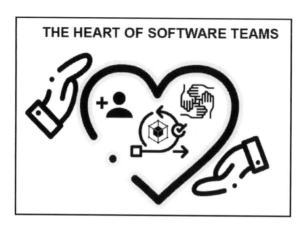

The goal is to build great software for as many users as possible and everyone on the team has to believe that it is doable as well as having the experience that will make it happen. When interviewing with a team or talking with management, attempt to get at the heart of their software design philosophy and process. I would recommend getting to the heart of whether they really care about their users as they make software decisions. It also wouldn't hurt to understand whether the HCI designers and developers work as a team in an agile environment. Ask a ton of questions to the team as there are many teams who are buzzword compliant, but in execution, do not actually follow through with the HCI and human-centered process aspect of the work.

If you find a team that lives up to the quality bar I have been trying to set, congratulations! Now you can grow that team's abilities with your own HCI skills. Let's discuss how you can hit the ground running with the HCI skills.

Team handoff and responsibility

As a result, the nature of software design and development work is both collaborative and individually executed. The HCI process is attempting to infuse human needs into all aspects of the software design process, which includes respecting the time and challenge each team member is working on. The agile design cycle requires all team members to be aligned with the same software goals:

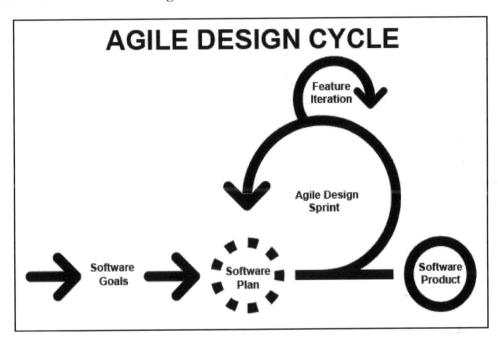

A plan to execute a feature, for example, requires validating whether the feature is actually needed by the users through user research. Next, a UX design solution as a prototype is created and iterated on as a UI/visual design composition which is then coded by a frontend dev/backend dev (if required) and tested at each stage of the process. When done best, this process happens in tight cycles that allow all team members to be involved in the agile feedback loop. The feedback loop is both from team members communicating their processes as well as implementing the feedback from users acquired through the testing of prototypes. Throughout the software design process, each team member is required to communicate and share with their colleagues. The better the team communicates and upholds the process, the faster the software solution can solve its users' problems.

Know as a team handoff, software solutions can be more accurately developed if, for example, the UI/visual designer shares development-ready assets with the frontend developer. Hopefully, those UI assets are a byproduct of a tested UX prototype that has been validated by your users. All of this requires using tools that help speed up moving from nothing to a full software solution. How teams communicate and share these designs and iterations is essential to growing your team's confidence, as well as to creating tighter feedback loops. The software design world moves quickly and the tools teams use to execute software prototypes need to be equally nimble. If a software tool is slowing your team down or hindering essential communication about how a prototype performed, then replace it in your team's process. There is no room for prioritizing a tool over the team's progress.

In the past, I worked with a visual designer who loved using Adobe Photoshop to create web design compositions. He was relatively fast and kind of stubborn about adapting to a different UI design tool. Other team members had experienced some bottlenecking with the work that was created but never equated it to the lack of using similar tools. As we grow the team and the UX team members continued to use Sketch to execute the vast amount of system wireframes, it became quickly apparent that the visual designer's unwillingness to use the similar software systems was creating friction and limiting the quality of our prototypes and our speed in producing them. The designer was having to duplicate a lot of work and was creating too many problems. In our case, we had to replace the designer due to his unwillingness to play as part of a team and share in the visual design responsibilities. It can be very hard to replace team members in the middle of the execution of a design system, however, getting teams using similar design processes and similar tools can help the team distribute the work and maintain quality over time. The software design process takes practice and getting everyone using similar tools allows everyone to collectively combine their skills together rather than leaning on one member or another to do one part of the process. Creating redundancy in tool usage, as well as familiarity with how to manipulate what is being shared between team members, both work to keep the process moving forward and can help a team avoid bottlenecking and conflicts in quality control.

The software design tools your team uses should be fundamentally built around prototyping and collaboration. The entire team should have access to the system they are designing. Sharing feedback on user issues uncovered during user testing or about bugs that need to be fixed should be captured and shared via a central hub that helps visualize and improve a software solution over time. Many tools exist for this purpose, including Atlassian Jira, GitHub, and Trello, among others. However, the feedback captured and the changes that need to be created should be realized and visualized in a shared prototype.

Tools such as Figma, Sketch + InVision, GitHub, and others help keep teams communicating and iterating their software solutions. Managing all this feedback and agile cycles should be a project manager's role but can also be supported through the tools we use as a team.

Communication tools – Zeplin, Figma/XD/Sketch, InVision

Software teams have built sophisticated systems across large teams. The ability to share documentation and details of how a system should be built is essential. Luckily, software communication tools have gotten better and gone are the days where a designer has to painstakingly document every last detail of their visual solution so that a developer will not miss aspects of their solution. Now, we have tools that speed up this documentation process and UI software tools that even generate basic pieces of code. Creating the ability to seamlessly share a working prototype or deliver an asset that is developer-ready is built into tools such as Adobe XD, Sketch, and Figma by using complementary development hand-off tools such as Zeplin.io.

Challenge 48 – Add a Zeplin.io project

Setup:

1. *Go to* `https://zeplin.io/`.
2. *Create an account and sign in.*

Zeplin.io project sharing:

- *Create a new project.*
- *Upload your Adobe XD/Sketch/Figma screens to your project.*
- *Explore how Zeplin.io converts the design file into dev CSS styles and sizing rules.*
- *Explore how Zeplin.io can connect to Jira and Slack.*

 Zeplin allows one free project so use it wisely while experimenting. Hopefully, the software team you will work with will be open to spending money on tools that speed up communication and development efficiency. Trust me, it is worth the ROI.

If you are continuing to use tools that make you work harder to hand off assets or code details, you will continue to create friction between the design and development sides of the software equation. The reality is neither side wants to repeat tedious, mindnumbing details, or sit through a meeting that could be made unnecessary with clear documentation. By using tools that bridge this gap you can free up both sides to do more designing, coding, prototyping, and testing rather than executing the documentation part of the software process.

Although tools like Zeplin.io exist, they are not foolproof and need to be overseen by the design and development teams, but they are a heck of a lot easier than the redlining and annotating solutions that we had to do in the past.

If you find a job or are working for a software team who values working hard over working smart with their tools or their treatment of people, go and find another opportunity. The software company that is unwilling to modify their design and development processes to remove the hassle of tedious work from the team is a company that will eventually fail, or at minimum, be taken over by other teams that do work and communicate effectively. Tools change a lot over time and software is created through a limited set of tools. Having many tools is both a good and bad thing – it's good because tools adapt to and are designed for the software systems we build, allowing the new tools to be more efficient, tailored, and responsive to the needs of a given software team.

For example, consider Sketch as an alternative to Adobe Photoshop, Illustrator, or Figma as an alternative to Adobe XD. The sheer amount of software tools with which to design and build software solutions is predicated on the fact that the software development process is constantly changing. How teams collaborate on a software solution is also different than it was in the past. Newer tools are fundamentally built around collaboration and the need to iterate as a team on a prototype helps.

The bad news is tools require new training and learning from the entire team. It can be hard to convert designers and developers to new tools, even if those new tools are better and align more closely to the design-build-test workflow within the prototype.

As we have discussed, software design is very hard but can be made even harder by using ineffective tools and communication processes. I recommend championing the idea that a team that communicates and works together tightly on a shared prototype is far better off than a team that prefers detailed documentation and tool rigidity over teamwork.

It is easy to champion teamwork, but in reality, actually building a great team is a much harder part of the equation. However, if you keep your eye out for the signs that a software team is following a design process, uses similar tools, and encourages a sound work/life balance, you will find software teams that hopefully are building great software. Trust me, they exist, and if they don't, you can bring your HCI skills into teams and help make them great.

Exploring how great solutions should be shared and scaled

Importantly, even software teams that are built around prototyping first and working with tight collaboration doesn't mean without a doubt that they will be successful. The reality is there is a ton of competition and making software solutions scalable is risky. For example, Microsoft Word is not going away anytime soon – even if a new software team invented a better word processor, the hold and longevity of Microsoft Word means it is staying around. There are many reasons why, but Microsoft Word is still the default. A 5-year-old in kindergarten is now learning to use a computer alongside their ABCs and I can bet you they use Microsoft Word software to write their first letters. The deep hooks in culture that software such as Microsoft Word has is profound, as that tool has achieved adoption on a massive scale. Its scale is achieved not just due to its use on computers; it has also reached such a scale culturally within education, business, and government usage. Microsoft Word is like Kleenex tissues, that is, it is ubiquitous for all the types of text-based software using word processing.

Challenge 49 – Software scale research

Setup

1. *Create a Google doc/Google Sheets file to capture your data.*

Software tools questions

1. *Ask ten friends or coworkers:*
   - *How would you write a long paper or letter?*
   - *If they say they'd use a computer, ask them, "What software would you use? Why?"*
2. *Document the answers.*
   - *Record each answer and mark what software was referred to.*

Gathering data manually will help you respect the time and effort a computer can save you.

Because of the reach of the internet, software has the ability to impact billions of people. Will every piece of software be used by 100 percent of the planet? No! However, if you are building software to solve human needs and designing it to address the widest audience possible, you can impact the lives of tens of millions or maybe more. It is a daunting thing that hundreds of millions of users could use your software solution; however, if we follow the goals of HCI and apply our skills, that is the goal. Whether your number of users is one or one billion, they are your users all the same and are worthy of our consideration when solving software problems. Failing one user doesn't contain the same risk as failing one billion users, but the concept is the same. Our software solutions should not fail anyone and that requires knowledge of where a system can fail.

The HCI design process is about determining and validating whether a solution will work with our users. Once we can prove it works, we can then scale those solutions with some level of confidence. Some solutions fail at scale; however, if you are testing along the way, hopefully your software team doesn't get to the point where they have one billion users they are failing.

Software solutions that are built for scale require a bit of nuance and should be carefully tested across a wide spectrum of users before deploying the solution for all. If you are working for a software company that is willing to modify its software for all its users on a whim, or because a CEO wants it to done, then be worried – that is not an effective way to scale your solutions. HCI skills and a human-centered ethos should not be so easily cast aside. If you are working to build scalable solutions, then everyone on the team, from the CEO to the unit tester, should care about solving user needs first.

As mentioned earlier, you are not the user! Your CEO is not the user, and your lead developer is not the user. Your user is your user – try not to confuse this. Use your HCI skills to solve your users' problems and then take the best solutions and push them to the masses. The best way to continue to improve and scale your software solutions is to keep learning and growing your team.

Evangelizing to your team and sharing common goals

As we discussed, software is not going anywhere; it literally runs the world. Because of this, we should be educating ourselves and our teams to be better. The very fact you have made it this far through the book speaks to the fact that you are willing to educate yourself. However, if you are the only one who gains from this knowledge, then it is limited. I am grateful you are learning but it is so much more powerful when the things you learn are shared and maintained by others. Because of the power of building software as a team that shares in the same canon of knowledge, the goal is to keep learning. Have you come across ideas in this book that you think will help your teammates? Share it. Great software teams are constantly consuming new knowledge and learning not only from their team process but from the processes of others.

We share a common passion, but there are many ways to solve problems, and scaling solutions to as many uses as possible is not easy. It gets a little easier when the software team you work with has common goals. As the HCI designer on a team, you can help forward the human-centered goals and champion knowledge-sharing about why it matters to other members of your team who might not know as much or care as much as you do about that goal. It is impossible to get a team to share in every goal equally, but you can communicate and educate everyone on a team that the goals have value and your role on the team is to maintain the quality bar for your users. By helping your team learn more from you, it also makes your role of maintaining quality for the users easier because others on the team are cued in, or at a minimum, understand and try to not make software that doesn't work for your users.

Challenge 50 – Educate yourself

Setup:

> *Create a Google Doc.*

Part 1: Practice learning from a team:

1. *Ask the biggest community of designers for advice* (https://dribbble.com/).
2. *Ask, "What is the key thing to learn when on a software team?" on a social media platform, such as Twitter/Quora/Facebook/Slack/Reddit/Snap, or any other.*
3. *See if anyone answers. Follow that person and thank them for their advice.*
4. *Ask any other questions about how a team educates itself.*

The technique of interviewing occurs again and again in HCI, simply because by asking questions, you can learn from your community of users and other HCI designers.

If you get a software team learning and sharing together, then they also back each other up and support each individual goal, which, when done right, adds together to help achieve bigger software goals such as scale or a return on investment for a business. Teams that learn together grow together and can continue to learn as new problems, new users, and new team members join in the quest to design great software.

Diversify your team's skills

As a result, while you continue to educate yourself and your teams, it is also essential to learn from others on your team. This is where the team should be as diverse as possible. If your software team is made up of all white males, all with the exact same educational background, all with the same skillsets and interests, you can create software solutions, but they are guaranteed to be inconsiderate of a large set of users. Software teams are better when they are heterogeneous:

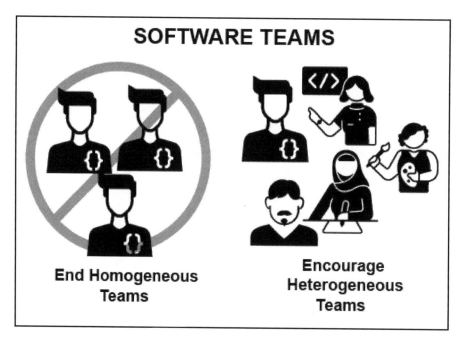

Unfortunately, the software world has an abundance of nerdy males who can write code, and I am in that category. However, that does not mean I want a software team that consists of a bunch of me. I want my software team to reflect in some way the users we are trying to serve by creating the software in the first place. This means building heterogeneous teams and collecting team members that have unique backgrounds, a variety of life experiences, different sexes, and hopefully diverse skills.

If you are a woman reading this, know that in 2020 you are still outnumbered in the software design world, but that number is changing. The more women, and the more of all types of people from all walks of life, that we get into software design, the better. Only a truly diverse set of practitioners designing and developing software as a team will be able to put their varied life experiences to good use in software design. Until then, we will have to encourage teams to diversify as much as they can. It makes for better software. Period! If you want to create great software, you will want to have a diverse set of ideas and opinions on the team and you will want to make sure that every team member truly cares.

Demonstrating how you care

Lastly, I can assume by this point that you already care, otherwise you wouldn't be reading this, nor would you be taking your knowledge of HCI out into the world. The reality is that, as a good team member, you also need to make sure the ethos of **caring about building great software** is contagious. Software design is a job and because of this, it is prone to the ailments of *clock in, clock out* thinking. Software development at some companies is treated very much this way, with a good example in Peter Gibbons at Initech in the movie *Office Space*.

 Check out the movie *Office Space*, written and directed by Mike Judge (`https://www.imdb.com/title/tt0151804/`).

Look out for software management, team members, or project managers that discourage you from caring about your user. They might say things like, *"That's not important; why should we listen to every user?"*, *"I did the minimum and then went home,"* or *"It's fine, I did most of what you asked for."* Team members who just don't care will drag down the team and will start to suck the potential life out of other team members who *do* care.

If you are looking to join a software team, ask questions that will help you gauge whether they do care. These questions could include *"What if you have a bunch of users complain about a feature, what does your team do?"*, *"How often do members of the team learn from each other?"*, *"Who prioritizes features?"*, or *"How does the team advocate for the user?"* When being interviewed for a software position, you are equally interviewing the team and company. If you leave an interview thinking, *"It doesn't seem like they really care about their users"*, then do not join that team! Doing HCI is hard enough, but being the team member who has to pull everyone else along and make them care is not fun.

Typically, teams who care build great software that is scalable, and if you can join a great team that does care, then software design can be endlessly fulfilling and fun.

Summary

To summarize, we discussed how HCI skills are valuable to a team and why we evangelize the value of human-centered design to every team member. The opportunities that teams small and large get is why HCI is a vibrant space and your practice of caring about the users and sharing that goal with your current team or a team you are looking to join is key to growing your HCI skills, but equally to demonstrating your value to users.

As we get approach the end of the book, and you prepare yourself to take these conversations and skills into the world, it is important to remember that you are part of a community and will join a team of designers. If you think about it, it is kind of remarkable that great solutions are designed by hundreds of people. The ability to share ideas and solutions and scale them around the globe is an opportunity, but also a challenge for you to continue to educate yourself and your team over time. As you grow your skills and extend them to your fellow team members, remember when it gets hard that you **care**! When your team members care as well, even hard days won't be so bad and you will know you have a process that you share with your team for making improvements.

In the next chapter, we will focus on the final chapter of *Learn HCI* by discussing the future of HCI.

12
The Future of HCI

By now, you should have picked up that HCI is intimately connected to people. Whether that be through the data we gather on users during research or throughout the software design process, the skills and experience we have been reviewing up to this point will allow you to extend your care for users. However, nothing is foolproof. You should not think that there is nothing more to learn even after completing a book; rather, you should see HCI as an opportunity for you to continuously gain new knowledge and skills. Because a computer is a great tool for gathering data, we design our software to capture data that allows a software team to capitalize on this feedback in order to understand our users and ultimately create better software solutions. The process is iterative and your role is continuous. The role that HCI designers play in this cycle is to improve the relationship between users and software solutions. The better the software team understands their users' needs, the better the software solution will be. The HCI design process never ends and it is our responsibility to extend this knowledge to those entering the HCI world and work at broadening the knowledge of HCI so that everyone has an understanding of why software matters and how they too can be involved in improving our collective user experience with computers.

In this final chapter, we will look at how to capitalize on the knowledge we have explored and use our own data to catapult us into the future. We've covered a lot of ground in terms of HCI, and to wrap it up, we'll discuss how we can extend HCI skills into a world that is primed to be more human-centered than it has been in the past:

- Designing software is an awesome responsibility
- Creating solutions that are net positive for culture
- Evaluating what is off-limits
- Empowering computers
- Designing software for the future

Designing software is an awesome responsibility

Technology and software's value and ability to scale has impacted every echelon of society, from the Pope down to the potter. Between the 1960s and 1980s, computers were devices for supplementing work and therefore took on work responsibilities with their software. This was dubbed "desktop computing" as the computer was a device used in an office on a desk to do "office" work. Desktop computer hardware continues to exist; however, the majority of users interacting with computers are now doing so through handheld devices. As we have discussed, these handheld computers have become powerful enough and have software designed for them that has altered the very nature of doing work. Consider the idea that doing "work" is fundamentally different in every industry because of technology, particularly the smartphone, which has untethered workers from their desks. On the one hand, this is great as a worker can more effectively address "work" on their own time using their technology effectively. On the other hand, it has radically blurred the lines between work life and personal life. The ability of technology (hardware and software) to change entire industries is just one of the big reasons why the people designing software should take this responsibility very seriously. I am talking about you!

Try to avoid the trappings of technological determinism, which is a theory that our social structure and cultural values are defined by technology. Technological determinism assumes a reductive path, resulting in the consolidation of software tools that ultimately constrain a user's abilities rather than expand them. Software can be fundamentally a positive force, but if we assume its use is inevitable, it can lead down a dangerous path. An HCI designer's role is not inevitable. We need to continue to fight for and advocate for our users; otherwise, software paths such as government-mandated facial recognition or always-on recording devices can and will produce unwanted and potentially destructive reactions.

I imagine right now that you have a supercomputer in your pocket, a device that can connect you to all of the world's knowledge at the push of a few buttons or, in most cases, a few glass screen strokes. It is remarkable and also kind of scary, the sheer scale of use that mobile technology has had in our world. The role that technology plays is fantastic and part of that is due to the ability of these devices to be transformed by the software that is executed on them. A smartphone is such a versatile device and has raised the expectation of what software can be and how it can impact our lives. As computer technology has become smaller, faster, and mobile, it has embedded itself into every nook and cranny of our lives. If you are traveling, it is your boarding pass. If you want to buy something, it is your wallet. If you want to get from point A to point B, it is your map. Need to be entertained on the train? Guess what: it can become your movie, TV, podcast, or videogame as well.

The ability of software and hardware to become whatever the user needs it to be can bring huge value to the user. The smartphone is addressing so many different aspects of the user's world. However, this also has a risk as more and more users are becoming 100% reliant on their technology to control and navigate their world. The reliance on mobile technology makes those devices keys both figuratively (access) and literally (keyless cars and homes). The issue with keys is that they can be lost or stolen, or worse, hacked and ransomed off. Smartphone technology requires power through battery life; however, if the value a phone provides when it is charged is greater than the inconvenience of being locked out of all your connected vehicles, homes, offices, and so on, we will see our software continue to embed itself into our lives.

An individual piece of software that exists on a smartphone is not solely responsible for this technology reliance; however, it does contribute. If one piece of software is designed with flaws that allow hackers to control your technology, all other software becomes hijacked by that lowest common denominator. The reality of the world is that as an HCI designer, there is a lot of competition, and the software you work on does not want to be the reason a user gets locked out of their phone. Therefore, work in teams that care and prioritize your users' needs for privacy and security.

In software design, every positive implementation has a negative catch. Let's take the example of a single sign-on feature, where the user signs in once and their login credentials are used to access multiple applications. The positive: from a user perspective, this has value as it diminishes the repetitive tasks of signing into multiple applications. The negative: if the feature is not designed securely and is hacked, the centralized sign-on service will have jeopardized every service that the user has connected the single sign-on to work with. We see this occur in our world far too often as service after service reports that their databases have been compromised and credential information has been leaked or stolen.

When we design any software feature, we should evaluate and consider such risks. A way to evaluate these risks is through a **SWOT (strength, weakness, opportunity, threats)** analysis. SWOT is a method of evaluating a software solution. Let's practice SWOTing our prototype challenges.

Challenge 51 – SWOT analysis of a software feature

Setup

Get out a sheet of paper or create a digital sketching space (`miro.com` *or* `mural.com`*).*

Part 1: SWOT a software feature for its opportunities

Create a SWOT matrix and evaluate one of your prototype features:

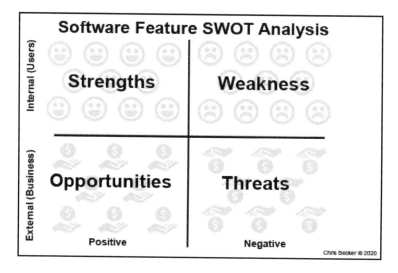

Part 2: Evaluate your prototype feature

1. *The feature you SWOTed should have more positives than negatives, or the positives should far outweigh the negatives.*
2. *If your feature has more weaknesses and threats than strengths and opportunities, identify it early and eliminate that feature.*

SWOT on a whiteboard with a few other team members, talking through your decision and debating each section for the best results.

If you have SWOTed your prototype, it can help reduce your team's chances of failure by showing you what you're lacking and pointing out hazards that would otherwise create more risk when left untended to. A software team needs to share in the responsibility for what they create and what impact it has on the world. Looking at weaknesses and the threats your solution may cause to your user or your business through an honest lens will hopefully help your team to avoid choosing ideas or solutions that foster more risk.

The global scale of technology also comes with a lot of responsibility as the needs of the world are always changing. Whether it be global supply chain logistics, mass communications, remote work, or automation, internet-connected software is at the heart of allowing users to understand and navigate these issues. The reality is that all these future job roles also come with a brand new set of complexities and user experience issues, which is why we are having this discussion in the first place. At the heart of why software technology has been so scalable is the fact that it fundamentally allows users to contribute to each other. Contribution is a human need and as a species, we have evolved to be socially connected. As social beings, our technology has allowed us to interact, collaborate, and solve problems together. Software is a key driver for human collaboration and iteration, which has an endless number of opportunities:

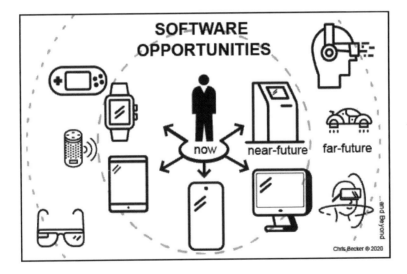

As we have discussed, humans are complicated and their needs are not static; as software burrows deeper and deeper into our lives, it also changes our opinions and our understanding of the opportunities that software can present. Although computer software is solving more and more problems each day, it is also creating new problems and new opportunities as new technologies and software capabilities become available, get invented, or are dreamed up by HCI designers like you and me. Because HCI designers have the skills to think about solutions for now, for the near future, and the far future, the skills we possess should be taken with great care. The idea that just because you can, you should, is false.

The role you play in the creation of software has deep roots and is not done alone. Since collaboration is essential to any software solution, the fact that it is messy and hard and can be used for good or evil should be discussed regularly as a team. If you work for a software team that is not deeply considering their impact on the world, here is your opportunity to change that conversation and reaffirm the value that an HCI designer can bring to the table. If you are looking to break into the HCI role and use the skills discussed in this book, awesome: make sure your efforts are put to good use. Ask the hard questions, make sure your team members care about and look for software opportunities that do not compromise the role of an HCI designer on their team.

I recommend avoiding any job description that uses "ninja," "rockstar," "fast-paced," "wear multiple hats," or has tons of slashes: "UX/UI/IxD/IA designer" (or worse, "UX/FE Dev"), as these businesses are trying to lure talent and combine roles rather than building out software teams that can care about users. Fundamentally, they don't really know what they are looking for, or worse, they are looking to overload a designer with too much responsibility in the hopes of capitalizing on the HCI designer's enthusiasm and human-centered skills. HCI has value but we need to hold businesses accountable for understanding and investing in humans to build human-centered software.

Creating solutions that are net positive for culture

Software design has informed the way we think about the world and, in turn, how we contribute to the world as well. For hundreds of millions (perhaps billions) of people, platforms such as Facebook, Instagram, YouTube, Reddit, WhatsApp, Twitter, Quora, TikTok, and others are a means of access and contribution to society. Of course, some users contribute to their communities more than others, but fundamentally, they are utilizing the same technology channels.

Both Pope Francis and Alex Jones use Facebook to communicate with their communities, albeit for very different ends, but the utilization of the software features is equal. How software and platforms are used as a vehicle for communication is then transferred to its users with little to no oversight or moderation. As software designers, we typically don't want to restrict our users from using our solutions; however, if a software team is finding that users are abusing our platforms, or worse, abusing each other, the role of a software team is to limit this behavior. Conceptually, there is a belief that communities using a piece of software will self regulate and if user A is stealing content or being belligerent, then the community will correct that bad behavior. As an HCI designer, I think software design teams should do a better job of educating their users about the software process, content rules, and what is acceptable community behavior. Alongside our education, another component is also enforcement. An HCI design should incentivize positive behavior before it gets to a point where a community of users has to be impacted by a bad actor. It is, of course, an imperfect process, but if a software team correctly considering all their users, they will attempt to anticipate and design for users who break the rules.

Unfortunately, up to this point in 2020, there has been a laissez-faire approach to users and how they are educated in, say, writing a tweet, or posting a TikTok, or rating a restaurant on Yelp. We hope that users will behave in a civil fashion. However, software platforms have amplified and in some cases encouraged poor behavior and misuse of platforms by mostly anonymous users. As HCI designers who care about their users, we don't have have to lean into this trend; we can recognize that software has been designed and executed with flaws and therefore try and fix it for the betterment of society.

Software teams have to walk a tricky path when it comes to moderating their users' interactions. If you are too restrictive – say, users only get to post three times a week or only upload 500 MB of video – your users will regard this restriction as a usability error or a reason to not use your software. But if your software is too hands-off, your users could upload thousands of inappropriate images or share copyrighted material without permission.

I highly recommend not setting arbitrary rules based on technical access but rather using the user research skills we have covered in this book to really understand what software rules and content restrictions make sense for your users. As I have been telling you, software can make an impact on your users:

Now, a risk in creating any piece of software is that once it is in the hands of the users, how they use it or abuse it is up to them. The reality is that this is true, but as software designers, we set the rules; if a user doesn't use a feature we created, it is not the user's fault. If the user abuses a feature we allowed them to use, that is also due to a lack of educating our users. The software designer is more culpable than we would like to think. In many cases where software features are abused by their users, it is due to an inherent faith that our users will use what we design positively. Unfortunately, that is not a reality and the role of an HCI designer is to funnel users into positive use of our systems.

For example, a few software companies used to have a motto that went like this: "move fast and break things." This was fine and good for a software company that used Agile design methods to iterate their platform for their users, but if you dig deeper, it was not all that responsible. Ideas have power, and building a software platform that touches billions of users while having what I believe is a cavalier motto allows bad decision making, especially when it comes to user data access. The amount of data they have on their users is fundamentally how they make money. However, this, in my opinion, creates a conflict of interest with its users. The business is incentivized to allow corporate and political spending to drive features that tap into user behavior rather than considering what users want first, which in most cases is not more advertising or targeted political content. At this point, social media platforms such as Facebook, Twitter, Snapchat, TikTok, and so on have had more impact on society than any other content maker.

If you are interested in working for social media software companies as an HCI designer, I would highly recommend that you evaluate the potential risks that your software decisions are causing. There is nothing wrong with making money, but if you are degrading the software experience for your users in order to make more money, then that power relationship should be evaluated, and hopefully, as a human-centered designer, you can advocate for making decisions that have a net positive outcome for your user. When your user wins, typically, your business will also be successful.

Evaluating what is off-limits

Here is a moment to be real with yourself. *What do you want to work on?*

As an HCI designer, you should think deeply about what is off-limits for you:

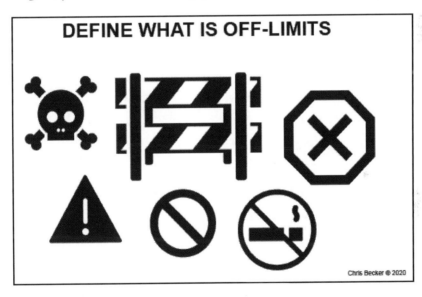

Software is involved in every aspect of society and therefore can be used by every industry. For instance, I do not smoke, I do not want to smoke, and because of the well-documented health issues, dubious marketing tactics, and other negative effects caused by the tobacco industry, I don't want to create software or websites that help their businesses. Because of my stance against smoking, promotion, websites, and software, it makes it easy for me to place them on the off-limits list. Having an off-limits list, or, at a minimum, knowing what is off-limits, will help you identify what is fair game or, even better, what you are passionate about from a software perspective. With your experience in HCI, let's practice defining some of your software interests.

Challenge 52 – Zones of interest and worthwhile pursuits

Setup

1. *Get out a sheet of paper or create a digital sketching space (miro.com or mural.com).*
2. *Draw four concentric circles representing you and three zones of interest.*

Part 1: You – Add some personal interests, cares, hobbies, and passions.

In the middle, put yourself and a few things that you care about personally.
- For me, it is "Chris Becker – Education, Arts, Creativity, User Experience, Writing, Nerds."

Part 2: Zone 1 – Add companies, brands, and software concepts that align with the things that you care about the most.

In the next circle, write down the companies, brands, and software concepts that align with the things you care about the most.

Part 3: Zone 2 – Add companies, brands, and software concepts that are somewhat interesting to you.

In the next circle, write down the companies, brands, and software concepts that are somewhat interesting to you but not as compelling as the ones you just wrote about.

Part 4: Zone 3 – Add companies, brands, and software concepts that you are opposed to.

In the next circle, write down the companies, brands, and software concepts that you are opposed to.

Part 5: Reflect – Review what your priorities and interests are.

Analyze your software interests zone by zone.

Part 6: Identify a software industry you want to pursue.

Use three stars to identify possible career paths.

 Designing your zones digitally will make it easier to make connections.

As we have been discussing, software design is really hard, and if you have the opportunity to work on a project or for a company where you are working on something that you are already passionate about, it can go along way in helping you to produce better software. Typically, software teams that care about their users, have a passion for their problems, and are supported by their businesses will, in turn, create great software solutions. Where software solutions are not very good, we typically see software teams that are either too small or time-poor, or the business prioritized their needs over the needs of their users. Work exists out there, and aligning your software interests with the interests of a business will help you be a better candidate for a role and hopefully design software solutions that you are proud of and willing to use yourself.

Not everyone will have the luxury of working in their dream role or with a dream team. Actually, it is far more likely that you will not. Not to be a contrarian, but the opportunities to work for dream teams and dream companies are highly competitive and some just don't become available that often. Because of this, you have the opportunity to help software teams that want to be great but haven't figured it out yet. Software design requires a lot of hustle, and if you find teams that are also willing to put in the hard work, you will be better off.

Empowering computers

It is important to highlight that our digital lives have become more complicated, but at the same time, they have never been so convenient. When you are considering software projects or companies that you want to work with, commit to working on solutions that embody the value that computers can bring to humans. Computers are really great at repetitive tasks, and more and more of our lives is being augmented by software. Your efforts to build software that speeds up tasks or frees its users from clicking through an interface represent time that you have given back to your user by allowing computers to do what they do best. Software should not be valued by the time a user spends using it, but rather by the time it gives back to them in their day or work schedule.

For example, take documenting meetings and sending a recap of a discussion via email. This is a valuable record but one that currently requires human intervention. However, a piece of software has a unique opportunity to speed up this process rather than requiring a worker to take notes, type out detailed notes, and send them to all those invited to the meeting. What if software could be used to record the meeting, automatically generate a transcript, and attach the assets to the email of the meeting invite?

This could be a highly useful feature for any video-conferencing application. As an HCI designer, you can recognize the advantages that technology supplies and implement solutions for users that maximize the capabilities of a computer. Computers are great at repetitive tasks that can be automated through software, ultimately making users more efficient.

An HCI designer can apply efficiency concepts to how software is designed and allow a computer to maximize a user's interactions, which will not only enable your software to do what computers do best but improve your users' understanding of the value software can bring to their lives. For example, do not force your user to save; a computer can be programmed to automatically save, and you can include a UI element to confirm that the saving process is being completed periodically by the computer. If the computer is auto-saving, create some form of message that shows the time and date of the last save. If a user wants to save manually, so be it, but a user should never be in a scenario where they lose a lot of work because a file is not saved. Furthermore, never allow a file to not be saved upon quitting. It is ridiculous that work doesn't save when you quit and that there's a modal alert – *do you want to save before you quit?* Yes, of course, I do! Stop making users select UI buttons unnecessarily. There are countless opportunities for the programmer to anticipate what the user wants to do and program computer software to address those needs. The important factor to remember is that computers are able to be programmed, and therefore we should program according to our users' needs. Don't force your user to think like a computer; on the contrary, the computer should anticipate how a user thinks and attempt to be as helpful and efficient as possible.

As an HCI designer, you have the opportunity to look at your digital world, evaluate where computers are highly useful and where they continue to cause repetitive, time-consuming, and busy work, and fix it. Caring about how your users interact with the entire system of a computer and all its software will help you focus on what your users need as well as how to improve what computers can do for them. By focusing on software that is designed for users, an HCI designer can continue to grow their skills and spread their influence across all software. Eventually, it could lead to no more bad software. Wouldn't that be amazing? In reality, there will always be bad software designed by people who don't care as much as HCI designers do. All we can do is take our skills and apply them across as many projects as we can over our careers, which is one of the takeaways from this book. By applying the skills you have gathered from this text and the many others you will read on your HCI journey, you have to opportunity to improve the future of software.

We started *Learn HCI* with a brief history that led us to this place in time and space. Let's wrap up this book with a review of how our HCI history can take us into the future.

Designing software for the future

Technology is not going anywhere; on the contrary, it is ushering in the future faster than we ever imagined. Like the management expert Peter Drucker said, *"The best way to predict the future is to create it"* (`https://www.drucker.institute/thedx/joes-journal-on-creating-the-future/`). Any new software is in the future. Now that we have the skills to create it, we should consider what our users really need from the future. We are always hurtling toward an undefined future destination; therefore, we might as well use the skills we have been discussing in this book to direct our trajectory and usher in a world of software that is designed by HCI designers and is more human-centered, with the ability to adapt to the new needs our users will have in the future.

Let's conclude our discussion by covering the future of software systems in six trajectories:

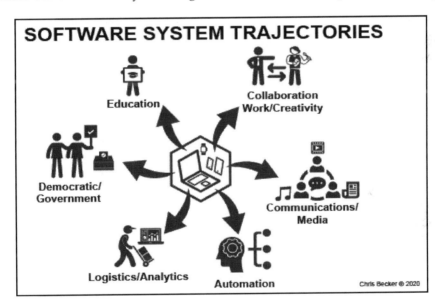

The six trajectories are as follows:

1. Education software systems
2. Collaboration software systems for work and creativity
3. Communication/media software systems
4. Automation software systems
5. Logistics/analytics software systems
6. Democratic software systems

Education software (embedded systems)

Computer software has impacted every aspect of education, from kindergarten through to adult learning. This is literally a human life span, and software is already touching each phase of the user's learning. Educational software has a unique opportunity to improve students' experience and therefore their education:

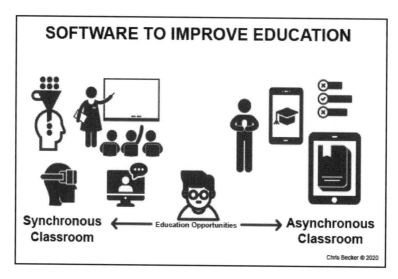

The role software can play in the future of education is profound. The question is not, "Should software be used for education?" but rather, "What is the best way software can be used for education?" There are thousands of educational software solutions all trying to capitalize on helping users to learn. One of the opportunities for education is that it allows us to design experiences that are embedded in our users' lives. A child does not distinguish whether they are using a tablet or a piece of paper when they are learning how to solve a math problem. The learning process is transcendent and math can be learned with or without computer software. However, software can be adaptive and customizable to the student exploring math problems. Software can then act as a support and intervention to encourage a student to extend their math learning through gamification or other tactics. Besides the ability of software to make learning math more engaging for a student, it also gathers learning data that can be automatically graded, communicated with parents or teachers, and used to improve a student's skills. Education software now allows an instructor or parent to access insights as to a student's progress rather than relying on the student to self-report or fail during exams for an instructor or teacher to intervene in learning. Educational software allows computers to do what they do best but also creates an opportunity to build students' confidence with math or literally any other subject.

Another huge opportunity that software creates in education is meeting students where they are at in terms of their learning style. In education circles, we have learned so much about how humans learn. Take the seven learning styles: visual (spatial), aural (auditory-musical), verbal (linguistic), physical (kinesthetic), logical (mathematical), social (interpersonal), and solitary (intrapersonal). Consider your users' learning styles:

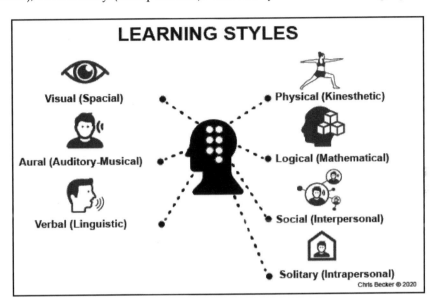

Educational software has the opportunity to be customizable and adapt to an individual's specific learning style. Although this customization represents more work for a software team as individual lessons need to be adapted to each learning style, software can learn how a student learns to help a student be more successful.

There is a meta-learning that goes along with using software to learn any topic. The process of using software is also a process of learning about software; as a student learns math through software, they also learn how to use a computer interface. Since computer software is so ubiquitous in our world, we take this experience for granted. A point of caution, though: a poorly designed learning experience is doubly damaging for a student trying to learn a skill. A student should not struggle with any UI usability issues when trying to learn a subject through software. In education, the opportunity for software to be the vehicle for learning new skills seamlessly is why the HCI skills we have been discussing are so relevant.

A student doesn't want to learn an interface on its own; they want to use an interface to execute a skill they are learning. Computer software should be so useful that it disappears into the task your user is attempting to accomplish. If you care about your users' needs, the software interface you design will match these needs and hopefully facilitate that task seamlessly. As we have been discussing, the goal in software design and education is that your solutions become indispensable in your users' lives.

Collaboration software systems for work and creativity (ubicomp and seamless interactions)

The future is collaborative. Hopefully, you have picked up that computer software is designed by teams and contributes to a broader community who also collaborate with their software. Software that increases human potential and efficiency will continue to show value and be useful for society:

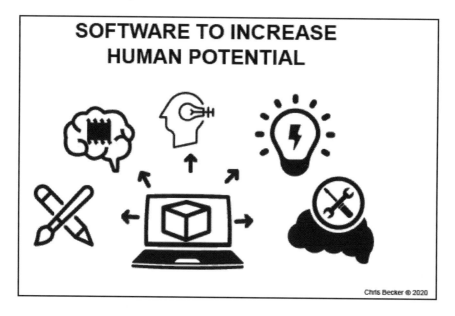

There is collaboration both in the creation of software (HCI/UX/UI/development teams creating software together, for example) and at the user's end (the users using the software tools as a community). Take tools such as Google Drive. Such software tools are not that much different from the Microsoft Office suite except for one key difference: the ability of users to collaborate simultaneously using tools in the cloud. The fundamental shift of software from an individual computer to the cloud and the enabling of interaction to happen collaboratively has produced a suite of software tools that allow users to co-create, share seamlessly, and distribute ownership not only of software files but also the content and ideas used to create software. The ability of computer systems to be connected to the internet, and, in turn, cloud infrastructure, does away with the idea of storing a computer file on your person and locking it away on an individual computer's hard drive. The concept of collaborative software has unique potential in creating software solutions that lean into how communities work, how they are created together, and the computer's potential to enhance creativity within a team.

Creativity is a core concern of humans, and software has the potential to help enhance a user's, team's, or community's creative capacity. Software and computers on their own are not that creative, but as tools, they allow a user to be almost infinitely creative. In the 20th century, cultures liked to highlight the maverick genius, the lone creative thinker that shone brighter than the rest: the Picassos, Einsteins, Plancks, and Bucky Fullers of the world. Now these individuals are highly credited for their unique contribution and creativity, and I believe that the world will still have a few; but because of systems such as the internet and collaborative software, we will see that focus now distributed among teams that are extraordinary in their creativity. The expectation that a human has to go alone to make his or her mark is no longer valid, and the future of collaborative software will empower humans to solve bigger and bigger problems as a community. The role that collaborative software plays is then in making sure that as many users as possible can interact and communicate together regardless of language, location, age, sex, creed, religion, and so on. Collaborative software has the potential to bridge gaps between cultures and should foster interaction rather than creating barriers.

Communication/media software systems (digital affordance and seamless interactions)

As we move into the future and software becomes an enabler for our users, the responsibility that we as HCI designers have is to amplify human potential. In order to improve problem-solving, you need to improve communication. Software that impacts user's communication will continue to drive demand:

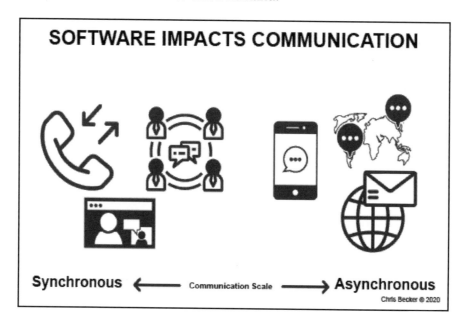

Computer software has radically impacted our ability to communicate, and much of the software innovation that has happened over the past decade has been dedicated to modifying, inventing, and adding modalities to our communication options. As HCI designers, we have a unique opportunity to identify the needs that our users have regarding communication and address the numerous problems that come with communicating across multiple channels, multiple devices, and multiple people. There is no perfect communication solution or software that fixes all of our problems (although some will try). There is, however, huge future potential in reconciling and generating software solutions that recognize the value of various communication styles, from synchronous communication (one-on-one phone calls, for example) to asynchronous styles (such as email), and everything in between.

Automation software systems (ubicomp and embedded systems)

As we have discussed, computers are great at repetitive tasks (such as doing math). As more and more jobs require a computer to get the job done, we will start to see more opportunities for where human interaction can be offset by computer automation. Software solves repetitive tasks and automates job processes, freeing up more time for users:

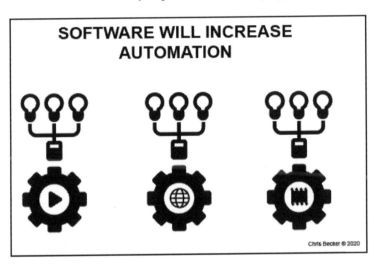

Consider the rise of the **automatic teller machine (ATM)**; consider the amount of software that has been created in order to eliminate a human job, the bank teller. The ATM was first introduced in 1969 and in the subsequent 50 years, the technology has not eliminated every bank teller job; however, it has fundamentally changed the role of a bank branch and what a bank teller's role is to customers. ATMs are now ubiquitous, but bank branches still utilize the high-touch customer-facing interaction of a bank teller. The automation of the ATM is valuable to users but can't solve every user's problem. Software is at the heart of the ATM, and it has been part of our culture for longer than I have been alive. It has been made highly efficient for users, which has in turn created value over time and trust from anyone who uses an ATM. For multinational banks, this ATM infrastructure and automation capability has enabled customers to trust banks from New York to Nigeria. The amount of computer software that has been created to support banking around the globe is astounding and represents tons of opportunities to innovate.

Automation has a wide range of applications, from the bad (the elimination of jobs at the expense of human capital) to the good (the automation of repetitive tasks to free users' time). As HCI designers, we should focus on caring about our users and the execution of automation features in software design. Our focus on the good part of automation will utilize the skills we have worked hard to gain. If our users are engaging in manual repetitive tasks and procedures, then we can identify them through research and design features, new processes, or computer assistance to help our users in their tasks.

Logistics/analytics software systems (knowledge data)

As we move into the future and software becomes an enabler for our users, the role of HCI designers is to amplify human potential and understanding. Software and the internet have ushered in the ability of companies to scale their operations and track their products around the globe. Software for logistics and analytics will continue to be in demand:

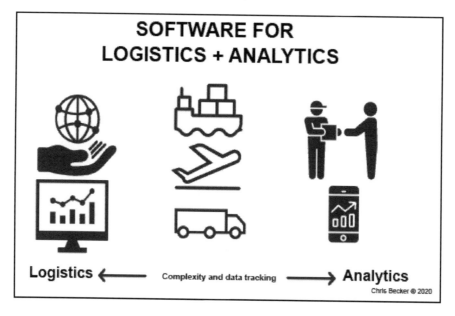

The opportunities that software can continue to provide in shaping the future are fundamentally linked to how it can make sense of massive amounts of data and produce meaning for its users through analytics.

Take Amazon, for example. When Jeff Bezos started Amazon as an online bookstore in 1994, many thought it would just be a bookseller website. However, as we have come to see, the dominance of Amazon's business in its early years, as well as today, is about establishing logistics in selling millions of products. The reality is that Amazon understood the power of the internet early on, not just as a global communication tool but as a global supply chain mechanism. Since no other business had created product connection software to this level of sophistication on a global scale, Amazon took off and sellers and buyers flocked to their service.

The opportunity for HCI designers to consider the future through design logistics software and analytics solutions is vast. Amazon is not alone in its ability to consider and quantify a global reach. As we discussed earlier, software can be scaled around the globe via the internet and because of this, software teams should be well versed in the implications of their solutions. As we move into the future, there will be more humans using more software, which will lead to more complexity. Without HCI designers and sophisticated software teams that can create solutions for globally scaling solutions, the value software can have will be diminished. Globalization is not a genie you can put back in the bottle; on the contrary, future software solutions should adapt to the wishes of the future and allow HCI designers and users to understand their global context more clearly.

Democratic power software systems (ubicomp and security)

Similarly, computer software has become so ubiquitous and relied upon that it is hard to see why it is not being used to greater societal ends by governments. Yes, every government relies on some aspect of software, whether it be websites to communicate policy, software to submit requests, or software to communicate with constituents. But software that enables democracy to thrive will also be in demand:

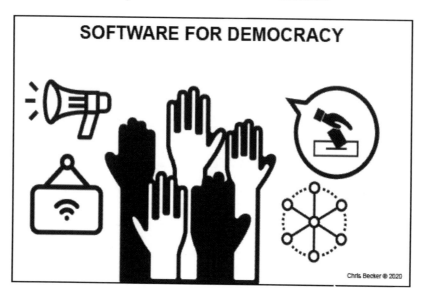

SOFTWARE FOR DEMOCRACY

Chris Becker ® 2020

Computer software is essential for operating any country and is even more important for democratic institutions. Full disclosure: I do not live under a totalitarian state and therefore cannot speak with any authority about how such a government uses computer software. On the other hand, I am an American and can discuss how software can and should reflect the values of a democratic society. The reality is that the human-centered ideal that underpins HCI is linked with the values of democracy. Consider the fact that as an HCI designer, you are representing users (people) just as an elected official is responsible for the voters (people) in their district. Although an HCI designer does not need to be elected by their users, they are in fact reliant on the HCI designer to have their best interests in mind. The act of designing through an HCI lens is a reflection of that.

The opportunities to create tools that empower a government to address constituents' issues more effectively are abundant. There are countless such opportunities, where the government is either behind the times or has created software that is so difficult to use that it defeats the purpose of having it at all. As we have been discussing, HCI designers can then identify these issues and work to solve them. Software has the ability to hold a representative government to account through participation that goes much deeper than just voting. Voting is a truly democratic act, and software in the future should find a way to make voting as convenient and trusted as Google Search. Although complicated, voting through software should allow users to vote effectively and not just wait on election day to determine who is "winning." When our representatives are more closely connected with the people they represent through technology, their roles and responsibilities can be defined more effectively. Helping constituents understand what is being worked on by representatives as well as allowing representatives to hear from and reflect the needs of their constituents is an opportunity to allow software tools to scale and distribute the vital task of decision making.

The reality is that hundreds of millions of users trust Facebook to document their lives with photos, events, cat pictures, and more, but very few trust a government to make voting digital. The irony is that Facebook has become a more powerful political tool than it was originally designed for, with it being designed at first to allow college students to connect, share, and possibly "hook up." As software grows in the number of users it reaches, it increases the power that the software can have over culture. Facebook quickly moved beyond college students and is now, for better or worse, a cultural driver and connection tool for a large number of users around the globe. The political power of Facebook's platform has resulted in both regulatory opportunities for the government but also stronger and more effective communication from our politicians. The ability of software tools to scale around the globe and be used by both democratic societies and dictators has to keep the designers at Facebook up at night, hopefully!

Regardless of the success or failures of our current software tools and their impact on government, the reality is that software is fundamentally looking to address users' problems, which will continue to be a valuable mission long into the future and will address more issues than those in education, collaboration, communication/media, automation, logistics/analytics, and government. Let's take this chance to mindmap the future opportunities of HCI and software.

Challenge 53 – Which software future?

Setup

1. *Get out a sheet of paper or create a digital sketching space (miro.com or mural.com).*
2. *Draw a circle in the middle.*

Part 1: Mindmap center – Choose a software future that you are interested in.

In the middle, write your software concept (education, collaboration, communication/media, automation, logistics/analytics, democratic software).
 - For example, for me, it is (Chris Becker - Education).

Part 2: Add future user needs around that software future.

1. *Document all the future needs you can think of.*
2. *Draw lines connecting the needs to the center of the mindmap.*
3. *If some user needs are related, cluster them together.*

Part 3: Add details about software or companies that are considering these needs today.

Review all the needs and connect the needs to the names of software or companies that are considering them today.

Part 4: Circle any unmet or highly underserved user needs.

Use a red marker to draw circles around user needs that are either not being considered or only have one connection.

Part 5: Review what is circled.

Reflect upon the mindmap and analyze your potential future opportunity space.

Be as realistic as you can. We all want to have our dream jobs or work at amazing companies, which is possible, but don't raise your expectations too high.

Summary

Throughout this final chapter, we dug deep into the responsibilities that HCI designers now take on and looked at the skills you have gained in HCI. The skills and tools used by small and large teams are the reason why HCI is such a vibrant space, but you also need to pay diligent attention to solutions and the impact your software can have on a community, society, and the globe. Software creation is an awesome responsibility that you should not just stop studying now that you have completed this final chapter. Since you will be taking the skills and ideas exposed in this book into the world and into the undefined future, I hope you will be able to faithfully apply your HCI skills, not just in your job but in the wider world.

In this book, we started by getting into some skills and activities that are foundational to HCI thinking. The book covered three key pillars:

1. **HCI skills, theory, and historical context**
2. **HCI activities and practical challenges**
3. **HCI community resources and source materials**

A refresher of the three HCI pillars we covered is shown here:

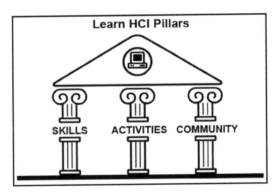

The interplay of these pillars is designed to hold you up and elevate your software solutions over time. As you continue to grow in your HCI experience, remember that there are many other ideas, activities, and communities that have impacted HCI, and I encourage you to keep learning. Congratulations on completing the book, you have now taken the initial steps towards becoming an HCI designer. The skills, activities, and community you have gained and been introduced to require diligent practice and teamwork, which hopefully you can bring to your companies and teams in order to create human-centered software that impacts our world as a positive force. Good luck!

Other Books You May Enjoy

If you enjoyed this book, you may be interested in these other books by Packt:

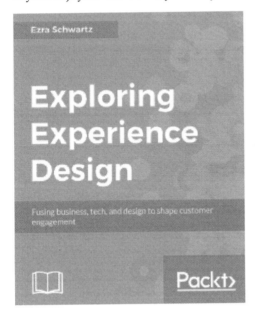

101 UX Principles
Will Grant

ISBN: 978-1-78883-736-1

- Use typography well to ensure that text is readable
- Design controls to streamline interaction
- Create navigation which makes content make sense
- Convey information with consistent iconography
- Manage user input effectively
- Represent progress to the user
- Provide interfaces that work for users with visual or motion impairments
- Understand and respond to user expectations

Exploring Experience Design
Ezra Schwartz

ISBN: Ezra Schwartz

- Understand why Experience Design (XD) is at the forefront of business priorities, as organizations race to innovate products and services in order to compete for customers in a global economy driven by technology and change
- Get motivated by the numerous professional opportunities that XD opens up for practitioners in wide-ranging domains, and by the stories of real XD practitioners
- Understand what experience is, how experiences are designed, and why they are effective
- Gain knowledge of user-centered design principles, methodologies, and best practices that will improve your product (digital or physical)
- Get to know your X's and D's—understand the differences between XD and UX, CX, IxD, IA, SD, VD, PD, and other design practices

Leave a review - let other readers know what you think

Please share your thoughts on this book with others by leaving a review on the site that you bought it from. If you purchased the book from Amazon, please leave us an honest review on this book's Amazon page. This is vital so that other potential readers can see and use your unbiased opinion to make purchasing decisions, we can understand what our customers think about our products, and our authors can see your feedback on the title that they have worked with Packt to create. It will only take a few minutes of your time, but is valuable to other potential customers, our authors, and Packt. Thank you!

Index

2

2x2 matrix challenge 99, 100, 101
2x2 opportunity matrix 181

A

A/B testing (split testing)
  A/B survey results challenge 152, 154
  about 150, 151
accessibility compliance 156, 157
accessibility
  about 237
  disability impairments 237
agile design
  about 104
  cycle 62, 105, 106
agile development 62, 107, 108
agile development cycles
  using 102
agile software development 82
Always Be Testing + Iterating (ABTI) 221
AngularJS (Google)
  URL 248
Apply
  URL 61
attention deficit hyperactivity disorder (ADHD) 239
auditory impairment 240
automatic teller machine (ATM) 291
automation software systems (ubicomp and
    embedded systems) 291, 292

B

Bootstrap (Twitter)
  about 248
  URL 248

C

call to action (CTA) 151
Cascading Style Sheets (CSS) 24, 79
clickable paper prototype
  building, with InVision app 113, 114
  challenges 189
clickable prototypes 112, 113, 187
clickable wireframe prototype
  challenges 190
coded prototypes 114, 115, 117, 118
cognitive impairment 238
collaboration software systems (ubicomp and
    seamless interactions) 288, 289
common goals
  sharing 269
communication/media software system (digital
    affordance and seamless interactions) 290
computer engineering 56
computer science 56
computer software
  used, for building software 68, 69
  used, for solving problem 66
computers
  history 19, 21, 22, 23
content delivery networks (CDNs) 24
continually better software
  designing 80, 82
continuous integration (CI) 81

D

data analytics
  using, in software design 128, 129
data collection
  qualitative data 130
  quantitative data 146
data, synthesizing into action

about 162
user insights 165
user research data analysis 162
democratic power software systems (ubicomp and security) 294, 295
design and development tools 73
design mindmap challenge 88, 90, 91
design strategy/systems design 59
design thinking 104, 107, 108
design/branding 56
development process 104
dot voting 180

E

education software (embedded systems) 286, 287
efficiency 233
ethnography and sociology 58
Extreme Programming (XP) 107

F

first computer experience challenge 92
fly-on-the-wall method
about 132, 133
micro-observations 134
formal user feedback, software hypothesis
critique feedback 213, 214
expert feedback 211, 212
formative assessment and user feedback 211
self-feedback and reflection 213
summary 214
formative assessment 211
frontend prototyping
about 192, 193
categories 192
challenges 193

G

General Data Protection Regulation (GDPR) 155
General Practioner (GP) 26
Google Forms
URL 148
Google search 40
graphical user interface (GUI) 22

H

HCI designer
balancing act 52
role 88
skills 50
HCI ethos
about 36
questions refresher challenge 36, 37
HCI interface, best practices
about 197
design guidelines 199
HCI interface, best practices 198
researching 197, 198
user interface guidelines, researching 200
HCI jargon
about 16, 17, 18
collecting 17
documenting 16
goals 18
highlighting 17
reference link 16
HCI principles 59, 60
HCI professions 30, 32
HCI sandbox
operating in 14, 15
HCI technology
about 37
accessibility factor 38, 39
time-on-task factor 40
usability factor 38
hearing impairment 240
hermeneutic loops 27, 28
How Might We (HMW) statement 176
human factors and ergonomics 58
human needs identification table challenge 48, 49, 50
human-centered software origins 70, 71, 72
Human-Computer Interaction (HCI)
about 11, 54, 56, 58, 59
areas of study 13
computer, implementing 283, 284
conceptual relationships capture challenge 11, 13, 14
culture solutions, creating 278, 280
design roles 74, 75

holy trinity (mirepoix) 40, 41
  need for 16
  off-limits, evaluating 281
  pioneers 14, 23
  professions 42, 43, 44
  software future 295
  software interests 283
  software, designing 274, 275, 285
  SWOT analysis 277, 278
hypertext markup language (HTML) 77, 78, 79
HyperText Transfer Protocol (HTTP) 24

I

informal feedback guerilla user testing challenge
    208
information architecture 58
interactive prototypes 112, 113
interfaces
  designing 242
internet 24, 25
Internet of Things (IoT) 25
intersection observation challenge 50, 51
interview candidate script challenge
  about 140
  one-to-one interview sessions 141
InVision app
  clickable paper prototype, building with 113, 114
iterative design cycle 61, 62
iterative loops
  used, for improving software 254, 256

K

key performance indicators (KPIs) 106

L

language/semiotics 57
Laseau's funnel 179, 180
lawnmower 30
learnability 233
logistics/analytics software systems (knowledge
    data) 292, 293
long tail of software design 93, 95, 96
low error rate 235

M

memorability 234, 235
Miller's law 239
Minimum Viable Culture (MVC) 252
Minimum Viable Product (MVP) 251, 252, 254
mobility impairment 239
moderated observation script challenge 135, 136
motion prototyping
  about 190, 191
  interface's behavior 191

N

native prototypes 114, 115, 117, 118
negative software example
  text messaging 67, 68
Node Package Manager (NPM)
  about 248
  URL 248
Node.JS
  about 248
  URL 248

O

object-oriented programming (OOP) 80
observation recording challenge 146
one-on-one interview challenge
  about 143
  one-to-many interview sessions 143
open source projects
  about 247
  AngularJS (Google) 248
  Bootstrap (Twitter) 248
  Node Package Manager (NPM) 248
  Node.JS 248
  React Native (Facebook) 249
  research 250, 251
  VS Code (Microsoft) 249
open source software culture 245, 247

P

Palo Alto Research Center (PARC) 22
paper prototypes 109, 110
paper prototyping
  about 182, 183

accountability opportunities 184
   sketching, challenges 186, 187
positive software example
   alarm 66, 67
POV mad lib challenge 170
POV mad lib iteration challenge 171, 172
product and software inspiration challenge 91, 92
professional interest challenge 44
prototype challenge
   about 111, 112
   iterating 222, 223
prototype usability testing challenge 221
prototype validation challenge 123, 217
prototyper (developer) 194
prototypes, types
   about 109
   clickable prototypes 112, 113
   coded prototypes 114, 115, 117, 118
   interactive prototypes 112, 113
   native prototypes 114, 115, 117, 118
   paper prototypes 109, 110
prototypes
   executing, as design ethos 108
prototyping solutions
   validating 215, 216
prototyping
   2x2 opportunity matrix 181
   about 176, 178
   dot voting 180
   idea/concept, generating 178, 179
   Laseau's funnel 179, 180
   paper prototyping 182, 183, 184
psychology 57

Q

qualitative data
   about 130, 131
   using 130, 131, 158
qualitative user research methods
   about 131
   fly-on-the-wall method 132, 133
   moderated observation 134, 135
   user interviews 136, 137
   user recording 144
quantitative data

   about 146, 147
   using 158
quantitative research methods
   A/B testing (split testing) 150, 152
   about 147
   accessibility compliance 156
   quantitative survey method 148
   usability analytics 154, 155
quantitative survey method
   about 148, 149
   quick-and-dirty survey challenge 149

R

React Native (Facebook)
   URL 249
research data
   on users, gathering 126, 127, 129
return on investment (ROI) 88

S

screen reader tool 241
semantics 77, 78
short tail of software design 96, 97
sketching challenge 111, 112
software design community, communication tools
   Figma/XD/Sketch 265
   InVision 265
   Zeplin 265
software design community, roles
   backend dev 260, 261, 262
   business 260, 261, 262
   frontend dev 260, 261, 262
   PM 260, 261, 262
   UI 260, 261, 262
   UX 260, 261, 262
software design community
   team handoff 263, 264
   team responsibility 263, 264
software design
   code 75, 76
   code development 73
   design 73
   developer's role, considering 97, 99
   for users, with universal design principles 228,
   229

roles 75, 76
tools 75, 76
software developers
  backend developers 99
  frontend developers 99
software development
  contributing, as collective community 258, 259
software experiences challenge 45, 46
software hypothesis
  about 205
  challenge 206, 207
  establishing 204
  formal user feedback 209, 210, 211
  formal user feedback challenge 215
  informal feedback guerilla user testing challenge 208
  informal user feedback 207, 208
  steps 205
software prototyping
  tools 201
software scale research challenge 268
software solutions
  iterating 221, 222
  prototype challenge, iterating 222, 223
software system trajectories
  automation software systems (ubicomp and embedded systems) 291, 292
  collaboration software systems (ubicomp and seamless interactions) 288, 289
  communication/media software system (digital affordance and seamless interactions) 290
  democratic power software systems (ubicomp and security) 294, 295
  education software (embedded systems) 286, 287
  logistics/analytics software systems (knowledge data) 292, 293
software team
  learning challenge 269
software
  caring ethos 271, 272
  improving, with iterative loops 254, 256
solutions
  aligning, to users 172, 174
  scaling 267

sharing 267
sprints 105
Survey Gizmo
  URL 148
Survey Monkey
  URL 148
synthesis 162
systems diagramming
  about 195, 196
  challenges 196

T
T-based person
  about 25
  evolving, into π person 25, 26, 27
team
  evangelizing 269
  skills, diversifying 270, 271
technology coding challenge 70
text editors 69
Typeform
  URL 148

U
Unified Modeling Language
  URL 195
universal design principles
  used, for designing software for users 228, 231
Universal Design
  URL 39
usability analytics
  about 154, 155
  data gathering challenge 155
usability tests
  executing 218, 219
  prototype usability testing challenge 221
usability
  applying, for users 231, 232
user experience (UX) 58, 198
user insights
  about 165
  identifying 165, 167, 169
  writing 169
user interface 57
user interviews method

about 136, 137
  open question types 137, 138
  probing question types 138
  probing questions types 139
user recording method 144
user research data
  analyzing 163
  categorizing 164
  clustering 164
  collecting 163
  mining 164
  organizing 163
  sorting 164
user research
  data, gathering on humans 60, 61
  examining 167, 168
user satisfaction 235
users purpose challenge 168, 169
users
  skills, enhancing 52, 54
  solutions, aligning to 172, 174
  validating with 118, 119
utility 236, 237
UX design
  about 11
  tools, URL 75

V

validating, with users
  about 118, 119
  idea validation 119, 120
  market validation 122
  usability validation 120, 121
visual impairments 240, 241
vocation 29
VS Code (Microsoft)
  about 249
  URL 249

W

waterfall design process 102, 103
waterfall development process 102, 103
Web Content Accessibility Guidelines (WCAG) 2.0
  URL 157
  used, for accessibility via ANDI testing 157
Worldometer
  URL 37

Z

Zeplin.io project, adding
  challenge 266, 267

Π

π person
  T-person, evolving to 25, 26, 27

Made in the USA
Columbia, SC
10 April 2021

35947125R00176